Topics in Sports Economics

NEW HORIZONS IN THE ECONOMICS OF SPORT

Series Editors: Wladimir Andreff, *Department of Economics, University of Paris 1 Panthéon Sorbonne, France* and Marc Lavoie, *Department of Economics, University of Ottawa, Canada*

For decades, the economics of sport was regarded as a hobby for a handful of professional economists who were primarily involved in other areas of research. In recent years, however, the significance of the sports economy as a percentage of GDP has expanded dramatically. This has coincided with an equivalent rise in the volume of economic literature devoted to the study of sport.

This series provides a vehicle for deeper analyses of the demand for sport, cost–benefit analysis of sport, sporting governance, the economics of professional sports and leagues, individual sports, trade in the sporting goods industry, media coverage, sponsoring and numerous related issues. It contributes to the further development of sports economics by welcoming new approaches and highlighting original research in both established and newly emerging sporting activities. The series publishes the best theoretical and empirical work from well-established researchers and academics, as well as from talented newcomers in the field.

For a full list of Edward Elgar published titles, including the titles in this series, visit our website at www.e-elgar.com.

Topics in Sports Economics

Thomas J. Miceli
Professor of Economics, University of Connecticut, USA

NEW HORIZONS IN THE ECONOMICS OF SPORT

Edward Elgar
PUBLISHING

Cheltenham, UK • Northampton, MA, USA

Published by

Edward Elgar Publishing Limited
The Lypiatts
15 Lansdown Road
Cheltenham
Glos GL50 2JA
UK

Edward Elgar Publishing, Inc.
William Pratt House
9 Dewey Court
Northampton
Massachusetts 01060
USA

Authorised representative in the EU for GPSR queries only: Easy Access System Europe – Mustamäe tee 50, 10621 Tallinn, Estonia, gpsr.requests@easproject.com

A catalogue record for this book is available from the British Library

Library of Congress Control Number: 2025933277

This book is available electronically in the **Elgar**online
Economics subject collection
https://doi.org/10.4337/9781035339396

MIX
Paper | Supporting responsible forestry
FSC® C013604
FSC
www.fsc.org

ISBN 978 1 0353 3938 9 (cased)
ISBN 978 1 0353 3939 6 (eBook)
ISBN 978 1 0353 9639 9 (ePub)

Printed and bound by CPI Group (UK) Ltd, Croydon, CR0 4YY

To the memory of my parents,
who were my first teachers and coaches.

Contents

Preface viii

1 Introduction to *Topics in Sports Economics* 1

PART I SPORTS AND BUSINESS

2 Sports teams as business firms 11

3 Pricing of sporting events 27

PART II THE ORGANIZATION OF COMPETITION

4 Leagues as economic organizations 46

5 The nature of competition on the field 66

6 Competitive balance 83

7 Rules and enforcement 112

PART III THE PLAYERS' LABOR MARKET

8 Player salary determination 135

9 Player contracts: risk sharing and incentives 165

10 Player training: the minor leagues 182

11 College sports 201

PART IV PUBLIC POLICY AND SPORTS

12 Policy issues 215

Answers to end-of-chapter exercises 245

References 251

Index 257

Preface

This book grew out of a one-semester course on sports economics that I have taught at the University of Connecticut over the past several years, but it is not principally intended as a comprehensive survey of the field nor as a standalone textbook.[1] My objective instead is to provide students with a new perspective on both sports *and* economics. With respect to sports, most students will readily accept the idea that economics can shed light on the business components of professional sports, and perhaps even amateur sports at the collegiate level. They may be skeptical, however, about what economics can teach them about other aspects of sports, such as the nature of the game on the field, how leagues are organized, how playing rules are formulated and enforced, and how owners and coaches make personnel decisions. My hope is that this book will reveal the pervasiveness of economic reasoning underlying these and many other decisions in the sports world.

More broadly, my hope is that the book will provide students with an expanded view of the scope of economics in general by demonstrating how principles of economic theory can be applied to understanding behaviors and institutions outside of the conventional market setting. It is my opinion that all undergraduate economics majors should take at least one course during their careers that studies environments other than traditional markets. Such a course, I believe, reveals the full power of economics to elucidate issues that will confront students in nearly all aspects of their lives. And for most students, at least those who are already sports fans, a course in sports economics will be an enjoyable vehicle for conveying this important lesson.

Pedagogically, the book can serve as the basis for a one-semester (14-week) elective course on sports economics or as a supplemental book for a more traditional introduction to the field. The order of the topics contained herein follows a certain logic, but it can be varied to suit the instructor's (or reader's) preference. The level of analysis is aimed at upper-division economics majors and, as such, it presumes reasonable familiarity with algebra and geometry, as well as an introductory-level understanding of calculus and game theory. I have endeavored throughout, however, to emphasize the intuition underlying the analysis, no matter how technical it appears, in an effort to make the book accessible to less mathematically-equipped readers. (Some more technical material is therefore relegated to appendices to the relevant chapters.) Consequently, the book may also be of interest to general readers interested in how economists look at the sports world or the world in general. Finally, because the book employs methods from a variety of fields in microeconomics, it could serve as a topic-oriented introduction to microeconomic theory generally, particularly for mathematically-inclined non-majors.

Most of the analysis in this book applies broadly to the world of sports, but I will confess a bias toward team sports, and to baseball in particular. This is partly due to personal preference and knowledge, but it also reflects the fact that much of the early research on sports economics was done in the context of baseball because of the wealth of data available. There is some discussion, however, of individual sports such as golf, and on how tournaments should be optimally structured.

The content and format of the book have benefited from the input of several cohorts of students, and I gratefully acknowledge their contributions. More than any other course I have taught, students are engaged with the topic and bring considerable personal experience, background knowledge, and interest to the classroom. Along the way, I have enjoyed the profound satisfaction of seeing students experience the pleasure and excitement of contemplating a familiar issue or idea from a new perspective.

I acknowledge the comments from anonymous reviewers on an earlier version of the manuscript and the encouragement and guidance of Nikhil Ghosh at Edward Elgar throughout the production process. Their input has definitely improved the final product. I also want to acknowledge the assistance and influence of Brad Humphreys, who graciously consented to collaborate with me when I was first venturing into sports economics and who educated me on many of the important issues in the field.

Finally, I wish to acknowledge the inspiration of my family in undertaking this project. Sports have provided an important source of connection between me and my two sons, and I thank them for their enthusiasm and tolerance of a well-intentioned but sometimes overly zealous coach/father. I also thank my wife for enduring countless hours at sporting events as I endeavored to make her into a sports fan while conducting my "research."

T.J.M., Summer 2024

NOTE

1. Students seeking such treatments should consult Berri (2018), Blair (2012), and Syzmanski (2009)—the first two being comprehensive textbooks, and the third being a non-technical but masterful introduction.

1. Introduction to *Topics in Sports Economics*

WHAT IS SPORTS ECONOMICS?

The world of sports comprises a wide array of activities, ranging from recreational and amateur to professional, and from individual to team competition. Sports economics is mainly, though not exclusively, about professional sports. It is about the business of sports, but it is also about decisions and behaviors by contestants and coaches on the field or in the arena of play.

In 1922, the United States Supreme Court exempted Major League Baseball from scrutiny under antitrust laws. Writing for the Court, Justice Oliver Wendell Holmes justified this holding by arguing that, while the business of major league baseball is to provide exhibitions of the sport, "the exhibition, although made for money would not be called trade or commerce in the commonly accepted use of those words."[1] To the modern ear, this argument seems at best quaint, and at worst absurd. It probably even strained credulity at the time. Nowadays, of course, there is no doubt that professional sports, and even some college sports, are big businesses, and as such, they are reasonable subjects for the application of economic analysis (and perhaps regulation).

But economics is about much more than business and markets; it is about rational choice in whatever context that takes place. In recent decades, for example, economic reasoning has been applied to decision making in politics, law, the family, and religion, to name just a few notable areas. So why not sports? Coaches, players, owners, and fans all make rational decisions,[2] both off and on the field of play, in the hope of furthering some goal or objective, and there is no reason to believe that the tools of economics cannot be used to understand those decisions and the consequences they entail. One purpose of this book is therefore to convince readers of the validity of this claim. Another purpose (a by-product of the first) is to demonstrate the versatility of economics for understanding broad categories of human behavior.

Sports economics is a relatively new field in economics, with most scholars dating it to the seminal article by Simon Rottenberg in 1956. Stefan Szymanski, for example, calls Rottenberg "truly the father of sports economics"

(Szymanski, 2009, p. xix). Rottenberg's article is principally about the baseball players' labor market, and particularly its unique aspects in light of the antitrust exemption as noted above (and it is explored in detail in Chapter 12). In terms of the field of sports economics, however, it is mainly remembered for two propositions. The first is the assertion that the distribution of talent in a sports league will be efficient, meaning that players will end up with the teams that value them the most, regardless of whether owners hold property rights to the players' labor services (as under a reserve system) or whether they are free agents. This "invariance proposition" actually anticipated its more famous cousin, demonstrated by Coase in the context of externalities, and later christened the Coase Theorem (Coase, 1960).

The other important contribution of the Rottenberg article is that it first advanced the so-called *Uncertainty of Outcome Hypothesis*, which is one of the core concepts in sports economics. The gist of this claim, later echoed in another classic paper by Neale (1964), is the assertion that consumers will only pay to attend sporting contests in which the outcome is uncertain. This argument, which will be discussed in detail in Chapter 6, is used to bolster league efforts to achieve and maintain competitive balance among member teams. Aside from this proposition, sports economics does not depend on any particular methodology or ideology, but instead draws insights from several sub-fields of economics, including price theory, industrial organization, game theory, law and economics, labor economics, and public finance. The concept of competitive balance provides a unifying thread.

In the remainder of this chapter, I will first review some key concepts of economic theory that will be important in the subsequent analysis. Students not well-versed in micro-theory may want to consult any intermediate microeconomics textbook for further details.[3] In the final section, I will provide a preview of each chapter.

ECONOMIC CONCEPTS

As noted, there is no special methodology needed to study sports economics; it makes use of the basic tools of microeconomics, which I review briefly here.

The first concept is *optimizing behavior* by individuals and firms, which means that the relevant decision-maker maximizes his or her objective function subject to the applicable resource constraints. The methodology by which they do that is called "marginal analysis." For individual consumers, the objective function is utility, which measures the level of satisfaction, or "happiness," that people derive from the consumption of goods and services. We will assume that fans derive utility from watching sporting contests, which forms the basis for the demand side of the market for those contests. On the supply side, team owners produce contests which they "sell" to consumers with the objective of maximizing profit (or possibly wins). Owners, in turn, are demanders of inputs used in the production of games, the chief of which is labor supplied by players.

The demand and supply sides of the market for games and for players' labor services are coordinated through the operation of the price mechanism, which determines *equilibrium* in the relevant market. Equilibrium exists when the quantity consumers demand equals the quantity producers supply at the prevailing price. The exact nature of the equilibrium depends on the market structure—specifically, whether there is a large enough number of suppliers or demanders, so that they act competitively (i.e., take the price as given), or if they interact in a strategic way. We will examine various structures in an effort to understand the nature of sporting markets, both for contests and for playing talent.

The concept of equilibrium can also be applied to the interaction of decision makers in non-market settings. *Game theory* provides the analytical tools for studying these types of strategic interactions. The key equilibrium concept in game theory is a *Nash equilibrium*, which describes a situation in which the strategy choices of the parties involved in the "game" are mutually consistent. This means that all parties are happy with their choices given the choices that everyone else has made. In other words, when a decision maker knows or observes what strategy the other decision makers are in fact employing, he or she will not want to alter his or her own strategy. Game theory has been applied to many types of social situations, including military conflicts, legal disputes, and voluntary contributions to public goods. The behavior of contestants or teams in a sporting contest represents an obvious application. (Indeed, as the name suggests, game theory was first developed to study the behavior of participants in games or contests.)

Finally, the study of decisions in the real world requires an appreciation of the role of *imperfect information* and *uncertainty*, both of which are potential sources of market failure. As noted above, uncertainty of outcome is a foundational principle in sports economics—in a real sense, it is the *raison d'être* of sports. Modern economics has developed sophisticated methods for incorporating these issues into economic models, and we will make extensive use of these methods throughout our study of the sports world. Principally, this involves the computation of expected values.

In addition to the preceding issues, I have already noted that sports economics draws on insights and methodologies derived from other fields of economics. To offer just a few examples, the discussion of the organizational structure of sports leagues employs models of market structure from the industrial organization literature; the analysis of the players' labor market employs tools from labor economics; the analysis of rulemaking and rule enforcement uses insights developed to study the economics of crime and law enforcement; and the discussion of publicly funded sports facilities draws on the field of public finance. It is this eclectic nature of sports economics that makes it an ideal elective course for economics majors because it provides a vehicle for bringing together various strands of analysis from prior coursework.

ORGANIZATION OF THE BOOK

This book is not intended to be an exhaustive survey of the field of sports economics. It is, rather, a selective treatment that nevertheless seeks to cover the major topics. The goal is to provide a rigorous analysis of those topics in a way that tells a coherent story about how economic theory can provide a unique insight into the nature and organization of the sports world. The book is divided into four parts. Part I (Chapters 2–3) focuses on sports teams as business firms; Part II (Chapters 4–7) considers the organization of competition on the field; Part III (Chapters 8–11) examines the labor market for professional athletes; and Part IV (Chapter 12) discusses various public policy issues related to the sports world. A brief preview of each chapter follows.

Chapter 2 begins by viewing professional sports teams as business firms. It first examines the assumption that teams, like ordinary firms, maximize profits by "selling" games, or sporting events, to consumers (fans). The consequences of this assumption are then compared with those that arise under the alternative assumption that teams maximize wins subject to a budget constraint. Not surprisingly, the analysis predicts that teams pursuing the latter objective will put a more talented team on the field, all else equal. It also predicts that teams in larger markets, which have a greater ability to pay for talent, will perform better on the field. Still, we show that small-market teams can compete with large-market teams if the former maximize wins while the latter maximize profits. The discussion concludes by considering the hybrid case of a team that makes business decisions to maximize profit, but simultaneously makes on-field decisions to maximize wins. This perhaps describes the behavior of most teams.

Chapter 3 turns to a more detailed examination of the pricing of sporting events. The focus is on price discrimination, which is the practice of charging different prices to different types of consumers by means of market segmentation. The primary examples are two-part pricing and quantity discounts, both of which are commonly utilized by sports teams. The chapter concludes by evaluating the practice of ticket-scalping—the resale of a ticket at a price above its face value. The focus is on why it happens and whether there is any economic justification for disallowing the practice.

Chapter 4 begins Part II by considering the interaction of teams within an organized league. The emphasis is on how the league, acting as a cartel, coordinates the decisions of teams with the goal of increasing their joint profits.

In contrast to ordinary markets, however, where this sort of cooperation is detrimental to consumer welfare, we suggest that some amount of coordination among teams is desirable. Indeed, some cooperation is essential, given that individual teams cannot stage contests. In this sense, leagues play an important role in maximizing consumer benefits. Whether or not leagues strike an optimal balance between cooperation and competition, however, is an empirical question, which from a policy perspective raises the issue of whether or not sports leagues should be subject to scrutiny under federal anti-trust laws. This point is pursued further in Chapter 12.

Chapter 5 turns to the study of competition on the field. The basis of the analysis is a conflict model that describes the interaction among competitors vying for a "prize," whether in the form of a first-place finish in a tournament or a league championship. The equilibrium of the model describes how competitors respond to the organization of the contest, such as how many competitors there are and what the magnitude and structure of the reward is. The discussion also considers the optimal structure of the contest under different objective functions. The conclusions differ depending on whether the goal of the contest is to maximize the profits of member teams (as under a cartel) or to achieve the greatest level of overall competition, reflecting the willingness to pay of consumers for a high-quality (action-filled) contest.

Chapter 6 undertakes a detailed analysis of the concept of competitive balance as embodied in the Uncertainty of Outcome Hypothesis (UOH) first proposed by Rottenberg. As noted, this hypothesis represents a cornerstone of sports economics. The chapter first investigates the basis of the UOH in consumer preferences. It suggests two approaches. One assumes that fans root for their favorite teams (i.e., that they are partisan) but that aggregate fan welfare is maximized when each team has an equal probability of winning. Another assumes individual fans value competitive balance *per se*. A hybrid model combines the two approaches. The chapter then discusses how economists actually measure competitive balance, and asks whether the available evidence supports the hypothesis that fans actually value it. It concludes by examining various policies, such as salary caps, revenue sharing, and reverse-order drafts, for promoting balance in professional leagues. As we will see, although these policies are aimed at counteracting differences in teams' ability to pay for talent, not all are effective in doing so.

Chapter 7 turns to the nature of rules governing sporting events and the optimal enforcement of those rules. It begins by suggesting that there is a useful distinction between intentional violations of rules (such as cheating or the use of banned substances) and accidental violations that arise as a by-product of ordinary play (such as fouls or penalties). We ultimately conclude, however, that this distinction is not especially useful for designing policies aimed at achieving optimal enforcement of rules. What matters instead is the ease of detecting violations and the harm that they cause. In making this argument, the discussion draws on insights from the economic theory of law enforcement. The general principle is that punishment should be harsher for violations that are more harmful or are more difficult to detect. The chapter next considers the evolution of rules, and how they change over time in response to changing technologies (such as the availability of video replay) and knowledge about the harmfulness of certain actions (such as head contact). We also argue that rules sometimes evolve to maintain a balance between offense and defense in team sports. The chapter concludes by examining how some rule changes, though well-intentioned, have unintended consequences that are not always desirable and may counteract the original intent of the rule.

Chapter 8 begins the analysis of the players' labor market, which is the subject of Part III. This initial chapter focuses on how salaries are generally determined, first in a competitive labor market and then in one where firms have monopsony power. In the latter case, which is descriptive of most sports labor markets (at least for players early in their careers), the prediction is that salaries will be set below players' value to their teams (their marginal revenue product). The chapter then reviews the research, pioneered by Gerald Scully, which seeks to measure the resulting "wage gap." The discussion next considers the determination of salaries in free agent markets, where players are free to negotiate with all teams in the league. The analysis uses simple auction theory to show that, although income-maximizing players will end up with the team that values them most, their salaries will nevertheless fall short of their value to the team because the winning bidder will offer, at most, the value of the player to the second-highest bidder. What's more, if the player has a nonmonetary preference for a particular team, his or her salary will fall further short of his or her maximum value. The chapter next discusses negotiations between a team and a player who is under contract or still subject to the reserve system. In that context, we specifically examine the effectiveness of a player's threat to hold out for a higher salary when so encumbered. (The answer is that it is not generally very effective.) The analysis then turns to the question of how aggregate spending on player salaries translates into winning. Actual data show that the link is positive but weak, reflecting the influence of other factors on winning, including chance, but also inefficiencies in the management of personnel. This last point leads to a discussion of the so-called "Moneyball Hypothesis," which concerns the use of statistical measures of performance to evaluate players. The rapid adoption of this approach by most professional teams following its initial successes prompts a discussion of the nature of innovation in sports markets and in markets generally.

Chapter 9 continues the discussion of player compensation by examining the role of formal contracts. The analysis uses the economic theory of the principal–agent relationship to study the optimal structure of contracts with an emphasis on two factors: risk-sharing and incentives. We argue that risk-averse players prefer long-term, guaranteed wage contracts to insure them against the unavoidable uncertainties associated with injury and poor performance, while teams prefer short-term, incentive-laden contracts to motivate players to exert effort. Actual contracts generally balance these considerations by promising a base salary augmented by bonuses for attaining certain standards of performance (incentive clauses). The chapter concludes by discussing the so-called "team production problem," which concerns the difficulty of measuring the contribution of individual players to a team's overall performance. We suggest that two mechanisms serve to overcome this problem in a sports context: peer monitoring and oversight by a coach/manager whose job security is tied to the team's performance.

Chapter 10 turns to the training of players, focusing specifically on the case of the minor league. This reflects the fact that baseball, more than any other sport, requires significant training beyond what players can acquire at the amateur level. The chapter begins with a brief history of the economic relationship between the major and minor leagues throughout the twentieth century. The predominant trend has been for major league teams to affiliate with minor league teams, either by buying them outright (vertically integrating with them) or by entering into long-term contracts that give the parent major league team considerable control over the operations of the minor league team, at least concerning its on-field decisions. The chapter then develops a theory of training which rationalizes that evolving relationship. The analysis specifically shows that as training became more important for a player to be successful in the majors, affiliation between major and minor league teams also became important as a means of giving the parent team control over player training decisions. When minor league teams are economically viable (as has been increasingly true in recent times), minor league team officials often take control over local business decisions, but the parent major league team retains control over baseball operations.

Chapter 10 next turns to the question of how training costs are financed. We argue that self financing by players is not feasible because of the high up-front costs and the unavailability of third-party lending for such a risky venture. Thus, teams foot the cost but then have to recover it from the small percentage of players who actually make the majors. As a result, player salaries have to be less than their full value to the team, at least for the early part of a player's career, during which time the player is bound to the team. This logic provides an important rationale for the persistence of a six-year reserve period in Major League Baseball. This limited reserve system is compared and contrasted with the system for financing college education, which generally involves self-financing by students, often by means of third-party loans. Finally, the chapter examines the screening function of the minor leagues and draws conclusions about the average quality of play on the field.

Chapter 11 turns to college sports with particular emphasis on the bundled nature of academics and athletics under the umbrella of the NCAA. Also emphasized is the role of college as a pseudo-minor league for certain professional sports (principally basketball and football). An important policy issue in this context is the perennial question of whether or not top college athletes should be paid. The discussion centers on the impact of the bundling of academics and athletics on the budgetary, allocative, and training aspects of college sports. The prevailing system is specifically examined in relation to a world in which academics and athletics are unbundled, and athletes are paid based on their contributions to the revenue generated by collegiate sports—so-called pay for play.

Chapter 12, comprising the entirety of Part IV, concludes by examining four public policy issues related to professional sports. These are the applicability of antitrust laws to sports leagues, the question of whether cities or states should subsidize some or all of the cost of building or renovating professional sports facilities, the relationship between sports and gambling, and discrimination in sports.

The discussion of antitrust law begins by reviewing how courts have treated sports leagues with respect to the issue of collusion. Picking up on a point that was raised in Chapter 4, the theoretical analysis argues that sports leagues are unique in the sense that, unlike ordinary markets, some collusion is essential for competition among member teams to occur. In addition, the discussion elaborates on the argument first made in Chapter 10 that barriers to entry are beneficial to fans because they maintain a minimum quality level of play.

Turning to the question of public financing for stadium construction, we argue that while there does exist a sound theoretical basis for some amount of subsidization, arising principally from the spillover benefits associated with the presence of a sports team, the magnitude of this benefit is an empirical question. The fact that much of this value may take a non-pecuniary form, such as civic pride from having a professional team in one's city, greatly complicates the computation of the full benefits of this use of public funds. Our review of the available evidence on this issue reveals little support for public subsidization.

We next consider the relationship between sports and gambling, which is and always has been an uneasy one. This is an especially important topic in light of the Supreme Court's recent ruling that the legality of sports gambling is controlled at the state level. We begin by reviewing the theory of gambling based on the traditional argument that it arises out of risk-preferring preferences on the part of some consumers. Using this theory, we examine the determination of odds in betting and the source of profits for bookies. We also propose other possible explanations for why people who are ordinarily risk-neutral or risk-averse may sometimes engage in sports betting. One of these is the likely correspondence between the demand for betting and the Rottenberg conjecture that people value contests with uncertain outcomes. We conclude by discussing the impact of sports betting on the integrity of sports leagues, which is the primary issue of policy concern.[4]

Finally, we examine the issue of discrimination in sports leagues. The first question concerns the measurement of workplace discrimination—whether racial or gender-based—which theoretically can be done using data on worker (player) salaries and performance statistics. The detection of salary differences across members of different racial or ethnic groups, or between male and female employees, that are not based on performance is evidence of discrimination. We next use economic theory to discuss how prejudice and discrimination impact outcomes in the labor market. Labor-market theory predicts that owners with prejudice against certain groups will hire fewer members of that group and will try to pay them less. Working against this, however, are two factors—first, competition in the labor market will limit wage discretion on the part of owners; and, second, teams whose owners exercise such prejudices will be less successful compared with those teams with unprejudiced owners, which may provoke fans of the former to demand a change in ownership. The discussion concludes with some comments on gender discrimination in sports.

NOTES

1. *Federal Base Ball Club of Baltimore v. National League of Professional Base Ball Clubs*, 259 US 200 (1922). See the further discussion of this case in Chapter 12.
2. Of course, not all fan behavior is rational—after all, the origin of "fan" is fanatic!
3. See, for example, Nicholson and Snyder (2017).
4. Another is the addictive aspect of gambling, which we will not address.

PART I

Sports and Business

2. Sports teams as business firms

This chapter and the next begin the application of economic analysis to the sports world by viewing professional teams as business firms. Specifically, this chapter examines the objective function of team owners, while the next focuses on various pricing strategies for sporting events.

Although most sports fans are only interested in the performance of their favored teams on the field, it is precisely that interest (which for many rises to the level of an obsession) that creates a market for sporting contests and thereby opens the door to the potential for teams to earn huge profits. In addition, we will see that the economic objectives of a team's ownership can have significant impacts on the team's performance on the field.

Like ordinary business firms, sports teams produce a "good" that fans are willing to pay for. The nature of that good is somewhat vaguely defined and will therefore be the subject of much discussion in this and subsequent chapters. For now, we simply assert that team owners will make rational management decisions, just as they would for any other type of business. Consequently, standard economic principles should be applicable. That perspective motivates the analysis in this chapter and the next.

As noted, this chapter specifically focuses on the objectives of teams in making their pricing and output decisions. To that end, we examine two possible objectives for team management. The first is the standard assumption that owners seek to maximize profit, while the second is that they maximize wins subject to a budget constraint. The latter objective resembles that often attributed to non-profit firms, such as hospitals or charitable organizations, which are generally assumed to maximize some measure of output subject to a zero-profit condition. After comparing the outcomes under these two approaches to team management, we suggest that some, perhaps most, teams might actually pursue a combination of the two objectives—specifically, that they maximize profit with respect to "business" decisions and maximize wins with respect to "on-field" decisions.

PROFIT-MAXIMIZING TEAMS

Consider first the view that professional sports teams are profit-maximizing business firms that sell "games," or "sporting events", to fans. In this context, we will use attendance, or ticket sales, as the measure of output. Let Q be the number of fans who attend a game, each paying a price P for admission. (If the time frame is a season, then Q is season attendance.) Total revenue (gate receipts) is therefore equal to PQ.[1] Price and quantity are related to each other through the demand function, which dictates how much fans are willing to pay for a game. The demand function is derived from consumer preferences for the particular good in question—here, sporting events. The "Law of Demand" says that as the price of a good increases, consumers will demand less of it. This logic should obviously apply to sporting events as well—as the price of admission increases, fewer fans will want to attend a game. As a result, P and Q are inversely related to each other. We will capture that relationship by defining the inverse demand function $P(Q)$, where P is a decreasing function of Q (that is, $dP/dQ < 0$).[2] This relationship is shown graphically in Figure 2.1.Total revenue, which is equal to $P(Q) \cdot Q$, represents the area of

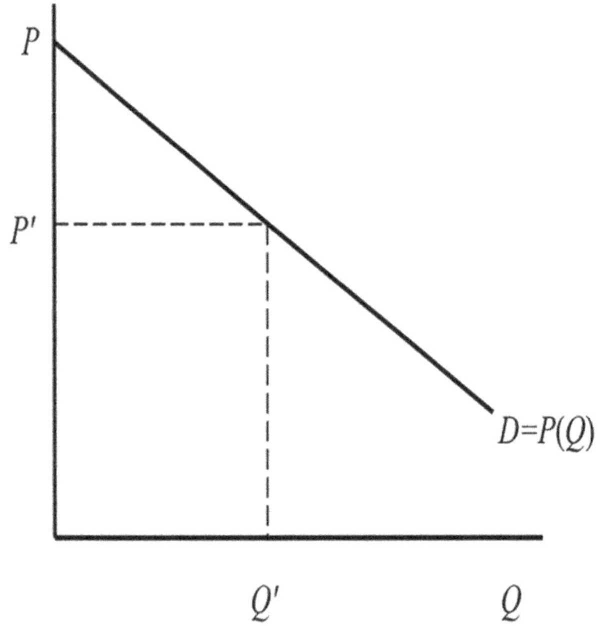

Figure 2.1 Demand curve for sporting events

the rectangle defined by any point on the demand curve. Thus, for example, if the price is P' and the corresponding output is Q', the resulting revenue would be $P' \cdot Q'$, as shown in Figure 2.1. The problem for a firm (team) facing the demand curve in Figure 2.1 is to maximize profit, which is equal to total revenue minus total cost:

$$Profit \equiv \pi = TR - TC$$

Given the above definition of total revenue, this becomes

$$\pi = P(Q)Q - C(Q) - FC \tag{2.1}$$

where total cost is decomposed into $C(Q)$, which represents variable costs (costs that vary with output), and FC, which represents fixed costs (costs that do not vary with output); these costs capture all the costs associated with providing sporting contests. These include labor costs (the salaries of players, coaches, scouts, grounds crew, officials, vendors, security, etc.), material costs (team equipment, uniforms, facility maintenance equipment, etc.), capital costs, and the owner's opportunity cost. Importantly, players' salaries are part of the team's fixed costs because they must be paid regardless of how many tickets are sold. We will discuss this in more detail below.

We will assume here that sporting teams have monopoly power regarding the sale of their "product." This is true because each team has the sole right and ability to sell games featuring its roster of players and its unique "identity." This monopoly power derives from several sources: (1) the loyalty of fans for their favorite team; (2) the spatial monopoly each team possesses, which is protected by the league's control of entry of new teams (as will be discussed further in Chapters 4 and 12); and (3) people's preferences for this particular entertainment option vis-à-vis other options in the local area (i.e., substitutes for sporting events).

As a monopolist, the team will maximize its profit in equation (2.1) by increasing output to the point where the last unit sold produces zero incremental profit. In other words, it will expand Q to the point where marginal revenue equals marginal cost:

$$MR(Q) = MC(Q) \tag{2.2}$$

Marginal revenue is defined to be dTR / dQ and marginal cost is defined to be dC / dQ. Given the definition of total revenue in equation (2.1), equation (2.2) becomes

$$P + (dP / dQ)Q = MC \tag{2.3}$$

According to the left-hand side of this equation, marginal revenue consists of two parts: the price earned from the last unit sold (the first term), plus the increment in lost revenue owing to the need to reduce the price for all previous units in order to sell one additional unit (the second term). The fact that $dP / dQ < 0$ implies that marginal revenue is less than the price over the range of positive output. (This assumes that all consumers must be charged the same price, an assumption we will relax in the next chapter.)

An alternative way to write equation (2.3) is to relate marginal revenue to the elasticity of demand, which measures the sensitivity of output to price. Specifically, the formula for elasticity is

$$\varepsilon = \frac{P}{Q}\frac{dQ}{dP} \tag{2.4}$$

which measures the percentage change of output relative to price.[3] Note that ε is negative, reflecting the negative slope of the demand curve. Using equation (2.4), we can rewrite equation (2.3) as

$$P\left(1 + \frac{1}{\varepsilon}\right) = MC$$

This expression can be rearranged to obtain

$$\frac{P - MC}{P} = -\frac{1}{\varepsilon} \tag{2.5}$$

which implies that $P > MC$. Equation (2.5) shows that the extent to which the monopolist is able to set prices above marginal cost is inversely related to the elasticity of demand. Specifically, as the demand curve becomes more inelastic (i.e., as output becomes less sensitive to price, or as ε becomes a smaller negative number), the price will exceed marginal cost by a larger amount. This is the case where the monopolist has a lot of market power because there do not exist good substitutes for the good it is selling. Strong fan loyalty will have this effect on demand, as will a larger distance to the nearest rival team. Both factors, therefore, allow a team to raise ticket prices.

Figure 2.2 shows the marginal revenue curve (labelled MR) that is associated with the demand curve from Figure 2.1. Note that it has the same vertical intercept but is steeper than the demand curve, and so for positive output levels, it is everywhere below the demand curve. The profit-maximizing output, denoted Q_M, occurs at the intersection of the marginal revenue curve with the marginal cost curve, MC, assumed here to be constant.[4] Note that the

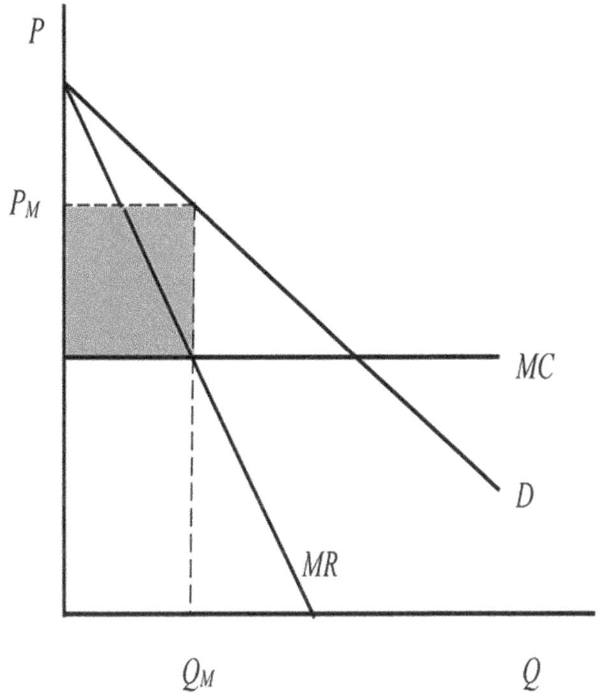

Figure 2.2 *Profit-maximizing output, price, and profit*

price, P_M, is determined by the point on the demand curve associated with the profit-maximizing output level. This represents the maximum price that the marginal customer is willing to pay. We will consider a more sophisticated approach to the determination of price in the next chapter. Profit (exclusive of FC) is shown by the shaded rectangle.

The preceding analysis obviously simplifies the nature of a professional team's business activities because it focuses solely on the production of games and ticket sales as the source of revenue. In reality, of course, teams generate revenue from multiple additional sources, including broadcast revenues, advertising rights, licensing fees, sales of merchandise, and concessions. The output and pricing decisions for each of these "products" would be made in the same manner as above, treating them as distinct markets.

Example 2.1: Calculating monopoly output, price, and profit.

Consider a linear demand curve of the form $P = a - bQ$, where a and b are positive constants, and let the monopolist's total cost be $TC = cQ$, where we assume that a > c. Total revenue is given by

$$TR = (a - bQ)Q = aQ - bQ^2$$

from which we can derive marginal revenue to be

$$MR = dTR / dQ = a - 2bQ$$

The monopolist's marginal cost is equal to $MC = dTC / dQ = c$. Equating marginal revenue and marginal cost and solving for Q yields

$$Q_M = \frac{a - c}{2b}$$

The corresponding price is found by substituting Q_M into the inverse demand curve to obtain

$$P_M = \frac{a + c}{2}$$

Finally, the monopolist's profit (again, exclusive of fixed costs) is given by

$$\pi = P_M Q_M - cQ_M = \left(\frac{a+c}{2}\right)\left(\frac{a-c}{2b}\right) - c\left(\frac{a-c}{2b}\right)$$
$$= \frac{(a-c)^2}{4b}$$

The Impact of Stadium Capacity

The analysis to this point has ignored the capacity of the stadium, which puts an upper bound, denoted by $\bar{Q}$, on game attendance.[5] In reality, the team maximizes profit in equation (2.1) subject to the constraint that $Q \le \bar{Q}$. However, we have so far been assuming that this constraint is not binding, or that $Q_M < \bar{Q}$. This means that there are unfilled seats in the stadium.

Figure 2.3 shows the outcome when the capacity constraint is binding; that is, when $Q_M > \bar{Q}$. In this case, the team's attendance maxes out at $\bar{Q}$, and so it sets the price at $\bar{P}$, the point on the demand curve corresponding to $\bar{Q}$. Here, paradoxically, a consistently full stadium indicates that the team is forgoing some potential profits. Thus, it would ideally like to expand the

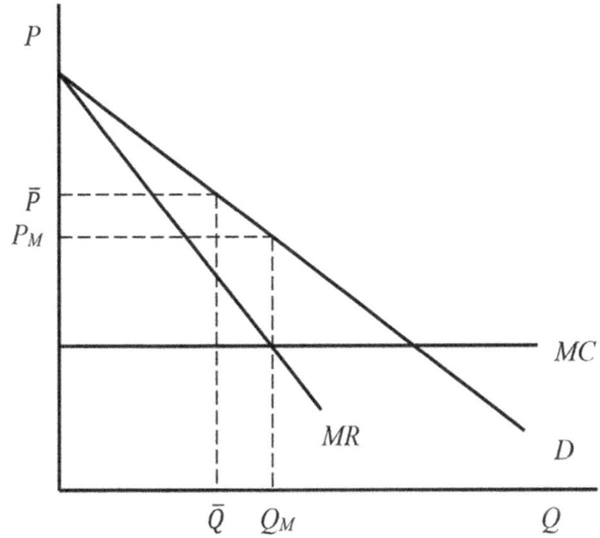

Figure 2.3 *Output and price when the capacity constraint is binding*

stadium's capacity. Such a situation will often arise when a team enjoys a long stretch of success, thereby causing its demand curve to shift outward over time, eventually leading to the outcome in Figure 2.3. The team may be able to respond in the short run by adding some additional seats, as the Boston Red Sox did when they installed seats above the Green Monster. However, if the situation persists, the team may consider building a new stadium with greater capacity. This is a risky venture, however, because the same thing can happen in reverse if the team suffers a prolonged period of losing. In general, this dilemma confronts any business that faces fluctuating demand—specifically, at what point is a change perceived to be sufficiently "permanent" to justify expanding or contracting capacity?

WIN-MAXIMIZING TEAMS

The assumption that ordinary business firms maximize profit is not especially controversial, but in the case of professional sports teams, there is another reasonable objective—namely, to maximize wins subject to a budget constraint. Teams that behave in this way are essentially acting like non-profit firms. To examine this objective, however, we first need to redefine the team's variable of choice from "output" (ticket sales) to winning percentage, denoted by *WP*. The assumption here is that fans value winning, not just games, and therefore will spend more for better teams. Thus, a team's total revenue will be an increasing function of its winning percentage, though it will most likely increase at a decreasing rate.[6] That is, the revenue function, written as $TR(WP)$, is concave. We will have more to say about the relationship between revenue and team performance later, but for now, we simply assert this as a reasonable specification.

Of course, a team cannot directly "choose" its winning percentage, as that depends on numerous factors, including the actions of other teams and chance.[7] What the team *can* choose is the composition of its roster and, in particular, how much to spend on its players, or "talent." We therefore define x to be the inputs of talent and assume that *WP* is increasing in x, though at a decreasing rate (reflecting the usual assumption of diminishing marginal productivity). Total revenue, therefore, becomes $TR(WP(x))$. We finally suppose that the team can acquire units of talent at a fixed wage equal to w.

Given this specification, a profit-maximizing team would choose x to maximize

$$TR(WP(x)) - wx$$

This would lead it to set x at the point where marginal revenue equals marginal cost, or where

$$(dTR / dWP)(dWP / dx) = w$$

In contrast, a team wishing to maximize wins subject to a budget constraint would choose x to

$$\text{Maximize } WP(x) \text{ subject to } TR(WP(x)) - wx \geq 0 \qquad (2.6)$$

These two outcomes are compared in Figure 2.4, which graphs revenue as a concave function in x, reflecting the above assumptions, and costs as increasing linearly in x, reflecting the constant wage rate for talent.

The profit-maximizing outcome is shown by x^*, which occurs at the point where the vertical distance between the revenue and cost curves is largest. (This is also the point where the slopes of the curves are equal, reflecting the equality of marginal revenue and marginal cost.) The win-maximizing outcome, by contrast, is shown by x^{**}, which represents the highest winning percentage (and hence the greatest total revenue) that the team can attain while not running a budgetary deficit. It is important to remember that both of these talent choices can only produce *expected* outcomes in terms of revenue, given the impact of other teams' choices and random factors on a team's realized winning percentage. We will revisit these issues in more detail in

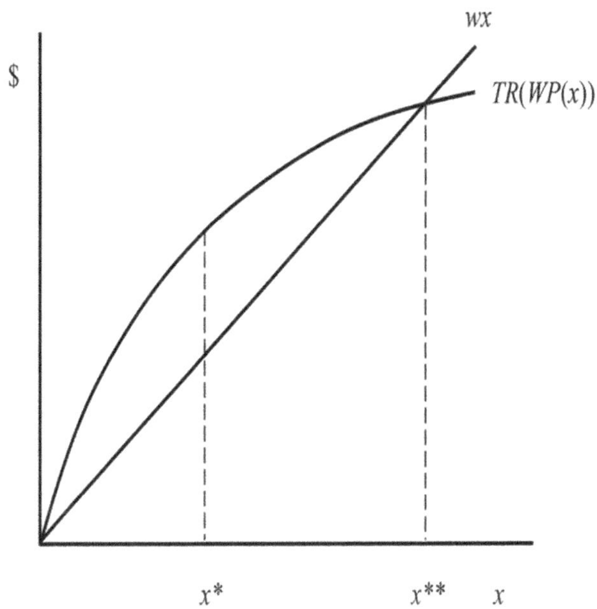

Figure 2.4 *Profit maximization versus win maximization*

later chapters. For now, the key conclusion is that the two objectives yield very different expected outcomes regarding team performance. Not surprisingly, the win-maximizing team will assemble a more talented roster of players and hence will likely win more games than the profit-maximizing team. Note that it will also generate more total revenue, though by construction its profit will be zero (at least in expected terms).

Varying Market Sizes

An important difference across teams in a league is the size of their markets. Teams that operate in large markets have an economic advantage over teams in small markets by virtue of their larger fan base.[8] This will have the effect of shifting both the demand curve and the total revenue curve upward for the large-market team. If everything else is equal (in particular, if costs are the same), the large-market team will generate more attendance, charge higher ticket prices, and earn larger profits compared with small-market teams, assuming teams are profit-maximizers.[9] This comparison is shown in Figure 2.5, where D_L and D_S are the demand curves for the large- and small-market teams, respectively.

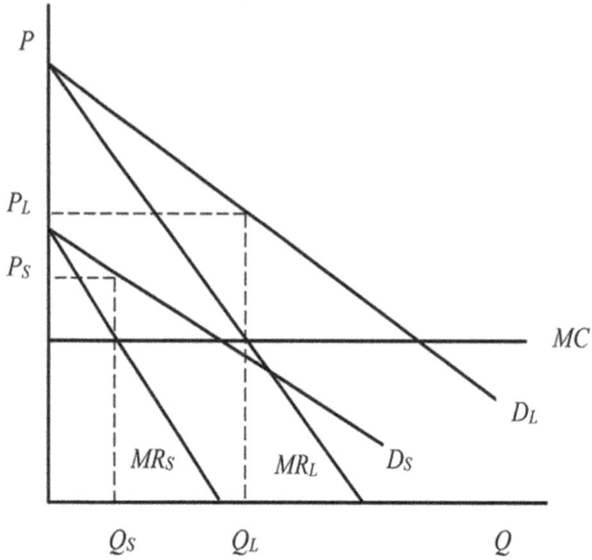

Figure 2.5 *Large and small market profit-maximizing teams*

As for the purchase of talent, the large-market team would be able to acquire a better roster of players, and hence would have a higher winning percentage, compared with the small-market team, assuming both teams are pursuing the same objective (i.e., maximizing profits or wins). But suppose that the large-market team is a profit-maximizer and the small-market team is a win-maximizer. This case is shown in Figure 2.6, where the revenue curve for the large-market team, TR_L, is rotated upward compared with the revenue curve for the small-market team, TR_S. Again, we assume they face the same costs of talent, wx. As drawn, the small-market team actually acquires more talent and, therefore, will have a higher expected winning percentage. Specifically, $x_S^{**} > x_L^{*}$ and so $WP\left(x_S^{**}\right) > WP\left(x_L^{*}\right)$. This will not necessarily be the outcome—it depends on the shapes and locations of the revenue curves—but the point is that a small-market team can compete on the field of play with a large-market team if the former pursues a win-maximization strategy while the latter pursues a profit-maximization strategy. This is not the only way a small-market team can be competitive in a league with unequal resources, however; Chapter 8 considers another possibility.[10]

As a final point, we have specified a team's total revenue here as depending on its own winning percentage, which seems to be a reasonable assumption, but is that the only thing fans care about? Certainly, fans who have a rooting

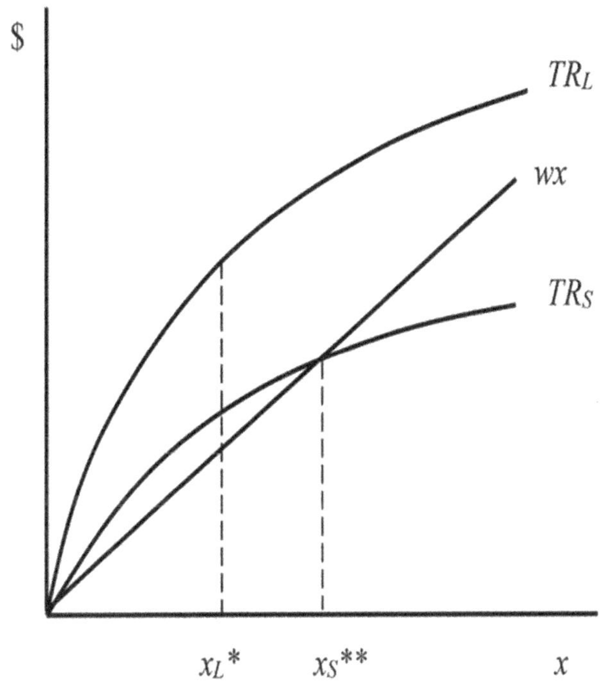

Figure 2.6 *Profit-maximizing, large-market team compared with win-maximizing, small-market team*

interest in a team want that team to do well, and there is abundant evidence that attendance increases with a team's performance on the field. However, the Uncertainty of Outcome Hypothesis (UOH) referred to in Chapter 1 contends that fan interest is highest when the outcome of a contest is uncertain (Rottenberg, 1956; Neale, 1964). Thus, the winning percentage of a team's opponents may also enter its revenue function. Further, since competition in sports is a zero-sum game, whenever one team wins, its opponent must lose, and so if one team acts to improve its winning percentage, the winning percentage of all other teams must collectively decrease. An implication of this interdependency is that from the league's perspective (reflecting the collective interests of teams), it will probably not be desirable for any one team or small group of teams to become too dominant. We pursue the implications of this idea in detail in Chapter 6.

TEAMS THAT SIMULTANEOUSLY MAXIMIZE PROFITS AND WINS

We finally consider the case of a "hybrid" team that simultaneously pursues the objectives of win *and* profit maximization.[11] To examine this possibility, let the total revenue of the team now depend on both output (attendance) and winning percentage, or $TR(Q,WP(x))$.[12] In other words, we combine the above approaches in recognition that teams make multiple choices that affect revenue, some concerning off-field decisions (marketing, concessions, scheduling) and some concerning on-field decisions (talent, training, coaching). If the team is a pure profit or win maximizer, it would proceed as above in choosing both Q and x. It seems entirely plausible, however, that a team would make its off-field decisions to maximize profit but its on-field decisions to maximize wins. How would this work?

First, write the expression for profit as

$$\pi = TR(Q,WP(x)) - C(Q) - wx \tag{2.7}$$

which includes both variable (game-related) costs, $C(Q)$, plus the cost of talent, wx, which is independent of Q. (Recall that wage costs were included as part of fixed costs, FC, in the analysis of ticket sales above.) Now maximize this expression with respect to Q, taking as given the composition of the roster, x. Proceeding as above, the team sets marginal revenue equal to marginal cost:

$$MR(Q,WP(x)) = MC(Q) \tag{2.8}$$

Note that the cost of talent does not enter this condition because it is additive and independent of Q. Condition (2.8) defines optimal output as a function of x, or $Q^*(x)$, where Q^* is increasing in x assuming that marginal revenue is increasing in x. In other words, this is the profit-maximizing level of attendance given a particular make-up of the team, and attendance increases as the talent level rises.

Now substitute $Q^*(x)$ into the profit expression in equation (2.7) to get *maximum profit* as a function of x:

$$\pi^*(x) = TR(Q^*(x),WP(x)) - C(Q^*(x)) - wx \tag{2.9}$$

Regarding the choice of x, we could imagine ownership of the team instructing the general manager (or whoever makes decisions about on-field personnel) to put the best possible team on the field, subject to a fixed budget. In this case, the general manager's problem would be to choose x to

$$\text{Maximize } WP(x) \text{ subject to } \pi^*(x) \geq \pi_0 \tag{2.10}$$

where π_0 is the minimum acceptable profit for the team, which may be zero or some positive amount. The solution to this problem depends on how $\pi^*(x)$ varies with x. The likely relationship is shown graphically in Figure 2.7, where profit is shown as first rising and then falling in x, with the maximum occurring at x^*.

Given this configuration of the profit function, if the team also made its on-field decisions to maximize profit, it would obviously choose point x^*.[13] This choice would maximize the overall profit of the team in the sense that it would be simultaneously choosing Q and x to maximize profit. If, however, the team chooses x to maximize wins subject to the budget constraint, it would pick point x^{**}, the largest value of x that just allows the team to meet its target profit level of π_0. A team that chooses x to maximize wins will therefore perform better on the field than one that chooses x to maximize profit. Further, the lower the target profit the team owner is willing to accept (i.e., the lower is π_0), the larger will be the budget for talent, and hence, the better the team's roster will be. Clearly, the economic objectives of the ownership of a team can significantly affect its on-field performance, as many fans no doubt can attest!

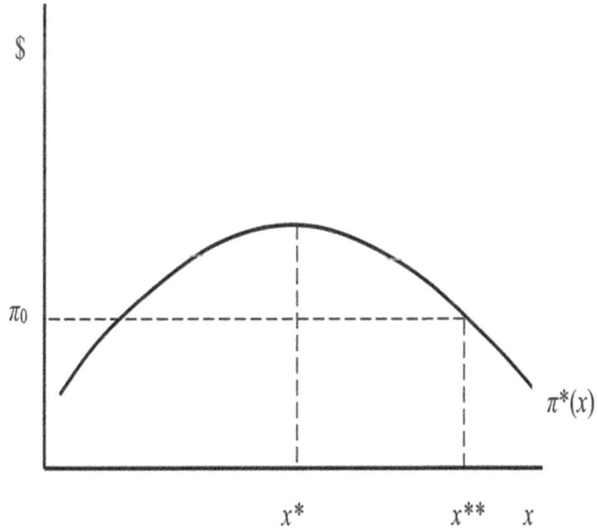

Figure 2.7 Talent choice of a joint profit- and win maximizing team

SUMMARY

This chapter examined the decisions of sports teams based on the assumption that they behave like business firms. We first assumed that teams maximize profit, and interpreted the choice variable of teams as "games supplied," or attendance. The economic theory of monopoly was used to describe the resulting behavior of such teams. We then considered the alternative possibility that the objective of teams is to maximize wins subject to a zero-profit constraint, rather than maximizing profits. In this sense, win-maximizing teams act like non-profit firms. We argued here that the appropriate choice is not games supplied, but winning percentage as determined by the team's investment in talent. Not surprisingly, we showed that win-maximizing teams will be more successful on the field than profit-maximizing teams, all else being equal. Thus, small-market teams that pursue win-maximization can compete with large-market teams that pursue profit maximization.

Finally, we considered a hybrid team that maximizes wins with respect to output and pricing decisions (off-field management) but maximizes wins with respect to talent acquisition (on-field management). Perhaps that model best reflects the behavior of many professional teams, which operate like businesses off the field while leaving on-field decisions to managers and coaches.

EXERCISES

2.1. Consider a team that chooses attendance Q (measured in millions) to maximize profit. Let the inverse demand curve be

$$P = 210 - 20Q$$

which has the associated marginal revenue function equal to

$$MR = 210 - 40Q$$

Also, let the total cost function be given by

$$TC = 200 + 10Q$$

for which the marginal cost is $MC = 10$. Find the team's optimal output, price, and profit.

2.2. Now, consider a team that chooses its winning percentage, WP. Let the team's total revenue as a function of WP be given by

$$TR = 100WP - 50WP^2$$

Also, let its total cost function be

$$TC = 60WP$$

The resulting marginal revenue and marginal costs are

$$MR = 100 - 100WP$$

$$MC = 60$$

(a) Find the winning percentage that maximizes profit.
(b) Find the highest winning percentage that just allows the team to cover its costs. Compare your answer to (a).

2.3. Finally, consider a team with a profit expression given by

$$\pi = 40WP \cdot Q^{1/2} - 10WP \cdot Q - 60WP^2$$

(a) Find the profit-maximizing level of Q. Does it depend on P?
(b) Using your answer to (a), derive the winning percentage that just allows the team to break even.

NOTES

1. Broadcast revenues will be ignored, but presumably can also be linked to output and thus can be examined in the same manner as ticket sales. See Blair (2012, Chapter 7) and Szymanski (2009, Chapter 5) for discussions.
2. This is referred to as the *inverse* demand because the price is written as a decreasing function of output. This reflects the convention that demand curves are usually drawn with price P on the vertical axis and quantity Q on the horizontal axis, as shown in Figure 2.1.
3. The use of percentage changes ensures that elasticity is free of the units by which P and Q are measured.
4. Thus, marginal cost equals average cost.
5. Season attendance is also limited by the fixed number of home games in the schedule.
6. This specification is consistent with the literature. See, for example, El-Hodiri and Quirk (1971) and Dietl et al. (2009).
7. We examine the strategic interdependence of team decisions in Chapter 5.
8. See Bradbury (2007, Ch. 6) for an assessment of the importance of this advantage.

9. Costs may not be the same. Although the market for players is national and hence should be the same for all teams, local costs (e.g., wages for non-player personnel and taxes) may be higher in larger market areas. If large-market teams also face higher costs, then their prices would still be higher, but their output and profit may not be higher compared with small-market teams.
10. See, in particular, the discussion of the Moneyball Hypothesis.
11. See, for example, Késenne (2000, 2006) and Dietl et al. (2009).
12. More specifically, we would write total revenue as $P(Q,WP)\cdot Q$, where the inverse demand curve $P(Q,WP)$ is decreasing in output but increasing in winning percentage. In other words, it is negatively sloped in output Q but shifts upward in winning percentage WP.
13. Formally, maximizing equation (2.9) with respect to x yields

$$d\pi^* / dx = (dTR / dQ)(dQ^* / dx) + (dTR / dWP)(dWP / dx)$$

$$-(dC / dQ^*)(dQ^* / dx) - w = 0$$

The first and third terms on the left-hand side drop out given profit maximization over the choice of Q (i.e., given equation (2.8)). That leaves the second and fourth terms, which are the marginal revenue and marginal cost of x, respectively. Together they equal zero at x^*.

3. Pricing of sporting events

This chapter expands on the previous one by examining in more detail the pricing of sporting events. The previous chapter focused on the pricing and output decisions of a monopolistic team under the differing assumptions of profit maximization and win maximization, subject to a budget constraint. Here, we delve more deeply into the pricing behavior of teams as business firms, focusing on a monopolistic market as compared with a competitive market, where the latter serves as a benchmark to assess the welfare losses from monopoly pricing.

We then turn to more sophisticated pricing policies by a monopolistic team, policies that are aimed at extracting greater profit from customers. These policies involve different forms of *price discrimination*, which means the charging of different prices for different types of consumers. There are several forms of price discrimination that differ depending on what differences the firm knows about or can observe across consumers, and how (or if) it is able to segment that market into distinct sub-markets based on these differences. Examples of price discrimination include senior citizen discounts, two-part pricing (an entry fee plus per-unit prices inside the stadium), and quantity discounts (season ticket packages).

The chapter concludes by examining the practice of ticket scalping, or the resale of tickets by consumers. The specific questions to be addressed are why it happens and whether or not it should be legal.

COMPETITIVE VERSUS MONOPOLISTIC PRICING

We begin the analysis of pricing decisions by distinguishing between competitive and monopolistic pricing in an ordinary market setting. Here, we only consider the setting of a single price. One reason for doing this is to motivate the use of price discrimination as a way of increasing profits.

As shown in Chapter 2, a monopolist maximizes profit by equating marginal revenue and marginal cost, which determines output, Q_M, and price, P_M. Figure 3.1 shows this outcome in comparison to the output (Q_C) and price (P_C) that would arise in a competitive market setting with the same

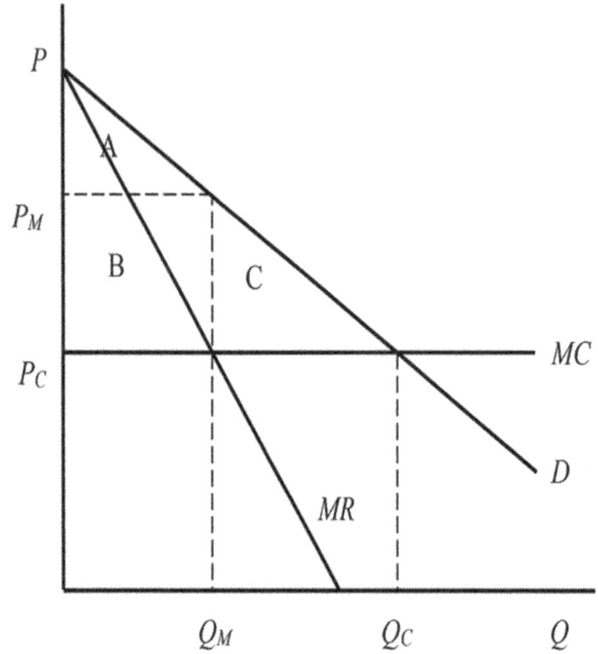

Figure 3.1 *Monopolistic versus competitive pricing*

demand and cost conditions. Clearly, output is higher ($Q_C > Q_M$) and price is lower ($P_C < P_M$) under the competitive market structure.

The graph also shows that social welfare is maximized under competitive pricing, as measured here by the *consumer surplus*, which is defined as the aggregate difference between what consumers are willing to pay for the good in question (as determined by the demand curve) and what they actually have to pay for it. In the competitive market outcome, that surplus is shown by the triangle comprising areas A, B, and C in the graph, which is the maximum potential amount. In contrast, under monopoly pricing, consumer surplus shrinks to the area shown by triangle A. Area B is now the monopolist's profit (exclusive of fixed costs), while area C is a deadweight loss, representing the forgone benefits from those units of output between Q_M and Q_C that are not produced under the monopolistic market structure. It is this loss, plus the transfer of consumer surplus to profit (area B), that motivates calls for the regulation of monopoly.

We argued in Chapter 2 that professional sports teams have monopoly power in part by virtue of barriers to entry that leagues have put in place. Despite the apparently detrimental effects of these barriers on fan welfare, courts have generally exempted professional sports leagues from antitrust laws. The next chapter, which examines league organization in detail, and later Chapter 12, which explicitly considers antitrust laws as applied to sports leagues, discuss some possible justifications for this exemption.

PRICE DISCRIMINATION

The analysis of monopoly in this and the previous chapters has assumed that the monopolist sets a single price for its output. However, in some cases, the monopolist can increase its profit by departing from this constraint and setting different prices for different types of consumers. This practice is called *price discrimination*. As will be clear from the examples, sports teams (and indeed most retailers) routinely do this, though often in ways that are not obvious.

Before proceeding, it is important to point out what is *not* price discrimination. If a team sets different prices for, say, bleacher seats versus box seats, that would not be price discrimination because the "product" being sold is different. Watching a game from the distant and cramped bleacher seats is a very different experience from watching it from spacious and comfortable seats close to the field of play. Another example is the differential pricing of seats in the sun versus the shade during daytime contests, as is often done for European sporting events. In contrast, giving senior citizen or child discounts for the same seats *is* a form of price discrimination because these consumers are being sold the identical product as consumers who are charged the full price. In this case, the price difference reflects differences in demand between different types of consumers.

The motivation for a monopolist to engage in price discrimination can easily be seen in Figure 3.1. As argued above, the single-price monopolist is able to convert some amount of the consumer surplus under a competitive market (areas A+B+C in the graph) to profit (area B) by restricting output from Q_C to Q_M and correspondingly raising the price from P_C to P_M. However, the monopolist is not able to capture areas A and C—as noted, area A remains as consumer surplus while area C is forgone. This is partly a consequence of the single-price assumption, which requires moving upward along the demand curve to raise the price for all consumers. However, the monopolist may be able to do better if it can set different prices for different consumers.

The most extreme form of this strategy would be the setting of a different price for every consumer, called *first-degree* (or *perfect*) price discrimination. Think of each point along the demand curve in Figure 3.1 as a distinct consumer, with the height of the curve representing how much that individual is willing to pay for a unit of the good. If the monopolist can observe that value for each consumer and can prevent resale of the good across consumers (i.e., can prevent purchasers of cheap tickets from reselling them to high-value consumers), then it could theoretically capture all of the consumer surplus by setting a unique price for each consumer corresponding to that person's willingness to pay. Under this solution, the monopolist would actually produce up to Q_C, the competitive (and efficient) level of output, with the entire area, A+B+C, becoming profit.

Of course, this outcome would be undesirable from the perspective of consumers, but it is also unrealistic because of the unobservability of individual consumer valuations. We will see, however, that there are feasible strategies that do allow the monopolist to capture some portion of areas A and C. These strategies involve *second-* and *third-degree* price discrimination strategies. We discuss some of these strategies in the following sections, beginning with third-degree price discrimination.

Third-degree Price Discrimination

Under what is called third-degree price discrimination, the monopolist is able to divide the market into distinct and observable segments and pursue a different pricing strategy within each segment. Senior citizen discounts are an example. The specific requirements for successful third-degree price discrimination are: (1) distinguishable market segments (enforced by the requirement to show a form of ID, say); (2) a different demand elasticity within each market segment (for reasons to be discussed); and (3) inability of buyers to resell the good across segments (enforced, for example, by issuing different colored tickets).

Let us consider a market comprising two segments whose inverse demand functions are $P_1(Q_1)$ and $P_2(Q_2)$. The total profit from serving both types of consumers, possibly with different prices for each, is given by

$$\pi = P_1(Q_1) \cdot Q_1 + P_2(Q_2) \cdot Q_2 - C(Q_1 + Q_2) \tag{3.1}$$

where $C(Q_1 + Q_2)$ is the cost of the overall output. For each segment, the monopolist will equate marginal revenue to marginal cost, or

$$P_i + (dP_i / dQ_i) \cdot Q_i = dC / dQ_i, \quad i = 1,2 \tag{3.2}$$

Because the marginal cost is the same for both segments (given that the good being sold to each segment is identical), it follows that the marginal revenues must also be equal:

$$P_1 + (dP_1 / dQ_1) \cdot Q_1 = P_2 + (dP_2 / dQ_2) \cdot Q_2 \tag{3.3}$$

We now apply the formula relating marginal revenue to elasticity as derived in the previous chapter (see equation (2.5)). This yields the condition

$$P_1\left(1+\frac{1}{\varepsilon_1}\right)=P_2\left(1+\frac{1}{\varepsilon_2}\right) \tag{3.4}$$

We next ask when it is optimal for the monopolist to set a different price in the two sub-markets, given that it is feasible to segment them. Let us conjecture that the higher price is set in market one, or $P_1 > P_2$. Then by equation (3.4), it must be true that

$$\left(1+\frac{1}{\varepsilon_1}\right)<\left(1+\frac{1}{\varepsilon_2}\right)$$

which implies that $\varepsilon_1>\varepsilon_2$, or, given that the elasticities are negative, $|\varepsilon_1|<|\varepsilon_2|$. This says that the demand in segment one is more inelastic, or less price-sensitive, compared with segment two. This makes intuitive sense. The monopolist should set a higher price in the market where consumers will reduce their demand less as the price rises. Notice, finally, that setting the same price in both (all) market segments is always a possibility under this strategy and would, in fact, be the optimal policy if $\varepsilon_1=\varepsilon_2$; that is, if the demand curves have the same elasticity. In this case, segmentation, even if feasible, would not be profitable.

Second-degree Price Discrimination

Suppose that the monopolist cannot divide the market for its product into distinctly observable segments, and indeed cannot observe any differences across consumers. Surprisingly, it turns out that price discrimination may still be possible. This strategy, referred to as *second-degree* price discrimination, requires the monopolist to induce different types of consumers to reveal their unobservable valuations by means of "self-selection." The monopolist accomplishes this feat by offering a price schedule, or menu, that includes multiple options from which consumers are free to choose. We will see that by appropriately structuring the options, the monopolist can segment consumers according to their demands. We will illustrate this by describing two commonly used examples of such a strategy: two-part pricing and quantity discounts.

Two-part pricing

Under two-part pricing, a consumer has to pay a fixed fee up-front for the "right" to purchase individual units of the good, which are then available at a set per-unit price. Such a pricing scheme is commonly used for amusement parks,[1] where there is an entry fee to get into the park, and then a fixed price is charged for each ride, event, or food item purchased within the park. Public utilities also sometimes use this sort of pricing scheme. Most big-time college basketball and football programs likewise charge fans large fees up front (sometimes euphemistically called "donations") for the right to buy individual game tickets.

To see how such a pricing strategy works, we write the total cost of purchasing Q units of the good in question as

$$TC = F + P \cdot Q \tag{3.5}$$

where F is the up-front fee and P is the price per unit of the good. Suppose the monopolist faces the downward-sloping demand curve in Figure 3.1, which, for the sake of argument, we will initially treat as the demand of a single consumer. Under a single-price policy as discussed above, which, in essence, involved setting $F = 0$, the monopolist maximized profit by setting a price equal to P_M and sold Q_M units to the consumer. In so doing, it earned a profit of area B but, as we saw, that strategy left areas A and C "on the table." The question here is whether, by optimally choosing F and P, the monopolist can capture some of that forgone profit.

Let us first conjecture that the monopolist sets $P = P_C = MC$; that is, it sets the competitive price for individual units of the good. After having paid F, the consumer will therefore purchase Q_C units, the amount that would be sold in a competitive market. Note that the monopolist earns zero profit from the sale of these individual units because P_C equals marginal (and average) cost, which leaves the entire triangle, A + B + C, as consumer surplus. Here is where the fixed fee comes in—because the consumer can only realize this surplus by paying the "entrance fee," F, she will be willing to pay *up to that amount for the right to purchase the good in question*. Thus, by setting F equal to area A + B + C, the monopolist is able to replicate the outcome under first-degree price discrimination. That is, it captures all of the potential consumer surplus as profit.

This outcome is unrealistic, however, because of the assumption of a single type of consumer. In reality, consumers will vary in their demand for the good, which complicates the optimal strategy for the monopolist. To see how, suppose now that there are two types of consumers whose demand functions are represented by D_1 and D_2 in Figure 3.2. We may think of consumer two as the higher demander because he or she is willing to pay more for each quantity

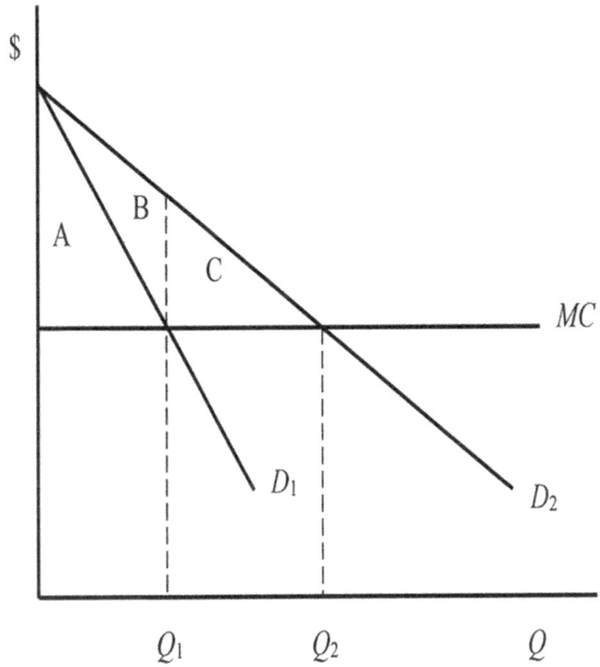

Figure 3.2 *Optimal two-part pricing with two types of consumers*

compared with consumer one. If the monopolist can distinguish the two types, it would set $P = MC$ for units of the good as above, but it would set a different entry fee for each consumer. Specifically, it would set F_1, the entry fee for a type-1 consumer, equal to area A in Figure 3.2, and F_2, the entry fee for a type-2 consumer, equal to area A+B+C. Under this scheme, the monopolist would again replicate the perfect discrimination result, and would thereby earn total profit equal to 2A+B+C.

But suppose that the monopolist cannot distinguish between the two types of customers, though we assume that it knows the number (or fraction) of each type in the population of potential consumers. In this case, it must set a single unit price, P, and an entry fee, F, for all consumers. Let us again suppose that the monopolist sets the same unit price as above; that is, $P = MC$.[2] Thus, low-demand (type 1) consumers, if they choose to pay the entry fee, will consume Q_1 units of the good, while high-demand (type 2) consumers, if they choose to pay the fee, will consume Q_2 units. According to the above logic, the maximum fee that each type of consumer will pay is his or her consumer surplus given these consumption levels. Low-demanders will therefore pay up to area A, while high-demanders will pay up to area A+B+C. However, the monopolist must set a single fee that applies to both types. It will therefore pick one of those two amounts.

Suppose first that the monopolist sets the single fee equal to area A. (Note that this is the lowest F that it would set.) In this case, both types of consumers will pay the fee, and, assuming equal numbers of each type (say, one of each), total profit will be 2A. Under this fee, low-demanders will be indifferent between entering and not entering, while high-demanders will enter and enjoy a surplus of area B+C. The total cost to low- and high-demanders, respectively, is $TC_1 = F + PQ_1$ and $TC_2 = F + PQ_2$, and the resulting cost per unit of output is equal to $TC_i / Q_i = (F / Q_i) + P$. This per-unit cost has the characteristic that

$$\frac{F}{Q_1} + P > \frac{F}{Q_2} + P \tag{3.6}$$

given $Q_2 > Q_1$. Thus, low-demanders pay a higher per-unit cost; it is in this sense that the strategy involves price discrimination.

Alternatively, the monopolist can set the fee equal to area A+B+C, the highest amount that would still attract type-2 customers.[3] In this case, only high-demanders will enter, and the total profit will be area A+B+C. In this scenario, the monopolist extracts all of the consumer surplus from high-demanders, but it forgoes the surplus from low-demanders (area A). Thus, price discrimination does not occur under this strategy.

Clearly, neither of these two strategies allows the monopolist to capture the full potential surplus from the two types of consumers. That is the cost of imperfect information, reflecting the monopolist's inability to distinguish between the two types. Further, either strategy may be profit-maximizing depending on the magnitude of the areas. In particular, setting F = A—that is, serving both types—is preferred if 2A > A + B + C, or if A>B+C; while setting F = A + B + C—serving only type-2s—is preferred if the converse is true. The choice depends on both the configuration of the two demand curves and, in the most general case, on the number of each type of consumer in the market. We have assumed an equal proportion of the two types, but a greater number of high-demand types will work in the direction of choosing the high-fee strategy, and vice versa.

As for social welfare, when F = A, there is no welfare loss because both types of consumers are in the market, so all potential gains are realized as profit or consumer surplus. However, when F = A + B + C, low-demanders are excluded, so area A for low-demand types is a dead-weight loss.

Quantity discounts

A second form of second-degree price discrimination consists of *quantity discounts*, such as when the monopolist offers customers pre-packaged bundles of the good at a set price, rather than offering any quantity at a fixed per-unit price. Think of soft drinks, for example, which are sold in containers of various sizes, with prices set by the container rather than by the ounce. A 12-ounce can might sell for $1.20, while a 64-ounce bottle might sell for $2.50. The price per ounce is therefore 10¢ for the can but a little less than 4¢ for the bottle. Thus, the consumer receives a quantity discount by purchasing the larger package, but is "forced" to buy more. This same principle obviously applies to season or multi-game ticket packages that offer discounts on a per-game basis. What makes this a potentially profitable strategy for the monopolist?

To answer this question, let us again consider two types of consumers of sporting events—those who value single games only, and those who value multiple games. Specifically, suppose that single-game fans are willing to pay a dollars for the first game and zero for any additional games, whereas multi-game fans are willing to pay a dollars for the first game, b dollars for the second game, and zero dollars for any additional games, where $a > b > 0$. Thus, both types of fans value the first game equally (a dollars), but the multi-game fan values the second game at a positive, though lesser, amount (b dollars). These demand curves are shown graphically in Figure 3.3. For simplicity,

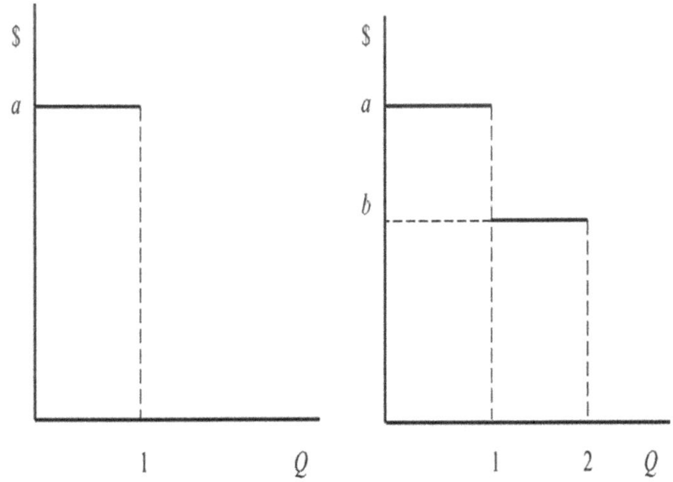

Figure 3.3 Quantity discount pricing

suppose that the marginal cost to the team of "supplying" games is zero.[4] The question is, how should the team price games?

Two single-price strategies are possible: $P = a$ and $P = b$. Under the first policy, fans of each type will attend exactly one game. Assuming one of each type (i.e., equal numbers), total attendance and profits from this strategy are 2 and $2a$, respectively. These are shown in the first row of Table 3.1. Alternatively, the team could set a single-game price of b, which is the highest price that would induce the single-game fan to attend one game and the multi-game fan to attend two games. This would result in attendance of 3 and profits of $3b$, as shown in the second row of Table 3.1.

Either of these strategies could yield greater profits; it depends on the relative magnitudes of a and b. Specifically, the high-price strategy (i.e., $P = a$) would be preferred if $a > 3b/2$ (again, assuming one of each type of fan), and the low-price strategy ($P = b$) would be preferred if the reverse is true. Finally, note that neither strategy allows the monopolist to capture all of the consumer surplus. Under the high-price strategy, the multi-game fan's value of attending a second game is forgone, while under the low-price strategy, both fans enjoy a surplus of $a - b$ from their first game, as shown in Table 3.1 in the column labeled *CS*.

Now consider a third possible pricing strategy: setting a single-game ticket price of P, and a season (2-game) ticket price of P_s. Obviously, the season ticket is targeted at the multi-game consumer, and so it should be set to extract the maximum willingness-to-pay from that consumer for two games. Thus, $P_s = a + b$. And since the single-game price is aimed at the other consumer, $P = a$. Note that this strategy resembles the soft-drink example from above in the sense that the per-game price of the season ticket, $(a + b)/2$, is less than the single-game price of a, thus representing a quantity discount.[5]

This combined pricing package yields a profit of $2a + b$, which strictly dominates either of the single-price options,[6] while the attendance of 3 is the

Table 3.1 Comparison of pricing strategies

Strategy	Attendance	π	*CS*	π +*CS*	*Efficient?*
Single-game price: $P=a$	2	$2a$	0	$2a$	No
Single-game price: $P=b$	3	$3b$	$2(a-b)$	$2a+b$	Yes
Single-game price: $P=a$ Season ticket price: $P_s=a+b$	3	$2a+b$	0	$2a+b$	Yes

same as under the lower single-price option. From the monopolist's perspective, the combined package clearly dominates because it succeeds in extracting all of the consumer surplus as profit (i.e., the monopolist's profit equals the total area under the two demand curves in Figure 3.3). Although this perfect-discrimination outcome will not generally be possible as the number of consumer types and the number of games increase, the firm can also expand its offerings in an effort to extract as much consumer surplus as possible. For example, most teams offer various multi-game ticket packages.

The welfare effects of monopolistic price discrimination, in whatever form it takes, depend on whether the chosen strategy extracts more surplus from consumers already in the market or attracts new consumers relative to traditional monopoly pricing. For example, welfare in the preceding example consists of the sum of the consumer and producer surpluses. Under the first single-price strategy ($P = a$), consumer surplus is zero, so welfare is simply the monopolist's profit of $2a$. However, the potential consumer surplus from the second game for the multi-game consumer is forgone, and so it represents a deadweight loss. Under the second single-price strategy $(P = b)$, by contrast, both consumers enjoy a surplus of $a - b$ for the first game, and the multi-game fan also attends the second game, though with no surplus. Thus, overall welfare is the monopolist's profit plus the total consumer surplus, or $3b + 2(a - b) = 2a + b$, which in this example is the maximum amount available. This outcome, therefore, maximizes welfare.

Finally, under the combined pricing strategy, there is no consumer surplus, so welfare consists entirely of the monopolist's profit, which in our example is equal to the maximum amount available. Thus, this strategy improves welfare over the first single-price strategy because it raises attendance from 2 to 3 by inducing the multi-game fan to attend the second game.[7] It does not improve welfare over the second single-price strategy, which is maximized, but instead extracts all of the surplus from the multi-game fan in the form of profit. Thus, welfare is maximized, but all of the gains are realized by the seller. These results are summarized in Table 3.1.

TICKET SCALPING

The final pricing issue that we examine is *ticket scalping*, which is defined as the resale of a ticket for a price greater than its face value. We specifically consider two questions regarding this practice: first, why would a fan pay more than the face value for a ticket (in other words, why is ticket scalping possible)? And second, why is scalping illegal in some jurisdictions? Not surprisingly, the answers to these questions turn out to be related.

Figure 3.4 shows the demand and supply for tickets to a particular sporting or entertainment event. As usual, the demand curve is downward sloping,

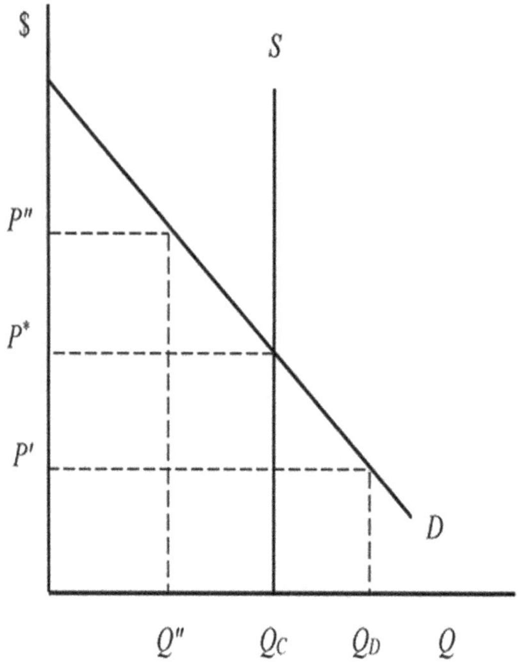

Figure 3.4 *Ticket scalping: P* = market-clearing price; P' = face value of ticket*

but the supply curve is now shown as vertical because it is fixed (in the short run) at the capacity of the stadium. The equilibrium price, P^*, occurs at the intersection such that the quantity demanded is exactly equal to the seating capacity, Q_C. At this price, every seat is filled, and no one who is willing to pay that price is turned away. Why, then, would the price ever deviate from this market-clearing level?

Consider first the behavior of a monopolistic promoter of the event in question. The situation resembles that discussed in Chapter 2 for a monopolist facing a capacity constraint. Assuming here that the marginal cost of admitting one more spectator is zero, profit is maximized when marginal revenue equals zero. This may occur at a Q that is either smaller or larger than the capacity, Q_C. If it is smaller, that point would be optimal, and the price would be set at the corresponding point on the demand curve. In this case, $P > P^*$, and the arena would not be filled (i.e., the capacity constraint would not be binding). Conversely, if the profit-maximizing Q is larger than Q_C, then the constraint is binding, and the optimum would occur at Q_C and P^*. The important point is that in neither case is P intentionally set *below* P^* by a monopolistic supplier.

Let us suppose, however, that for some reason the price *is* set below the market-clearing price, say at P', resulting in an excess demand of $Q_D - Q_C$. We will consider possible reasons for this "mispricing" shortly. In practice, this situation will manifest itself in waiting lines for admission, with the limited number of tickets typically being allocated on a first-come, first-served basis.[8] In other words, rationing by waiting replaces price rationing.

Now consider a consumer on the segment of the demand curve between Q_C and Q_D who values the ticket more than the price she actually has to pay, P', but values it less than anyone on the demand curve to the left of Q_C, some of whom were not able to get a ticket. (This must be true because, for each person to the right of Q_C who gets a ticket, there must be one to the left who does not, given the fixed supply.) Consider, for example, the person at Q'', who is willing to pay P'' for a ticket. It should be clear that there is room for a mutually beneficial bargain whereby the person at Q'' buys a ticket from the person to the right of Q_C who obtained one. Indeed, anyone to the right of Q_C who acquires a ticket can always find someone to the left of Q_C who values it more, and if all such transactions actually happen, all of the tickets will end up in the hands of consumers on the demand curve to the left of Q_C.[9] As a result of these secondary market sales, an efficient equilibrium is achieved whereby the tickets are all allocated to the highest-valuing consumers. In other words, the outcome that would have occurred if the price had initially been set at P^* is in fact attained through scalping. This process of market equilibration through resales is called arbitrage.

The preceding analysis answers the question of why someone would pay a price above the face value of the ticket. It is because the face value is below the market-clearing price of P^*, which makes resale profitable. The analysis also shows that ticket resale serves a potentially useful allocative function; namely, it corrects for the price having been set too low initially. This conclusion, however, makes laws against ticket scalping somewhat puzzling. Before attempting to resolve that puzzle, we first need to ask why the price of the tickets (the face value) may have been set too low in the first place, thus triggering the need for resale. We suggest two possible reasons.

The first is that it may have been done accidentally because demand is uncertain, and so the price had to be set before actual demand could be known. If this is the reason, then we would expect that, given the fixed stadium capacity, the price would sometimes be set too high (resulting in unused capacity) and sometimes too low (resulting in excess demand). Restaurants face the same problem given the time-varying demand for their product. Consequently, there are empty tables at some times and waiting lines at others. Restaurants try to address this problem by varying their staff during the day (i.e., altering their labor input) and by offering off-peak pricing (for example, "early-bird" specials). However, menu costs and the fixed capital input (i.e., the size of the establishment) prevent a perfect solution.

Given this logic, if restaurant-goers could purchase and then resell table access over time, an efficient inter-temporal solution to the "restaurant problem" could be possible. Of course, this is not done in practice, precisely because the "good" being sold is not identical—that is, people do not equally value meals at different times of the day, which is what causes peak and off-peak demand in the first place. In contrast, the good being resold in the ticket scalping example *is* homogeneous—namely, a seat in the arena for a particular event. The exact analog to ticket scalping in the restaurant example would be if diners arrived at their ideal time and, finding the restaurant full, bribed an already-seated party to give up their table.

The preceding argument just reinforces the puzzling nature of laws against ticket scalping. What possible justification could be advanced for preventing the resale of tickets as a way to equilibrate the market in the face of uncertain demand? A possible answer is dissatisfaction with the market outcome. In order to make this argument, it is first necessary to review what price rationing really means.

When there is a scarce resource (such as stadium seating) that needs to be allocated among competing users, some mechanism must be devised to determine which of the demanders gets the resource. This is the fundamental economic problem in the presence of scarcity. Price rationing accomplishes this by splitting the demand curve into two segments: those who value the resource at least as much as the price, and those who value it less. The former thus gain access to the resource while the latter do not. This mechanism works perfectly in allocating the resource provided that the price is set so that the number of demanders whose value exceeds the price exactly equals the number of units of the resource available. Of course, this is accomplished at the market-clearing, or equilibrium, price, given by P^* in Figure 3.4.

The problem with price rationing, however, is that it determines who gains access to the resource in question based solely on willingness to pay (as embodied by the demand function), which is dependent in part on consumers' *ability* to pay (i.e., their income). Thus, low-wealth consumers disproportionately comprise the set of consumers who are on the excluded segment of the demand curve and therefore do not gain access to the resource. This is why society often departs from price rationing for certain goods deemed to be necessities, such as food, health care, education, and housing. For these types of goods, governments enact policies that depart from pure price rationing as a way to allocate them in a "fair" way.

What does this have to do with ticket scalping? One argument for making scalping illegal is to ensure that some consumers on the demand curve on the segment to the right of Q_C can get tickets *and actually use them* rather than turning around and reselling them. Which consumers will, in fact, get tickets under this rule will depend on what type of non-price rationing mechanism is used. Under rationing by waiting, for example, one supposes that those consumers who are willing to wait the longest will tend to be lower-income individuals (for example, because they have lower time costs), thus ensuring that at least some fans from the lower end of the demand curve will actually get into the stadium.[10]

Purely profit-maximizing teams or concert promoters, however, are presumably unconcerned with the make-up of those fans that attend games in person, and so would endeavor to set their price as close as possible to the market-clearing level. This ensures that the seller, rather than scalpers, captures the profit from ticket sales. Demand uncertainties will nevertheless lead to some underpricing (as well as some overpricing), and making scalping illegal will allow (require) some low-income consumers to acquire and use tickets. For the case of big-time college sports, and possibly some altruistic entertainers, profit-maximization may not be the controlling factor, and so a conscious strategy of setting the price below the market-clearing level and thus relying on non-price rationing may be a way of generating a more diverse, and perhaps more raucous, audience.

SUMMARY

This chapter focused on the pricing decisions of teams as business firms whose sole objective is to maximize profit. We first examined the difference between competitive and monopoly pricing as a means of depicting the welfare effect of monopoly pricing. This consisted of a transfer of consumer surplus to profit, plus a deadweight loss arising from the restricted output of the monopolist. The chapter then turned to an analysis of various forms of price discrimination by a monopolist, which involves setting multiple prices based on differences across consumers. We showed that the firm's objective in undertaking this strategy was both to capture more consumer surplus and to recover some of the deadweight loss under the single-price policy.

We first examined third-degree price discrimination, which involves segmenting the market based on observable features of consumers that are thought to be correlated with variations in the elasticity of demand. The result is that the price is set higher in the segment where demand is more inelastic under the condition that resale of tickets is not possible. Such a strategy underlies policies such as senior citizen discounts.

The discussion then turned to second-degree price discrimination, which involves offering consumers a "menu" of pricing options (a "price schedule") from which consumers choose their most-preferred option. The menu is structured so as to induce consumers with different demands to sort themselves (i.e., to self-select) in a way that enhances the seller's profit. We explicitly examined two examples of this strategy: two-part pricing and quantity discounts, both of which are often used in the pricing of sporting events.

The chapter concluded by examining the practice of ticket scalping, or the resale of tickets by consumers at prices above face value. We first derived the basis for the practice, and then discussed the desirability of laws preventing ticket scalping. We concluded that allowing ticket scalping may, in some cases, be a socially desirable way to use non-price rationing as a means of allowing lower-income fans access to sporting events or other entertainment venues. Consequently, this is not a strategy that profit-maximizing providers would be likely to pursue in a conscious way.

EXERCISES

3.1. Consider a team that can segment its fan base into distinct markets whose inverse demand functions are given by

$$P_1 = 25 - .0001Q$$

$$P_2 = 50 - .0002Q$$

The relevant marginal revenue functions are given by

$$MR_1 = 25 - .0002Q$$

$$MR_2 = 50 - .0004Q$$

Also, suppose that the firm's total cost is $TC = 5Q$, which makes its marginal cost $MC = 5$.

(a) Assuming that the team can segment the two markets and prevent resale between them, calculate the optimal quantities, Q_1^* and Q_2^*, and prices, P_1^* and P_2^*, for each market segment.

(b) Use the formula

$$\varepsilon = \frac{dQ}{dP} \cdot \frac{P}{Q}$$

to calculate the elasticities of demand at the optimal price and quantity in each market. How do they compare?

3.2. Suppose a team has 105 potential fans who may choose to attend one or more of the team's five home games in a season. Suppose that 100 of the fans would pay up to $25 to attend a game, but would pay nothing to attend a second game. The remaining five fans, however, each have the following demand schedule:

Value of 1st game: $25

Value of 2nd game: 20

Value of 3rd game: 15

Value of 4th game: 10

Value of 5th game: 5

Assume the team has zero marginal cost of supplying games.

(a) What will the team's home attendance and total revenue be if it sets a single-game price of $25?

(b) What is the maximum amount that multi-game fans would pay for a season ticket entitling them to attend all five home games?

(c) Suppose the team sets the single-game price at $25, but offers season tickets at the price you calculated in part (b). What will the team's attendance and total revenue be under this pricing scheme? Compare this to your answer in part (a).

3.3. Ten potential attendees of a sporting event have valuations that can be arrayed from the most to the least in $1 increments, starting from $10. Thus, the highest valuer is willing to pay $10 for a ticket, the next highest, $9, and so on down to $1. Suppose that the stadium only seats 5.

(a) What is the market-clearing price? (Assume that the price must be in whole dollar amounts.)

(b) Suppose the price is set at $3. How many consumers will desire to attend the event? How will the five available tickets likely be allocated?

(c) Suppose a consumer with a willingness to pay of $5 or less acquires a ticket for the $3 selling price. Describe the side transaction between this consumer and one who values the ticket at $6 or more but did not get one.

NOTES

1. This pricing scheme was first studied by Oi (1971).
2. This would not necessarily be optimal, but to keep matters simple, we will assume it is done.
3. Some reflection should convince you that the monopolist would never set F strictly between A and A+B+C.
4. The results would be the same if there were a positive but constant marginal cost for games as long as it is less than b.
5. Specifically, $(a+b)/2 < a$ because $a > b$.
6. Clearly, $2a + b > 2a$, and $2a + b > 3b$ given that $a > b$.
7. Bradbury (2007, p. 215) similarly notes that price discrimination in sports improves overall welfare, though it does so by increasing team revenue rather than consumer surplus.
8. Another rationing mechanism could be a lottery.
9. In fact, even some people to the right of Q_D, who value a ticket less than the price they would have to pay for it, P' may nevertheless buy one in anticipation of being able to resell it for a higher price, P'' say.
10. See Goldfarb (2013, pp. 282–283) for some evidence on this.

PART II

The Organization of Competition

4. Leagues as economic organizations

The previous two chapters examined the business decisions of individual teams in the exercise of their monopoly power. The next several chapters turn to the interaction of teams within a league structure. The emphasis in this chapter is on how the league, as an economic organization (or market), coordinates the behavior of teams, effectively allowing them to behave as a cartel in their business decision-making. In an ordinary market setting, this sort of collusion would allow the teams as a group to increase their profits at the expense of their customers, and would therefore trigger scrutiny under government anti-trust laws. This chapter considers whether that logic should also apply to sports leagues by asking whether cooperation among teams, as facilitated by the league, is necessarily detrimental to the interests of fans.

The analysis begins by studying the economics of imperfect competition using standard models of oligopoly, or competition among a "few" firms when there are barriers to entry. It then considers collusive behavior based on the economic theory of cartels. Although the theory predicts that cartel agreements are difficult to sustain, sports leagues have been largely successful in maintaining their monopoly position because of their formal structure. The final issue concerns the benefits of cooperation among teams in a sports league. In contrast to ordinary markets, where cooperation (collusion) is detrimental to consumer welfare, we will see that some amount of coordination among teams in a sports league is essential for the production of games. Thus, an optimal sports league involves a balance between competition and cooperation. An important welfare question, therefore, concerns whether actual league policies achieve that balance.

MODELS OF IMPERFECT COMPETITION

The preceding chapter examined the pricing and output decisions of monopolistic firms acting in isolation from one another. In reality, rival firms (teams) are in competition with one another, both on the field in pursuit of a league championship (sporting competition) and off the field in pursuit of profits (economic competition). Of course, these two objectives are intertwined, as profits generally reflect team success.[1] Further, some coordination among teams is necessary because teams cannot produce "games" in isolation. Thus, league organization is essential by the very nature of sports. But that sort of essential cooperation will unavoidably seep into the economic decisions of teams acting as profit-maximizing firms, which is where concerns about collusive business practices arise. The focus in this chapter is on how teams interact economically ("outside the lines") within the context of a multi-team market setting. Chapter 5 then turns to the nature of team interactions regarding play on the field or in the arena ("inside the lines").

Several models have been developed to portray the behavior of multiple firms within a market setting, all of which predict price and output behavior that falls somewhere between the competitive and monopolistic extremes discussed in the previous chapter. The specific outcomes of these models, however, depend on the particular assumptions that each makes about how firms compete with one another for the customer base; that is, how they interact strategically. We examine three specific models of this: the Cournot model, the Bertrand model, and a "spatial" version of the latter. Although the emphasis in this discussion will be on traditional economic theories of competition, the insights that we gain from how rival firms (teams) interact in this context will inform our treatment in the next chapter of how they interact when engaging in on-field competition.

The chapter next looks at sports leagues as cartels aimed at promoting cooperation among firms (teams). The focus will be on the question of how leagues are able to maintain a cartel when traditional theories predict that such arrangements are inherently unstable. Finally, we consider the role of leagues in facilitating "essential" cooperation among member teams.

The Cournot Model

The Cournot model of oligopoly is sometimes characterized as a model of "quantity competition." In the model, each of several firms (at least two) seeks to share the demand for a homogeneous good that they all supply. In the sports context, the good is "sporting contests," which fans can attend at each of the home arenas. For current purposes, we will assume that each firm (team) retains its entire gate receipts, that games staged by different teams are identical, and that travel costs are negligible. Thus, fans only care about price. We will relax all of these assumptions later. We first illustrate the equilibrium in this market for the case of two firms, and then generalize it to n firms. The latter analysis will allow us to show that the outcomes under perfect competition and monopoly studied in the previous chapters emerge as special cases of the Cournot model, which is one of the attractive features of that model.

Let the overall inverse demand curve for contests be given by the simple linear form

$$P = a - bQ \tag{4.1}$$

where Q is aggregate output (fan-games), and a and b are positive constants. The individual output levels supplied by the two firms are Q_1 and Q_2, so that $Q = Q_1 + Q_2$. Finally, we assume that each firm has variable costs equal to $TC_i = cQ_i$, which means that marginal cost (which equals average cost) is a constant, c.

Each firm is assumed to choose output to maximize its own profit, taking as given the output of the other firm. Thus, firm 1 chooses Q_1 to maximize

$$\pi_1 = \left[a - b\left(Q_1 + Q_2\right)\right]Q_1 - cQ_1 \tag{4.2}$$

where the term in square brackets is the price, written as a function of the summed output of the two firms. The first-order condition defining firm 1's optimal choice of Q_1 is

$$\frac{d\pi_1}{dQ_1} = a - 2bQ_1 - bQ_2 - c = 0 \tag{4.3}$$

This equation defines firm 1's *reaction function*, which determines the firm's profit-maximizing choice of Q_1 for any choice of Q_2 by firm 2. Firm 2 will solve an identical problem, which will define its reaction function to firm 1's choice of Q_1. In the Cournot equilibrium, the reaction functions must be mutually compatible, meaning that the output level that firm 1 expects firm 2 to produce is what it actually produces, and vice versa. This outcome arises when the reaction functions intersect. Analytically, the solution is found by simultaneously solving equation (4.3) along with the corresponding first-order condition for firm 2 for the two unknowns: Q_1 and Q_2.

In the simple two-firm example with identical firms, the equilibrium will be symmetric:

$$Q_1^c = Q_2^c = \frac{a - c}{3b} \tag{4.4}$$

It follows that overall industry output and price are

$$Q^c = Q_1^c + Q_2^c = \frac{2\left(a - c\right)}{3b} \tag{4.5}$$

$$P^c = a - bQ^c = \frac{a + 2c}{3} \tag{4.6}$$

It is worth comparing this outcome to the monopoly solution, which would be obtained if a single firm served the entire market with the identical demand curve. As Example 2.1 in Chapter 2 showed, this yields

$$Q_M = \frac{a-c}{2b} \tag{4.7}$$

$$P_M = \frac{a+c}{2} \tag{4.8}$$

Overall output is therefore less ($Q_M < Q^c$), and the price is higher ($P_M > P^c$), as compared with the Cournot equilibrium, a finding that makes intuitive sense. We can also compare these outcomes to a hypothetical competitive market in which the price would be bid down to marginal cost, or $P^* = c$. Setting the right-hand side of equation (4.1) equal to c and solving for Q yields equilibrium output in the competitive market setting:

$$Q^* = \frac{a-c}{b} \tag{4.9}$$

Figure 4.1 compares the various outcomes just derived, showing that the Cournot duopoly outcome is intermediate between the monopolistic and competitive outcomes, which is exactly what one would expect of a model of imperfect competition.

To gain further insight into the nature of the strategic interaction among firms implied by the Cournot model, we can derive the equilibrium for the case of n identical firms. In that case, overall output is given by $Q = Q_1 + Q_2 + \ldots + Q_n$, and the inverse demand curve is therefore

$$P = a - b\left(Q_1 + Q_2 + \ldots + Q_n\right)$$

Firm 1 now chooses Q_1 to maximize profit, taking as given $Q_2, Q_3, \ldots, Q_n$. The resulting first-order condition, corresponding to equation (4.3), is given by

$$\frac{d\pi_1}{dQ_1} = a - 2bQ_1 - b\left(Q_2 + \ldots + Q_n\right) - c = 0 \tag{4.10}$$

which defines firm 1's reaction function. In this case, the n reaction functions would have to be solved simultaneously to derive the equilibrium output levels for the n firms. For the case of identical firms, however, we can use the symmetry of the equilibrium to rewrite equation (4.10) as

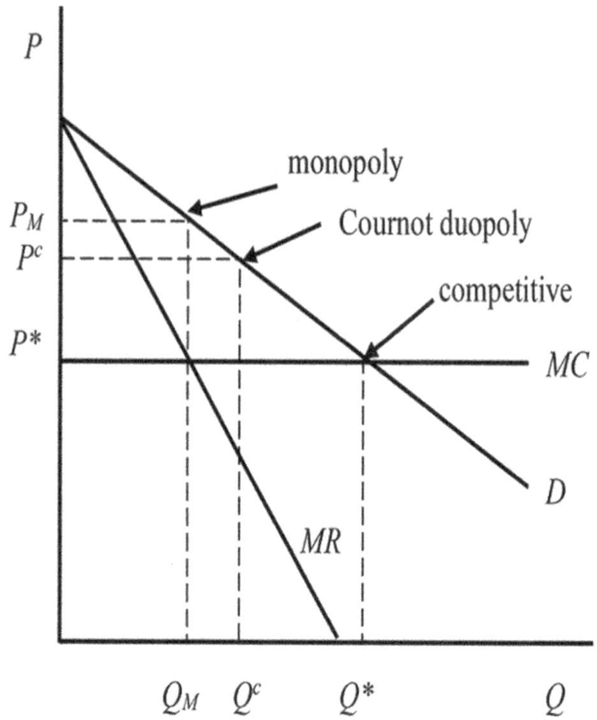

Figure 4.1 *Comparison of the monopoly, Cournot duopoly, and competitive outcomes*

$$a - 2bQ_i^c - b(n-1)Q_i^c - c = 0 \tag{4.11}$$

and this single equation can be solved for the common output level

$$Q_i^c = \frac{a-c}{(n+1)b} \qquad i = 1,\ldots,n \tag{4.12}$$

The resulting aggregate industry output ($= nQ_1^c$) and price are

$$Q^c = \frac{n(a-c)}{(n+1)b} \tag{4.13}$$

$$P^c = \frac{a + nc}{n+1} \tag{4.14}$$

Now observe that if we set n=1 in equations (4.13) and (4.14), we immediately get the monopoly output and price as shown in equations (4.7) and (4.8).

Likewise, if we set n=2, we get the two-firm Cournot output and price in equations (4.5) and (4.6). Finally, if we take the limit as $n \to \infty$, Q^c converges to the competitive output level in equation (4.9), and price equals marginal cost, or $P^c = c$.[2] In this way, the generalized Cournot model includes monopoly and perfect competition as limiting cases. More generally, as n increases in Figure 4.1, the equilibrium point moves down along the demand curve from the monopoly outcome toward the competitive outcome. This is a very appealing feature of the Cournot model because it depicts a gradual impact of economic competition as entry occurs.

The preceding analysis has shown that in this simple model of quantity competition among identical firms, limiting the entry of competing firms is beneficial to existing firms because it increases their profits. This provides a rationale for the league to limit entry as a way of improving the economic well-being of member teams. The impact on consumers is exactly the opposite: the entry of new teams would erode team profits and correspondingly increase consumer surplus. Thus, in the simple Cournot model of identical firms and a homogeneous product, the interests of firms and consumers are in direct opposition. This conclusion reflects the benefit to consumers of "economic" competition, and hence provides the basis for anti-trust scrutiny of entry barriers and other collusive practices in ordinary markets. It therefore raises the question of why sports leagues have typically been exempted from such scrutiny. As we will see, the subtlety of this question becomes evident as we alter or relax some of the assumptions of the simple oligopoly model.

The Bertrand Model

Despite the attractiveness of the Cournot model, it is likely that most competition does not actually take place over quantity but rather over price. Consider, for example, competing gas stations across the street from one another. With their prices clearly displayed, they undoubtedly compete in that dimension. Competing sports teams in the same city, say, would presumably behave in the same manner, team loyalties aside. The *Bertrand Model* of oligopoly describes the outcome of this type of "price competition."

As in the Cournot model, we initially consider two identical firms with a constant marginal and average cost of c. The firms supply an identical product, and so consumers view them as perfect substitutes. Thus, they will purchase from the firm charging the lower price. If the firms charge the same price, we assume that they will split the market evenly. It turns out that the unique Nash equilibrium in this setting is for both firms to charge a price equal to the common marginal cost; that is, $P_1 = P_2 = c$. As a result, the Bertrand model with only two firms yields the competitive outcome.

It is easy to see the intuition for this conclusion. Suppose initially that firm 1 sets P_1 above marginal cost in an effort to earn profits. If firm 2 matches that price, the firms will share the market evenly, and both will earn a positive profit. However, firm 2 can do better by slightly undercutting firm 1's price, thereby capturing the entire market and taking for itself nearly all of the joint profits that the two firms were previously earning. This process will continue as each firm tries to undercut the other until price equals marginal (and average) cost, at which point profits are zero. Once this outcome is reached, neither firm has an incentive to raise or lower its price: lowering the price will result in a loss, and raising it will result in no sales.[3] Thus, a price equal to marginal cost is the unique Nash equilibrium.

It is notable that the implications of the Bertrand model are very different from the Cournot model with respect to consumer welfare: whereas the latter implies that a small number of firms can successfully earn positive profits to the detriment of consumer welfare in equilibrium, the former suggests that as few as two firms will compete away all profits and thereby replicate the competitive outcome. This conclusion, however, only applies to the case of identical firms supplying homogeneous goods, which is not descriptive of actual sports markets where teams are not identical. The next section, therefore, takes a step towards a more realistic characterization by introducing product differentiation.

The Spatial Model of Differentiated Products

The preceding models are limited in that both assume all firms sell identical products, which in the sports context means that games hosted by one team are perfect substitutes for games hosted by any other team. This, of course, is unrealistic as it fails to capture varying team loyalties, differing market sizes, and costs of travel to competing venues. A somewhat different approach to modeling oligopoly, based literally on varying locations in space, tries to capture these factors. As we will see, the spatial element can be interpreted either literally as distance, reflecting costly travel, or figuratively as consumer "loyalty."

The analysis is based on a simple model of location choice first studied by Hotelling (1929). Imagine two sellers of an identical product that are located at opposite ends of a straight line (a road, say), and that potential consumers are distributed uniformly along that line. Each consumer wants to purchase at most one unit of the good, which, if acquired, yields a gross benefit of V.

To make a purchase, however, a consumer must "travel" from his or her location to one of the sellers at a cost of t dollars per unit distance. If the distance traveled is x, then the total cost of purchasing one unit of the good at price P is $P + tx$. The situation is depicted in Figure 4.2.

Suppose that firm A is located at point 0 and firm B is located at point 1, and their prices are P_A and P_B, which are to be determined. A consumer at point x ($0 \leq x \leq 1$) will therefore incur a total cost of $P_A + tx$ to buy a unit of the good from seller A (i.e., he has to travel x units leftward to point 0), and a cost of $P_B + t(1 - x)$ to buy a unit from seller B (i.e., he has to travel $1-x$ units rightward to point 1). Given our assumption of identical goods, the consumer will purchase from the seller for whom the total cost (price plus travel cost) is lowest. The location at which a consumer is indifferent between patronizing the two sellers, denoted $\bar{x}$, will therefore satisfy

$$P_A + tx = P_B + t(1 - x) \tag{4.15}$$

Solving this equation for x yields

$$\bar{x} = \frac{1}{2} + \frac{P_B - P_A}{2t} \tag{4.16}$$

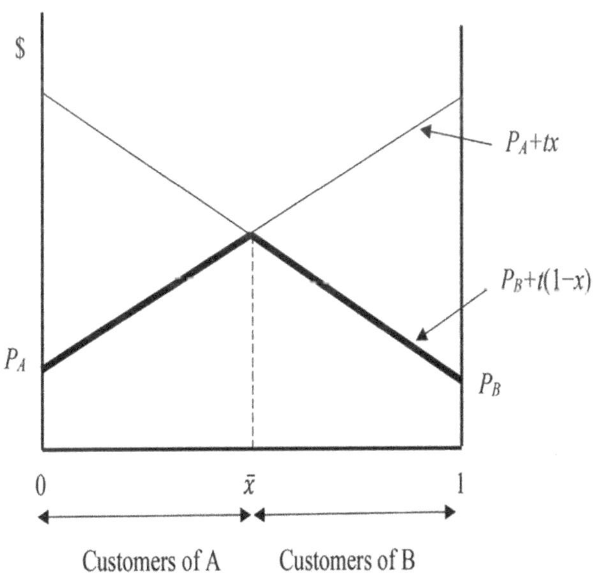

Figure 4.2 Equilibrium distribution of consumers between A and B

This is the dividing point between those consumers who will go to A (those for whom $x < \bar{x}$) and those who will go to B (those for whom $x > \bar{x}$). Thus, $\bar{x}$ is the demand for seller A, which is decreasing in P_A and increasing in P_B. Correspondingly, $1-\bar{x}$ is the demand for seller B, which is increasing in P_A and decreasing in P_B.

In Figure 4.2, the left-hand side of equation (4.15) is represented as the upward-sloping line (the cost of buying from A), and the right-hand side as the downward-sloping line (the cost of buying from B). The darkened segments show the least-cost option and the resulting customer base for each firm.[4] Note that, in contrast to the Bertrand model, setting a price below one's competitor does not allow a firm to capture the entire market. This is due to the impact of travel costs, which affect consumer choices by introducing a difference between the two firms based on their locations.

To determine the prices that the two firms will actually charge, observe first that firm A's total revenue is equal to its total demand, $\bar{x}$ (i.e., the number of consumers it serves), multiplied by its price, P_A. Now, assume for simplicity that the marginal cost of production is zero so that profit coincides with total revenue. Thus, firm A chooses its price to maximize its total revenue, $P_A\bar{x}$, or, substituting from equation (4.16),

$$TR_A = P_A\left(\frac{1}{2} + \frac{P_B - P_A}{2t}\right) \tag{4.17}$$

Maximizing this with respect to P_A yields the first-order condition

$$P_A = \frac{t}{2} + \frac{P_B}{2} \tag{4.18}$$

which defines firm A's reaction function. Since firms are symmetric, $P_A = P_B$ in equilibrium. It follows from equation (4.18) that in the Nash equilibrium,

$$P_A = P_B = t > 0 \tag{4.19}$$

According to equation (4.16), the two firms share the market evenly in equilibrium; that is, $\bar{x} = ½$. However, in contrast to the Bertrand model, firms are able to set their prices strictly above marginal cost, which in this case is equal to zero.[5]

Difference in Market Size

It is now possible to use this model to capture differences in market sizes. Suppose that the two firms are not located at opposite ends of the line, but that firm A is at x=1/3, while firm B remains at x=1, as shown in Figure 4.3. Note that this gives firm A an inherent advantage because of its closer proximity to all consumers to the left of x=1/3. Thus, A's share of the overall market, again given by $x \leq \bar{x}$, will comprise more than half of the line, as the graph shows. This reflects a situation where, for example, A is in a larger city.

Proceeding as above, we in fact find that the equilibrium is no longer symmetric. In particular, we can derive the equilibrium prices to be

$$P_A = \frac{10}{9}t \quad (4.20)$$

$$P_B = \frac{8}{9}t \quad (4.21)$$

which implies that $P_A > t > P_B$. Thus, even though the firms are selling identical products, firm A is able to charge a higher price by virtue of its superior location (i.e., larger market area).

An important consequence of this conclusion is that teams having an *economic advantage* will be able to acquire better players, and so will also have an advantage *on the field*. This reveals the inherent relationship between economic competition and sporting competition, and provides a rationale, explored in detail in Chapter 6, for league efforts aimed at equalizing the economic status of teams.

Travel Distance as Team Loyalty

So far, we have shown that introducing "travel costs," interpreted literally as distance, allows firms engaged in price competition to charge prices above marginal cost and thereby to earn profits (in contrast to the homogeneous-good Bertrand model). Further, firms in larger markets are able to charge higher prices than firms in smaller markets for the same good.

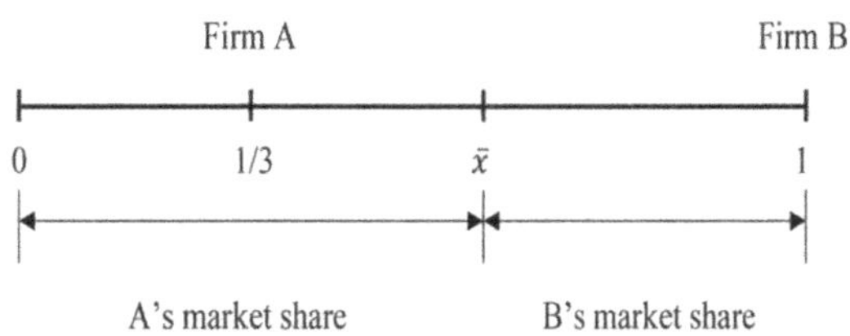

Figure 4.3 Spatial model with unequal market shares

We now use the current model to introduce one more element of reality into the analysis—namely, the possibility of *product differentiation* and *brand (team) loyalty*. Most ordinary products exhibit some amount of differentiation (think of soft drinks and automobiles), and it is certainly the case that sports teams are differentiated products. Most fans have a rooting interest in a particular team, and so would be willing to pay more to attend that team's games, all else equal. This sort of partisanship is another way that teams acquire some degree of market power.

To capture this factor, we will interpret "distance" in the above model, not as literal distance but as a measure of a fan's loyalty to his or her favorite team. Think, for instance, of two teams, A and B, located at opposite ends of the above line (as in the first version of the above model), and suppose that fans are distributed along the line according to the intensity of their affinity for each of the teams. Thus, more avid fans are located closer to a given team and less avid fans farther away.

We further allow the "gross" value that fans derive from rooting for their favorite team to be different. Specifically, let V_A be the maximum amount that the most devoted fan of team A would pay to attend a game played by that team. Such fans are located exactly at point 0. A fan located at some distance away, say at point $x > 0$, values games played by team A at $V_A - tx$, where t is the rate at which willingness-to-pay decreases per unit distance away from zero. In this case, however, x is not interpreted as the literal distance one has to travel to a game, but as how much one's devotion to the team declines compared with the most avid fan. In other words, fans at $x > 0$ are less devoted in terms of their willingness to pay to attend a game.

Similarly, let V_B be the maximum amount a fan of team B, the one located at point 1, values attending a game played by B. A fan located at point x would therefore value a game played by team B at $V_B - t(1-x)$, where $1-x$ is the fan's "distance" from the most avid fan of team B. The difference between V_A and V_B could reflect differences in the nature of the market the two teams play in or differences in the intensity of the commitment of the most avid fans of the two teams. Some teams, for example, have a longer history or simply have more devoted fan bases. The difference could also reflect differences in team quality. In any case, we assume that fan intensity declines with distance at the same rate, t, for both types of fans.

A fan located at any point x can attend a game for either team. (We ignore games in which they play each other.) Which team he or she chooses will depend on his or her inherent loyalty—measured by $V_A - tx$ for team A and $V_B - t(1-x)$ for team B—but also the price of a ticket. The point of indifference is determined by the equation

$$V_A - P_A - tx = V_B - P_B - t(1-x)$$

Solving this for the indifference point yields

$$\bar{x} = \frac{1}{2} + \frac{(V_A - V_B) + (P_B - P_A)}{2t} \tag{4.22}$$

As above, $\bar{x}$ demarcates the division of fans between the two teams and hence determines their market shares. This should not be interpreted as a literal geographic division (though it could be), but rather as a division of loyalties. Some teams, for example, have national fan bases (the New York Yankees or Dallas Cowboys, for example), so their fans are scattered geographically, while others are purely regional. Note that equation (4.22) reduces to (4.16) when $V_A = V_B$. In this case, the fan base tilts toward the team with the lower price, given an equal inherent intensity of fan loyalty.

Like travel costs, teams can exploit fan loyalty to exercise market power. Think about two teams in the same city with divided fan bases (for example, Yankees–Mets or Cubs–White Sox). Travel costs are negligible, so in a pure Bertrand model with homogeneous products, the prices for games of either team would fall to their marginal costs (which in the current model are zero). Team loyalties, however, create a source of market power.

To see this, consider team A's optimization problem. Given equation (4.22), which defines its demand, team A will choose P_A to maximize its revenue, given by

$$TR_A = P_A\left(\frac{1}{2} + \frac{(V_A - V_B) + (P_B - P_A)}{2t}\right) \tag{4.23}$$

Proceeding as above, we obtain team A's reaction function:

$$P_A = \frac{t}{2} + \frac{(V_A - V_B) + P_B}{2} \tag{4.24}$$

Note that this reduces to equation (4.18) when $V_A = V_B$. Symmetrically, we obtain the following reaction function for team B:

$$P_B = \frac{t}{2} + \frac{(V_B - V_A) + P_A}{2} \tag{4.25}$$

Solving equations (4.24) and (4.25) simultaneously yields the equilibrium prices:

$$P_A = t + \frac{V_A - V_B}{2} \tag{4.26}$$

$$P_B = t + \frac{V_B - V_A}{2} \tag{4.27}$$

Thus, assuming $V_A > V_B$, we have that $P_A > t > P_B$.[6] More intense team loyalty among fans therefore has the same effect as a larger market size in terms of its effect on prices and profits.[7] Specifically, it allows the team with the more loyal fan base to raise its prices relative to teams with less loyal fans, all else equal, and hence to earn higher profits. This will improve the economic fortunes of such teams, which can translate into more spending on players, potentially resulting in a snowball effect. Such is the genesis of sports dynasties.

LEAGUES AS CARTELS

From an economic perspective, professional sports leagues have many of the characteristics of a cartel, in the sense that they facilitate cooperation among teams, both on and off the field. As we have noted, in purely economic terms, this is detrimental to the interests of consumers because it allows teams to extract monopoly profits. Below, we ask whether there is an offsetting rationale for cooperation with respect to on-field activities and policies. First, however, we present the theory of cartel formation and demonstrate the inherent instability of cartels. We then offer explanations for how sports leagues nevertheless seem to sustain cooperative behavior.

Consider the case of two firms, A and B, selling an identical product and having equal marginal costs of c. Suppose the market demand is given by equation (4.1) with $Q = Q_1 + Q_2$ being aggregate output. The objective of a cartel agreement is for the two firms to act as one; that is, to coordinate their choices of output so as to maximize their joint profit, which is given by

$$\pi = \left[a - b\left(Q_1 + Q_2\right)\right]\left(Q_1 + Q_2\right) - c\left(Q_1 + Q_2\right) \tag{4.28}$$

One consequence of the assumption of constant and equal marginal costs is that as long as the aggregate output of the two firms is chosen to equate marginal revenue to marginal cost, the specific amounts that each firm contributes to this total are indeterminate. For ordinary goods, this would imply that the aggregate output could be arbitrarily assigned to the two firms.[8] In a sports league, in contrast, output (games) must be equally divided among teams according to the fixed schedule.

Both the Cournot and Bertrand models showed, to varying degrees, that equilibrium in the absence of coordination among competing firms will fall short of the cartel outcome. As a simple illustration of the instability of a cartel agreement, consider the following example involving two firms that enter into such an agreement. Suppose that if both firms adhere to the agreement, aggregate profits would be $100, with each firm receiving half of the total, or $50. In contrast, if they mutually engage in competition by increasing their outputs or reducing their prices relative to the agreed-upon levels, they each would earn only $30. However, if one firm "cheats" on the agreement while the other adheres to it, the cheating firm would earn $60 while the compliant firm would earn $20. (Note that aggregate profit in this case is therefore less than under dual compliance.) The resulting payoffs from the various strategy combinations are shown in Table 4.1.

Table 4.1 Payoff matrix for cartel game

	Firm B – Comply	Firm B - Cheat
Firm A – Comply	$50, $50	$20, **$60**
Firm A – Cheat	**$60**, $20	**$30, $30**

To derive the equilibrium of this game, consider firm A's strategy. If firm A believes that firm B will comply, A's best option is to cheat because it earns $60 rather than $50. If instead A believes B will cheat, A's best option is again to cheat, as that yields $30 rather than $20. Firm A, therefore, has a *dominant strategy* of cheating, meaning that no matter what it expects firm B to do, cheating is its best option. And since the payoffs are symmetric, the same logic applies to firm B's behavior. Thus, the unique Nash equilibrium is for both firms to cheat.[9] This result is indicated by the bold entries in the table, which show the optimal strategies for each firm given the other firm's choice. The equilibrium outcome is the cell where both entries are bold.

Some readers may recognize that the game played by the two firms in this case is a Prisoners' Dilemma, which is known to produce an equilibrium in which the players fail to sustain a jointly optimal outcome. In the current context, the failure of the firms to sustain a cartel, while detrimental to their joint interests, is actually conducive to consumer welfare because the equilibrium is closer to the competitive outcome.

The preceding demonstration of the non-sustainability of a cartel suggests that collusion among firms in ordinary markets may not represent a serious policy concern. To the contrary, sports leagues have been remarkably successful in organizing member teams into cartel-like arrangements that involve limited entry and other coordination practices, such as revenue sharing, that look a lot like a cartel. This raises two questions: first, how have leagues been able to sustain this sort of cooperation in light of the instability argument just offered? And second, is such cooperation necessarily bad for consumers of professional sporting events?

As to the first question, sports leagues sustain cooperative behavior in a number of ways. The first is through repeated interaction over time. The above Prisoners' Dilemma approach to the instability of a cartel represents a one-shot interaction between the two firms, while in reality, firms interact repeatedly over a long time horizon. Thus, failure to cooperate involves long-term costs that far exceed those reflected by the one-time payoffs in Table 4.1. When the relevant parties know that they will interact repeatedly, and there is no known end date,[10] an important result in game theory, sometimes referred to as the "folk theorem," suggests that a cooperative outcome is sustainable as the equilibrium. The theorem specifically says that the present value of gains from continuing cooperative play in the above game (i.e., \$50 each) exceeds the present value of the payoffs from cheating (i.e., a one-time profit of \$60 plus \$30 in all subsequent periods) as long as the discount rate is not too high. In other words, as long as firms care enough about future income, cooperation is sustainable.

A second way that sports leagues enforce cooperation is by delegating decision-making to a strong commissioner, who acts on behalf of team owners. In this way, individual teams effectively "tie their hands" to reduce the temptation to give in to strategies or actions that promise short-term gains but would undermine the overall collective interests of the league. "Rogue" owners will sometimes attempt to get around such policies, and some commissioners will prove stronger than others at enforcing the collective interests of owners, but, generally speaking, the hierarchical structure of league governance has proven quite effective in restraining such behavior.

Finally, because teams cannot unilaterally produce "games," some amount of cooperation among teams is inherent to sports as a consumer product, and hence is "built-in" to the league structure. Although a subset of teams could defect, that probably would not succeed in attracting a lot of fans. After all, fan loyalty to their favorite teams only makes sense in relation to other teams in the league rather than their existence as independent entities. In a real sense, "rooting" for a team is meaningless without the existence of other teams. This is different from most consumer products, which can be enjoyed in isolation from competing brands. Think of Coke versus Pepsi, where customers of one brand don't care how many drinkers of the other brand there are. This is obviously not true of sports rivalries.

LEAGUES AS PROVIDERS OF PUBLIC GOODS

Although maintenance of a cartel among teams risks off-field decision-making that is detrimental to consumer welfare, there are also significant benefits of cooperation, principally with respect to on-field decisions, which are unique to the production of sporting events as consumption goods. It follows that in an optimal sports league, there must be a balance between competition and cooperation. Indeed, it is a paradox of sports as an economic good that some amount of cooperation off the field is necessary to ensure optimal competition on the field. This balancing act presents a difficult challenge with regard to economic policy towards sports; namely, how to prevent beneficial cooperation with respect to on-field matters from spilling over into off-field economic policies that would be detrimental to consumer interests. This will be a theme that runs throughout this book.

In this light, we suggest an alternative function of sports leagues: namely, to provide public goods to member teams. In economics, public goods have the characteristic that once produced, their benefits cannot be denied to any consumers, including those who have not contributed to the cost. This so-called *free rider problem* undermines efficient market provision of these goods. It therefore serves as the rationale for the government to take over the provision of public goods, such as highways and law enforcement, and to finance them through taxation of beneficiaries. Sports leagues can be interpreted as serving a similar purpose.

Some examples of public goods in sports leagues include predictable scheduling of games, structuring of playoff formats, standardizing rules regarding equipment and player eligibility, ensuring the viability of teams, maintaining the quality of play, and promoting competitive balance. We will examine many of the issues in greater detail throughout this book; here, we simply catalog some ways that leagues seek to pursue these goals, leaving until later an evaluation of their efficacy.

First, as regards acquisition and compensation of players, leagues structure amateur player draft rules, which typically involve allowing the lowest placed teams to draft first, or at least to enter a lottery for early picks. The goal, of course, is to balance the distribution of talent in the league. Leagues also limit the ability of drafted players to negotiate with other teams (i.e., to become free agents), at least for a set time period. Historically, major league baseball actually prevented players from *ever* negotiating with other teams, even after any contractual obligations had expired, and no matter how long they had been in the major leagues. This rule, called the *reserve system*, was in place from the beginning of professional baseball in the 1870s up to 1975, when courts finally struck it down, ushering in the era of free agency.[11] Even today, however, players can only become free agents after six years of major league service. In other words, full free agency does not exist, despite a strong players' union.[12] Other league policies aimed at equalizing team quality are salary caps, luxury taxes, and revenue sharing, all of which are designed to offset the economic advantages that teams in larger markets enjoy.

Leagues also exercise control over the entry of new teams and/or the relocation of existing teams. On the face of it, these restrictions would seem to be contrary to the interests of fans as they limit off-field competition. As shown in the above generalized Cournot model, entry (an increase in n) moves the equilibrium price and output down the demand curve toward the competitive ideal. In contrast, barriers to entry protect team profits. In the sports market, however, the matter is not so simple. Free entry of firms in ordinary markets is conducive to consumer welfare because new firms are assumed to be able to replicate exactly the product being sold by incumbents and thus compete with these firms. Aside from team loyalties, this is also theoretically possible in sports markets in the sense that new franchises can supply games just like existing teams. The key difference, however, is that an essential input in the supply of professional sporting events is the quality (skill) of participants, which is a scarce resource. New teams are limited to choosing from the same talent pool as existing teams. Thus, the entry of new teams will necessarily require dipping deeper into that pool, with a consequent erosion in the average quality of games.

Some expansion is nevertheless desirable to exploit new profit opportunities, but it is a balancing act because, as argued in the previous chapter, team revenue depends not just on quantity but on the quality of play.[13] League governance plays a key coordination role here because individual teams (or prospective teams) will have an incentive to enter in pursuit of profit, and cities will then welcome entry, but overall league quality will decline as a result.

Another important function the league plays is the promulgation and enforcement of standardized rules, both regarding play on the field and the behavior of players off the field. In this capacity, leagues create a kind of law enforcement system that defines violations ("crimes") and specifies penalties for violations, including monetary fines and suspensions.[14] Leagues constantly refine and revise these rules in response to changing technology, knowledge, and fan preferences, thereby ensuring that the league supplies the best possible product while maintaining safe playing conditions.

SUMMARY

This chapter shifted focus from the decisions of individual teams to leagues as economic organizations whose purpose is to coordinate the behavior of teams. The chapter began by using traditional industrial organization models of market structure to describe the strategic interaction of teams. We first considered the standard Cournot and Bertrand models of firms selling homogeneous products, and then extended the analysis by introducing a spatial model of product differentiation to explicitly account for both travel costs and fan loyalty.

We concluded the chapter by offering two perspectives on sports leagues. The standard cartel model views the league as acting to coordinate the behaviors of member teams in a way that enhances their profits. This principally involves enforcing output quotas or prices, as well as restricting the entry of new teams to prevent excessive competition. This function of a league is clearly detrimental to the welfare of fans. The second model, by contrast, views leagues as serving the benevolent purpose of coordinating team decisions to achieve essential forms of cooperation, such as structuring schedules and playoffs, organizing drafts, enforcing league rules (both on and off the field), and engaging in joint marketing activities, all of which have public good characteristics. These activities are generally beneficial to fans because they contribute to the provision of well-organized competition. In truth, leagues simultaneously serve both of the above functions, and it is an empirical question whether, from the perspective of fans, the nature and degree of cooperation is optimal.

EXERCISES

4.1. Let the inverse demand curve for contests in a particular league be given by $P = 200 - Q$, and let the marginal cost of supplying contests be $MC = 50$.
  (a) Derive the output and price under a monopoly, a Cournot equilibrium with two firms, and a competitive market.
  (b) Draw a graph of the resulting outcomes.
  (c) What would the outcome be under a Bertrand model with two firms?

4.2. Consider a city with two teams in a sports league. Call them the Reds and the Blues. The total population of fans is 150,000, which is equally divided into three groups: devoted Reds fans, devoted Blues fans, and fans who are indifferent between the two teams. All fans are willing to pay at most \$50 to attend a game, but devoted fans will only attend games of their favored team, while indifferent fans will attend games of the team with the lower price. (If the price is the same, they will evenly divide it between the two teams.)
  (a) Suppose that both teams set a price of \$50. Calculate the total attendance and the total revenue for each team. Also, calculate the total aggregate revenue.

(b) Now, suppose that the Reds unilaterally lower their price to \$40. Again, calculate the attendance and revenue for each team, and the aggregate revenue.

(c) What do the results from parts (a) and (b) show about the joint gains from collusion in setting the price of games? What do they show about the incentives of individual teams to undercut each other in setting prices?

NOTES

1. Recall that we examined this interdependence in Chapter 2 when considering a team's choice of output (games supplied) and talent (player quality), both of which were assumed to affect total revenue.
2. To see this, multiply the numerator and the denominator of equations (4.13) and (4.14) by $1/n$. This yields

$$Q^c = \frac{a-c}{\left(1+\frac{1}{n}\right)b}$$

and

$$P^c = \frac{\frac{a}{n}+c}{1+\frac{1}{n}}$$

Now take the limit as $n \rightarrow \infty$. Since $1/n \rightarrow 0$, we obtain $Q^c = (a-c)/b$ and $P^c = c$.
3. Although no sales and zero profits are technically equivalent, we presume that a firm would rather be in business than not.
4. It is possible that if the cost of travel is too high, some consumers in the middle will forgo purchases altogether. We ignore that possibility here by assuming that the gross value of consumption, V, is large enough that in equilibrium, it exceeds the total cost of purchase for all consumers.
5. As noted, we are assuming that all consumers along the line purchase the good. The consumer who must travel the farthest, and thus incurs the highest overall cost, is the one at $\bar{x} = 1/2$, given equal prices. The total cost for that consumer is thus $t + t\bar{x} = 3t/2$. It therefore must be true that $V > 3t/2$.
6. As above, we are assuming that both V_A and V_B are large enough that all fans are in the market. If some are not, the resulting "gap" in the line between the two fan bases would allow each team to act like a monopolist.
7. It turns out that at these prices, the point of indifference as defined by equation (4.22) is exactly ½; that is, the market is evenly divided. Thus, the team with the inherent advantage fully captures that advantage in the price.
8. In contrast, if firms had different cost structures, output would optimally be allocated among firms such that their marginal costs of production are equal.

The allocation of profit would presumably be proportional, though no set arrangement is required.

9. Presumably, the argument for the instability of cartels only becomes stronger when more than two firms are involved.
10. If the final period is known, the equilibrium of the repeated game is the same as in the one-shot game—that is, there will be mutual cheating in all periods. This result arises as a consequence of unraveling when players solve the game by backwards induction.
11. See Miller (1991) for a first-hand account of the events leading up to free agency in baseball.
12. We will offer an explanation for this seeming puzzle in Chapter 10.
13. We elaborate on this idea in Chapter 12.
14. See Chapter 7, which deals with rule enforcement.

5. The nature of competition on the field

The previous chapters have focused entirely on the business dimension of professional sports by developing various ways of thinking about competition among teams off the field. This chapter turns to competition *on* the field and asks what economic theory can say about how that is (or should be) structured. It may not be obvious that economics has anything to contribute here at all. It is, of course, true that the rules of the game or contest, and how winning is defined, are not economic issues *per se*. However, once the contest has been devised, individual competitors or teams, in formulating a strategy, presumably have the goal of maximizing their chances of winning or the proceeds from participating, both of which involve marshalling their scarce resources in the most productive way possible. This surely *is* an economic problem. Also important is how the contestants respond to one another in a strategic way—this is the on-field counterpart to economic competition among teams, as examined in the previous chapter. The analysis in this chapter focuses first on the actions of individual competitors (teams), and then on the objectives and decisions of the league organizer.[1] The discussion will center on what I will call the "conflict model" of sports.

THE CONFLICT MODEL OF SPORTS CONTESTS

We study a simple model of a sporting contest in which a group of n competitors each seeks to capture a fixed "prize" valued at V.[2] This can be literally interpreted as describing a tournament such as golf or tennis in which individual competitors vie for a monetary prize, with the winner taking home the full amount—i.e., a "winner-takes-all" contest. (Later, we will consider different structures that allow prizes of decreasing amounts for second place, third place, etc.) Alternatively, the model could describe a team sport in which a team's attendance, and hence profit, is proportional to its winning percentage (as discussed in Chapter 2). In this interpretation, the prize can be thought of as total fan expenditure across the entire season, which teams divide based on their performance on the field.

We assume that each competitor expends some "effort" to win the contest, the combined effect of which, in conjunction with the rules of the contest, determines each side's probability of winning. To be specific, let x_i be the effort level of competitor *i* and let *i*'s probability of winning be given by $p_i(x_1, x_2,...,x_n)$, where we assume that a competitor's own effort increases his or her probability of winning, while the effort of all other competitors reduces that probability. This is referred to as a *conflict function*, or a *contest success function*.[3] Further, because one competitor must win,[4] the probabilities have to sum to one:

$$\sum_{i=1}^{n} p_i = 1 \tag{5.1}$$

I will refer to this as the "zero-sum constraint."

The problem for each competitor is to choose effort to maximize his or her net gain. Specifically, competitor *i* chooses x_i to maximize:

$$p_i V - x_i, \qquad i = 1,\ldots,n \tag{5.2}$$

where the marginal cost of effort is taken to be \$1 (i.e., x_i is measured in dollars). At the optimum for competitor *i*, the marginal benefit of effort must equal the marginal cost, or

$$\frac{dp_i}{dx_i} V = 1 \tag{5.3}$$

which defines *i*'s optimal effort, x_i^*. This outcome is shown graphically in Figure 5.1, where it is assumed that the marginal benefit of effort is decreasing.[5]

The optimal point defined by equation (5.3), and depicted in Figure 5.1, determines x_i^* as a function of the effort levels of all other competitors, which *i* takes as given. (Each of these effort levels enters the dp_i / dx_i term in equation (5.3).) The overall equilibrium for the league must therefore reflect the interdependency among competitors. We explicitly illustrate this interdependency with an example involving two competitors.

For the case of two competitors, the probabilities of winning are $p_1(x_1, x_2)$ for competitor 1, which is increasing in x_1 and decreasing in x_2; and $p_2(x_1, x_2)$ for competitor 2, which is decreasing in x_1 and increasing in x_2. Further, equation (5.1) implies that $p_2(x_1, x_2)=1-p_1(x_1,x_2)$. To make further progress, we will employ an explicit functional form for these probabilities. A commonly used form is given by the following expression:

$$p_1 = \frac{x_1}{x_1 + x_2} \tag{5.4}$$

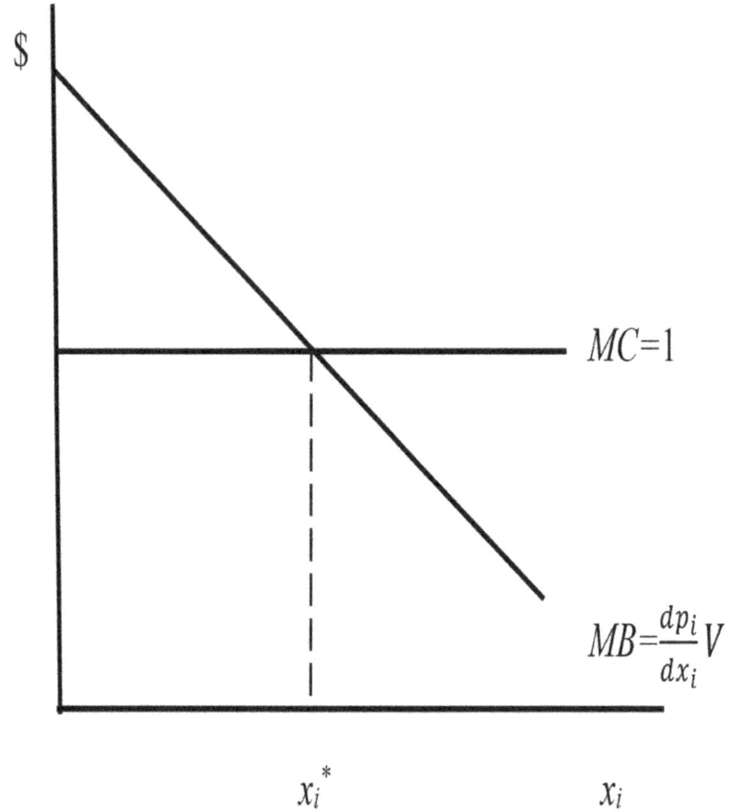

Figure 5.1 *Competitor i's optimal effort*

It follows that

$$p_2 = \frac{x_2}{x_1 + x_2} \tag{5.5}$$

It is easily verified that these formulations for p_1 and p_2 satisfy the stated properties (i.e., they are increasing at a decreasing rate in own-effort, decreasing in the opponent's effort, and they sum to one). Using equations (5.4) or (5.5), as appropriate, we obtain the first-order conditions for x_1 and x_2, respectively, as follows:

$$\frac{x_2}{(x_1+x_2)^2}V=1 \tag{5.6}$$

$$\frac{x_1}{(x_1+x_2)^2}V=1 \tag{5.7}$$

These equations represent the reaction functions for the two teams. As in the Cournot model, they define the optimal effort for each competitor as a function of the opponent's effort.

Equations (5.6) and (5.7) must be solved simultaneously to find the Nash equilibrium effort levels, x_1^* and x_2^*. This yields:

$$x_1^* = x_2^* = \frac{V}{4} \tag{5.8}$$

Using these results, we can solve for the equilibrium probabilities of victory for the two teams and their expected returns, as follows:

$$p_1^* = p_2^* = \frac{1}{2} \tag{5.9}$$

$$p_i^* V - x_i^* = \frac{V}{4}, \qquad i = 1,2 \tag{5.10}$$

The fact that the probabilities of victory are equal for the two contestants obviously reflects their symmetry—the fact that neither starts with an inherent advantage. Also note that individual effort in equation (5.8) and the value of participation in equation (5.10) are both increasing in the value of the prize, as we would expect. (The fact that they are equal is just a coincidence.)

One last point here: suppose that instead of engaging in the competition to determine who would receive V, the two parties agreed beforehand to split it evenly, or award it by a flip of the coin. The expected return from these methods for each contestant would be $V/2$, which is greater than the expected value in equation (5.10). The reason for the difference is that "consensual" division would save the expenditure of x by both sides. This approach would be a desirable substitute for actual competition in other conflict settings because it would avoid the wasteful nature of spending x—what economists call rent-seeking—but it obviously defeats the entire purpose of sports competition, which is what fans value. In this sense, sports competition is very different from, for example, political campaigns, legal contests, or outright warfare, where it would be better to award V without the need for actual conflict.[6] In sports, it is the conflict itself that people value.

The preceding model can be generalized to n competitors, where

$$p_i\left(x_1,\ldots,x_n\right)=\frac{x_i}{\sum_{j=1}^{n} x_j}, \qquad i=1,\ldots,n \tag{5.11}$$

which is increasing in x_i and decreasing in all the other x_j's ($j \neq i$). The first-order condition defining competitor i's optimal effort (corresponding to equations (5.6) or (5.7)) is

$$\frac{\sum_{j\neq i} x_j}{\left(\sum_{j=1}^{n} x_j\right)^2} V = 1, \qquad i=1,\ldots,n \tag{5.12}$$

In order to solve this equation for the equilibrium effort levels, we make use of the fact that in a symmetric equilibrium, $x_1^*=x_2^*=\ldots=x_n^*$. In that case, equation (5.12) can be solved as a single equation in a single unknown to obtain the common effort level x^*:[7]

$$x^* = \frac{\left(n-1\right)V}{n^2} \tag{5.13}$$

It follows that the equilibrium probability of winning and the expected return for each competitor, respectively, are

$$p^* = \frac{1}{n} \tag{5.14}$$

$$p_i^* V - x_i^* = \frac{V}{n^2} \tag{5.15}$$

It is easily verified that these results reduce to those in equations (5.8)–(5.10) for the case of n=2.

The following conclusions can be derived from the foregoing analysis. First, an individual competitor's effort increases with the size of the prize (V), but decreases with the number of competitors (n). Competitors, therefore, devote more effort when more is at stake, but less effort when they are competing against a larger field. Note that this latter point provides an interesting reason why leagues may want to limit entry. We argued in the previous chapter that limiting entry prevents talent dilution; the current result shows that it may also enhance the level of competition. However, as the fan base grows—meaning that V, defined as potential league-wide revenue, increases—entry of competitors (expansion) will not necessarily dilute competition (though it may still dilute talent).

Second, the probability of winning is equal for all competitors, reflecting symmetry, but it is decreasing in the number of competitors. The equal probabilities of victory reflect *perfect competitive balance*, a foundational concept in sports economics, which we will explore in detail in the next chapter. In the current context, however, that balance is a consequence of the assumption of symmetric competitors, which will not always be the case. Finally, the expected return for each competitor (equation (5.15)) is increasing with the magnitude of the prize and decreasing in the number of competitors. Thus, as in the Cournot model from Chapter 4, entry erodes profits. New competitors may therefore be less willing to join an already large league unless the value of the prize is correspondingly raised. Thus, expansion becomes feasible (or desirable) only as new markets emerge.

GRADUATED REWARD SCHEMES

The analysis so far has focused on a "winner-take-all" reward scheme, but in many tournament settings, such as in professional golf and tennis, graduated prizes are routinely awarded to competitors. The analysis in this section will first demonstrate the effect of this sort of reward scheme. It will then discuss possible reasons for adopting it over a winner-take-all scheme.

Let us return to the simplest possible setting where there are only two competitors and two prizes, one for first and one for second. Let V_1 and V_2 be the value of the prizes, where, for the sake of comparison with the winner-take-all case above, we assume that $V_1 + V_2 = V$; that is, the total purse is fixed at the same amount. For competitor 1, the probability of winning—coming in first—is given by equation (5.4), while the probability of losing—coming in second—is given by equation (5.5). (The reverse is obviously true for competitor 2.) Thus, competitor 1 chooses x_1 to maximize $p_1V_1 + (1 - p_1)V_2 - x_1$, or

$$\frac{x_1}{x_1 + x_2}V_1 + \frac{x_2}{x_1 + x_2}V_2 - x_1 \tag{5.16}$$

The resulting first-order condition, which defines competitor 1's reaction function, is given by

$$\frac{x_2}{\left(x_1 + x_2\right)^2}\left(V_1 - V_2\right) = 1 \tag{5.17}$$

A symmetric condition defines competitor 2's reaction function. Solving these conditions simultaneously yields the common effort level for each competitor (again, owing to symmetry):

$$x_i^* = \frac{V_1 - V_2}{4}, \qquad i = 1,2 \tag{5.18}$$

Comparing this with equation (5.8), the corresponding outcome under a winner-take-all reward scheme, we see that equation (5.8) is a special case of equation (5.18) when $V_1 = V$ and $V_2 = 0$.

It follows immediately from equation (5.18) that the competitors only exert positive effort if $V_1 > V_2$; that is, if the first prize exceeds the second prize. This makes intuitive sense since if both prizes are the same, winning means nothing. Further, we can show that the *level* of effort here is lower than that in the winner-take-all contest, given equal total prize money. To see that, use equations (5.8) and (5.18) to show that $V - (V_1 - V_2) = V - V_1 + V_2 = 2V_2 > 0$ given that $V = V_1 + V_2$. Thus, both individual and overall effort decline under the graduated scheme. This raises the question of why a contest organizer would give non-winners any prize money at all, given that competition is the principal reason for staging the tournament in the first place. Why structure the prize to *dampen* competition?

One explanation is to ensure that the participation constraint of competitors is satisfied. To see this, note that under the graduated scheme, the expected profit for each competitor (the equilibrium value of equation (5.16)) is given by

$$\frac{1}{2}V_1 + \frac{1}{2}V_2 - \frac{V_1 - V_2}{4} = \frac{V_1 + 3V_2}{4} \tag{5.19}$$

(Note that symmetry again implies that $p_i^* = 1/2$ under this scheme.) Now compare this with the expected profit under the winner-take-all scheme in equation (5.15):

$$\frac{V_1 + 3V_2}{4} - \frac{V}{4} = \frac{V_1 + 3V_2}{4} - \frac{V_1 + V_2}{4} = \frac{V_2}{2} > 0 \tag{5.20}$$

Thus, the graduated scheme makes entry more attractive. This makes sense since competitors invest less effort, and therefore there is less dissipation of profits. This factor—the need to attract competitors—was especially important in the days before endorsement contracts and appearance fees when, for example, competitors in golf tournaments relied solely on prize money to make a living. In that setting, a graduated reward scheme was probably necessary to attract a large enough field of competitors. A related explanation is that if one of the competitors in the tournament has a substantial advantage and only one prize is awarded, other competitors may have little reason to enter, thus undermining the purpose of the contest. Think, for example, of the days when Tiger Woods, Jack Nicklaus, or Annika Sorenstam were dominating their respective professional golf tours. A final explanation for a graduated scheme is risk aversion on the part of competitors, since a "flatter" reward scheme is less risky in terms of income. In other words, the difference between winning and losing is smaller.

It remains to determine the difference between V_1 and V_2—that is, the "steepness" of the prize money gradient. As we have just seen, this involves a trade-off between overall competitor effort and the expected returns of entry. Specifically, the steeper the gradient, the more effort competitors will expend, but the less attractive the tournament will be, thus possibly cutting down the size of the field. From a pure profit perspective, less competition and fewer participants both reduce aggregate revenue. Thus, the optimal scheme will balance the offsetting effects of these factors, given the total prize money to be given out.

THE OPTIMAL CONTEST

The preceding model of competition among rival contestants or teams can now be used to think about the optimal structure of a sporting contest. The relevant choices for the contest organizer are the number of competitors, n, and the overall size of the prize, V. For purposes of this discussion, we will focus only on a winner-take-all contest, where the first-place finisher gets the entire prize. (The structure of the reward scheme would be chosen based on factors mentioned in the previous section.)

We will consider three types of contests: (1) a free-entry contest, (2) a contest set up by a profit-maximizing entrepreneur, and (3) a professional league. In all cases, we first need to determine the identity and objective of the organizer.

Free-entry Contests

The first contest we consider—what I will call a "free-entry" contest—is one that is organized collectively by the contestants themselves and is open to all comers as long as they pay an entry fee of F. This describes all sorts of tournaments involving individual and team sports, including golf, soccer, and softball tournaments; fishing derbies; and even poker tournaments.

Self-financing requires that the prize and entry fee satisfy the balanced-budget condition $V = nF$, or

$$F = \frac{V}{n} \tag{5.21}$$

Given the announced values of V and F, contestants will enter as long as they expect a positive net benefit. If we suppose that their motives are purely based on monetary gain, this would imply that entry should occur to the point where $p_i^* V - x_i^* = F$, where x_i^* and p_i^* are derived as above. There is a problem with this, however. Using equations (5.21) and (5.15) we find that

$$p_i^* V - x_i^* - F = V / n^2 - V / n = \frac{V}{n}\left(\frac{1}{n} - 1\right) < 0 \text{ for } n > 1 \tag{5.22}$$

Thus, a break-even tournament *necessarily promises a negative expected return for all participants.* Intuitively, with the prize being constrained to equal the aggregate entry revenue, the gross expected return for each entrant must simply equal the entry fee itself. Thus, once the contestants' effort is accounted for, the net expected return must be negative.

Why, then, would anyone enter such a tournament, absent an outside subsidy? The likely explanation is that contestants derive utility from the competition itself, and/or from the right of the winner to claim the title of "champion." In other words, contestants are maximizing utility rather than wealth. A related explanation is that some tournaments of this sort are set up as fundraisers, and so contestants derive utility from contributing to the charitable cause in addition to participating in the competition. In this case, the expected return to competitors would be even lower because it would be necessary to set $F > V / n$, with the surplus of fees going to the charity.

Alternatively, people may have risk-preferring preferences. The logic is similar to the predominant explanation for why people gamble or buy lottery tickets, even though the expected return from those activities is negative. This is likely the reason, for example, why people enter poker tournaments. We pursue this point further in Chapter 12 in the discussion of sports gambling.

Entrepreneur-run Contests

The second type of contest we consider is one set up by a profit-maximizing entrepreneur who puts up the prize money and then takes the gross gate receipts as income. This is the case, for example, of professional golf and tennis tournaments that have corporate sponsorships, and it is the situation studied by Szymanski (2003). In this interpretation, total revenue (gate receipts) is assumed to be an increasing function of aggregate "competition," as measured by the sum of the competitors' efforts. As noted above, this captures the desire of fans to pay to watch the competition itself.

Specifically, let total revenue be defined by

$$TR = R(X) \tag{5.23}$$

where R is an increasing and concave function of aggregate competition, X. Further, from equation (5.13) we have

$$X = \sum_{j=1}^{n} x_j^* = \frac{(n-1)V}{n} \tag{5.24}$$

Thus, X depends on n and V. The organizer's problem in this case is to choose n and V to maximize its net profits, which are given by

$$R(X) - V \tag{5.25}$$

subject to the constraint that competitors are willing to participate:

$$p_i^* V - x_i^* = \frac{V}{n^2} \geq \bar{\pi}_i, \qquad i = 1, \ldots, n \tag{5.26}$$

Here, $\bar{\pi}_i$ is the return for competitor i in his or her next-best activity (i.e., their opportunity cost of participating).

Consider first the choice of n, the number of contestants in the tournament. Total revenue is increasing in n given that revenue is increasing in aggregate competition (i.e., $dR / dX > 0$), and aggregate competition, X, is increasing in n.[8] Thus, from a pure revenue perspective, the league organizer would like to have as many competitors as possible. However, as competitors enter, the expected return for each competitor decreases, which eventually causes the participation constraint in equation (5.26) to bind (that is, to hold with equality). This point determines the optimal tournament size, as shown in Figure 5.2.[9] The graph also shows that n^* increases with V. Specifically, an increase in V causes the downward-sloping curve to shift upward, as shown by the dashed curve, thereby shifting n^* rightward. Intuitively, a larger award will attract more contestants.

Finally, consider the choice of V, the total prize money. As shown in Figure 5.3, the optimum occurs at the point where marginal revenue, $MR = dR / dV$, equals marginal cost (which in this case is \$1).[10] This reflects the assumption of diminishing marginal revenue.

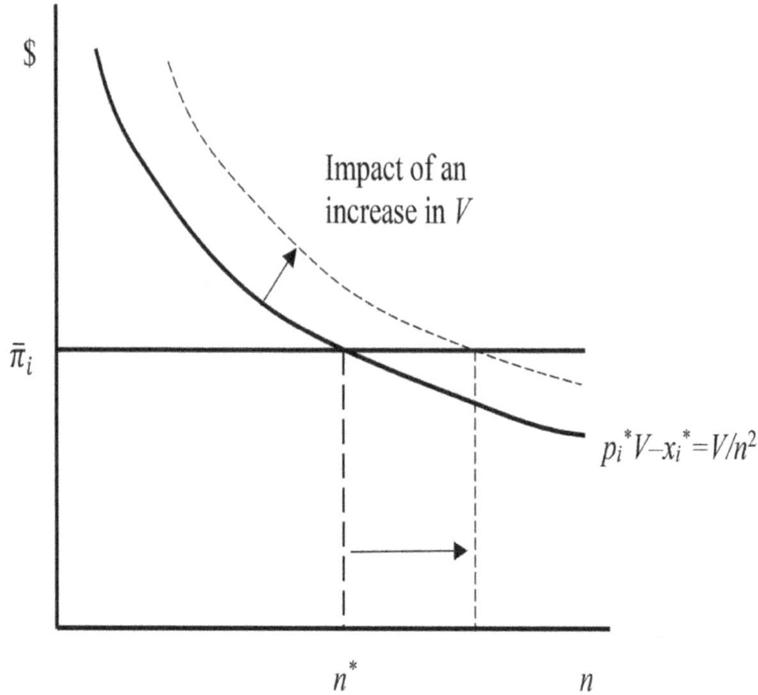

Figure 5.2 Optimal tournament size

Professional Leagues

The preceding model does not really reflect the behavior of professional leagues in team sports, whose policies are generally set collectively by league members rather than by an entrepreneurial third-party organizer. In reality, such leagues seek to maximize the overall profit of member teams, with revenue coming from aggregate gate receipts paid by spectators.

To capture this situation, we set the prize equal to aggregate revenue, or

$$V = R(X) \tag{5.27}$$

In effect, teams compete for the largest possible share of this revenue.[11] Notice, however, that according to equation (5.24), aggregate contestant effort, X, is itself a function of the "prize" through the effect of on-field competition among teams, and this in turn is dependent on the number of teams. Thus, equation

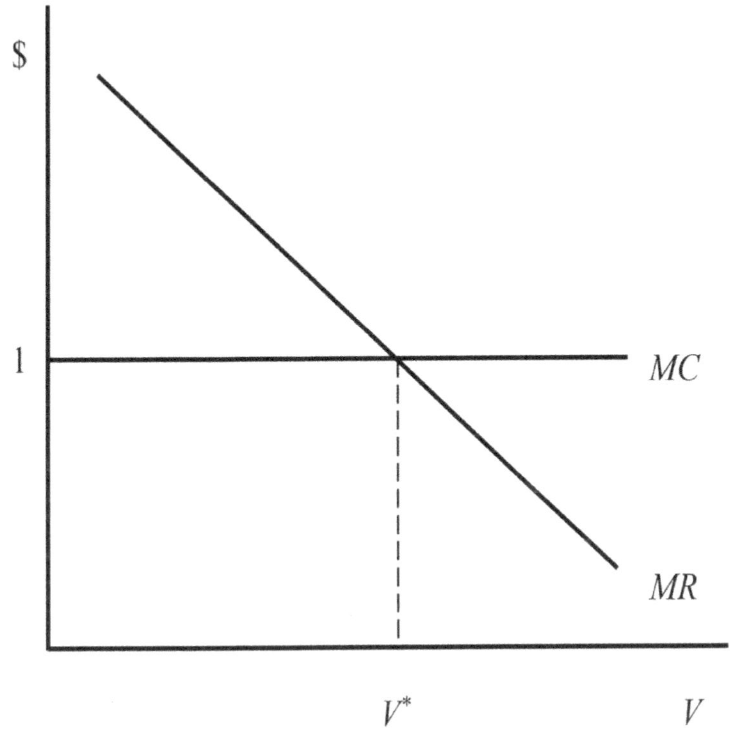

Figure 5.3 *The optimal magnitude of the prize*

(5.27) along with (5.24) jointly define a function $V(n)$ according to the implicit equation

$$V = R\left(\frac{n-1}{n}V\right) \tag{5.28}$$

Intuitively, more overall competition increases aggregate revenue, which raises the prize, which further increases competition, and so on. Assuming an equilibrium exists and that it is stable,[12] the resulting function $V(n)$ is increasing in n. That is, more teams increase aggregate revenue.

We assume that the goal of the league is to maximize total revenue per team, which is equal to $V(n)/n$. That is, $V(n)$ is shared equally among teams (given competitive balance). An interior solution in which $n^* > 0$ thus requires average revenue first to rise and then fall with the number of teams in the league,

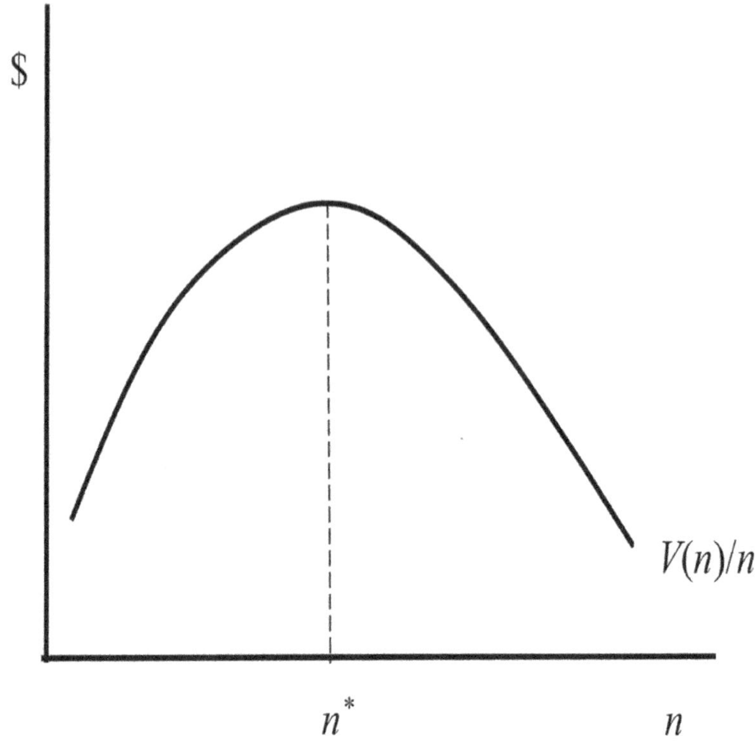

Figure 5.4 Optimal league size

as shown in Figure 5.4. This will be true if total revenue is initially rising at an increasing rate but eventually experiences diminishing marginal returns. The league's maximization problem, as described here, is similar to that facing a labor-managed firm, whose goal is to maximize the share of revenue for each worker (Meade, 1972). It is well-known in that context that at the optimum, marginal revenue from the last worker should equal average revenue, or, in the current context, $V'(n) = V(n)/n$. This condition is assumed to be satisfied at n^* in Figure 5.4.

OVERLOOKED ISSUES

This section discusses several issues that have been overlooked in the above models, most of which concern aspects of team performance. First, the analysis has abstracted from the inherent quality (ability) of competitors, which will generally vary based on the talent or skill of individual contestants and the unequal make-up of teams. Superior skill would give competitors an advantage in the above conflict models, which, not surprisingly, would result in asymmetries in the equilibrium outcomes such that more skilled competitors/teams would have higher chances of winning. We have also previously noted that if skill or talent is a scarce resource, it will influence the league's entry policy so as to avoid talent dilution. We pursue this point further in Chapter 10 in the context of the screening function of the minor leagues.

The models in this chapter have also assumed that there is a single decision maker for each competitor, who chooses effort to maximize the overall expected return. This is realistic for individual contests where competitors are in effect "sole proprietors," but it does not fit the situation for team sports where there are multiple competitors, all of whom are "employees" of the team. While the team owner makes certain economic decisions and assembles the team, it is the players and the coach/manager who ultimately make the on-field effort choices. As employees, however, they will not necessarily choose their individual effort levels to maximize the team's fortunes, except to the extent that their compensation is tied to that performance. Evaluating the performance of employees of an organization is studied by economists using the *principal–agent model*, where the principal is the employer (the team owner, manager) and the agent is the employee (player). The theory underlying this model is that the performance of agents depends, at least in part, on the nature of the contractual arrangement between them and the team owner. For example, to what extent is compensation tied to performance (such as by incentive clauses) rather than being a fixed salary? Chapter 9 studies these issues in detail.

Complicating the assessment of individual player performance is the so-called *team production problem*, which concerns the measurement of the separate contributions of individual members of the team to that team's overall performance. This problem arises in any employment situation in which multiple employees combine to produce a single final output. An assembly line or a road crew offers classic examples. The issue is how to assign responsibility for the value of the final output to the individual members of the team for purposes of paying compensation or for identifying shirkers. This same issue provides endless fodder for sports fans and commentators as they try to evaluate the contributions of individual players to a team's success or failure. The plethora of performance statistics actually makes this problem somewhat easier in sports than in most business settings, but all fans know that numbers alone can lie or at best tell half-truths. They also ignore such factors as leadership and team chemistry, which are vital contributors to the success of most championship teams. The aphorism in sports that such things as intangibles and team chemistry matter epitomizes the team production problem. We also return to this point in Chapter 9.

A further complicating issue is assessing the role of the coach/manager in team success. From the perspective of the principal–agent model, coaches are simultaneously the principal with respect to players and an agent with respect to ownership. If anything, however, their contribution to team success or failure is even harder to assess than that of players, yet they routinely bear the blame for a team's poor performance.[13] Most observers recognize, however, that this simply reflects the ease of firing a coach rather than a sign of his or her actual culpability. Still, incentive contracts for coaches can be used as mechanisms for eliciting the best possible performance from them, whatever that involves.

Finally, the preceding model has ignored the allocation of risk that is inherent in sports, reflecting both the risk of failure (poor play) and of injury. Economists usually assume that people are averse to risk, meaning that they prefer a predictable stream of income as opposed to income variability. However, if income is tied to performance in sporting contests, as the above models specified, then variability is an inherent element of the activity. In the extreme case of individual competitors whose sole income is prize money in tournaments, income will necessarily fluctuate from contest to contest. Indeed, that was one explanation we offered for why the professional golf tours and other individual sports leagues often embrace graduated reward schemes. As we saw, however, the price for that reward structure is weakened incentives to exert effort. For team sports in which players are employees of a team, player income usually takes the form of a salary that is at most weakly tied to team performance. Risk-averse players prefer that situation because it insures them against risk, but owners do not like it because, like graduated rewards, it blunts incentives for players to exert maximum effort. It is therefore an ongoing source of conflict between ownership and players' unions as to how much player contracts should be based on incentives and how much should take the form of guaranteed salaries. This age-old issue in economics is also addressed in Chapter 9.

SUMMARY

This chapter turned to the application of economic analysis to the game on the field. The basis for this approach was a conflict model, which describes how groups of contestants (individuals or teams) compete with one another for a prize. Each contestant invests in a level of "effort," which, in conjunction with the effort choices of the other contestants, determines the winner according to the specific rules of the contest (for example, most points scored, longest jump, fastest time, etc.). The result of the model was an equilibrium that described how much effort each contestant invested as a function of the parameters of the contest, parameters which, in the simplest setting, are the number of competitors, the value of the prize, and how the prize is structured (i.e., whether the winner receives the full amount of the prize or it is somehow apportioned). Given this result, we examined the design of the "optimal" contest, which depended on the objective function of the contest (or league) organizer. We considered various objectives, including free entry and maximization of revenue from gate receipts (which was assumed to depend on aggregate competition). Not surprisingly, the conclusions were very sensitive to the specified objective. We concluded the chapter by noting that the simple model overlooked several issues, many of which will be taken up in subsequent chapters.

EXERCISES

5.1. Consider a contest between two competitors, A and B, for a prize totaling \$50. Holding the effort of contestant B constant, consider the decision by contestant A between "high" effort, costing \$7, and "low" effort, costing \$4. Suppose the probability that A will win is 0.60 if she chooses high effort, and 0.40 if she chooses low effort.

(a) Suppose first that the reward scheme is "all or nothing." That is, whichever contestant wins receives the entire prize of \$50. Show that contestant A will choose high effort.

(b) Now, suppose a graduated prize is put in place, where the winner receives \$30 and the loser receives \$20. Show that contestant A now chooses low effort.

NOTES

1. Much of the analysis in this chapter is based on Szymanski (2003). See Chapter 2 of Szymanski (2009) for a non-technical treatment.
2. The first formal model of a sports league using this approach was El-Hodiri and Quirk (1971). Their model drew on the seminal paper on rent-seeking by Tullock (1967). Also see Fort and Quirk (1995) and Vrooman (1995).
3. Similar approaches have been used to study competition for political office, legal disputes, and military conflicts. See Garfinkel and Skaperdas (2007) for a survey.
4. We ignore ties.
5. Specifically, $d^2 p_i / dx_i^2 < 0$
6. Another mechanism that saves on the costs of all-out conflict in the case of warfare is for each side to choose one representative and allow them to fight it out. The biblical story of David and Goliath is an example.
7. Specifically, write (5.12) as $\frac{(n-1)xV}{(nx)^2} = 1$, which can be solved for x to get the expression in (5.13).
8. Specifically, from (5.24) $dX / dn = V / n^2 > 0$.

9. Mathematically, the constraint in (5.26), written as an equality, can be solved to obtain $n^* = \sqrt{V / \bar{\pi}_i}$.
10. Given the binding participation constraint, the first-order condition for an optimum is $R_X\left(\frac{\partial X}{\partial n}\frac{\partial n}{\partial V}+\frac{\partial X}{\partial V}\right)-1=0$. The second-order condition requires *MR* to be downward sloping at V, which means that the first term in this equation must be decreasing in V.
11. In later chapters, we will encounter team revenue functions that resemble this formulation.
12. Stability requires that $R'\left(\frac{n-1}{n}\right)<1$.
13. See Bradbury (2007, Ch. 5) for an effort to assess the impacts of a coach on player success.

6. Competitive balance

Sporting contests are, above all, about competition—two or more individuals or teams vying for a prize or championship. What are the specific elements of this competition that fans value? They presumably include (1) the quality of play on the field (i.e., the skill level of the contestants); (2) a rooting interest for one of the teams/participants (i.e., partisanship); and (3) uncertainty regarding the outcome of the contest (i.e., the excitement of the game itself). The previous chapter was about the first of these. The focus of this chapter will be on the third—the uncertainty of outcome—with some recognition of how it interacts with the second, partisanship.

Common sense suggests that if dominant teams consistently won games or championships, even partisan fans would eventually lose interest, and league revenues would decline. For this reason, all sports leagues are concerned about ensuring uncertainty of outcome, or competitive balance, among teams or competitors. Sports commentators commonly refer to this situation as "parity," though it is a testament to the subtlety of this issue that the attainment of parity is not always seen in a positive light; sometimes, it connotes universal mediocrity. Furthermore, the existence of some dominant teams can create fan interest in rooting for underdogs. Indeed, much of the national attention given to the annual NCAA basketball tournaments centers on the emergence of so-called "Cinderella" teams.

From an academic perspective, the concept of competitive balance is foundational to the economic approach to sports. Indeed, it is the one concept that is unique to the field. This chapter is therefore devoted to the various economic aspects of competitive balance. It first defines the concept, and then discusses its origin and theoretical foundation, the goal being to provide a firm basis in consumer preferences for the idea. The discussion then turns to measures of competitive balance with the objective of assessing the degree to which leagues actually attain it. Finally, we assess different policies leagues have adopted as a means of attaining or preserving competitive balance. The focus there will be on comparing the various policies and assessing their efficacy.

ORIGINS OF THE CONCEPT OF COMPETITIVE BALANCE

Organizers of professional leagues have undoubtedly been aware of the importance of competitive balance since the inception of professional sports. In the early days of professional baseball in the United States, for example, team owners instituted the *reserve system*, which tied a player to his team for life. Even if a player's contract with his current team had expired, he could not negotiate with other teams. His only alternative to re-signing with his current team was to leave professional baseball altogether. We will discuss the reserve clause later in this chapter (and indeed throughout this book); the point here is that owners believed (or at least publicly argued) that the reserve clause was necessary to prevent the richest owners from acquiring all of the best players, thereby undermining competitive balance. The logic sounded compelling, though as we will see, it turns out to be fundamentally flawed.

It has nonetheless become accepted as a truism that competitive balance is a critical aspect of the economic success of professional sports leagues. In the literature on sports economics, this assertion was first explicitly put forward by Simon Rottenberg (1956) in a classic article on the baseball players' labor market. According to Rottenberg, "uncertainty of outcome is necessary if the consumer is to be willing to pay admission to the game" (p. 246). Neale, in another foundational article in the field, likewise argued that "receipts depend upon competition among the sportors [sic] or teams … the more sporting competition the greater the profits" (Neale, 1964, p. 2).[1] This assertion, that profits depend on equal competition, has become known in the sports economics literature as the Uncertainty of Outcome Hypothesis (UOH). There has been, however, little theoretical foundation laid for this claim; usually, it is asserted to be self-evident. The next section therefore seeks to ground the concept in consumer preferences.

PREFERENCES FOR COMPETITIVE BALANCE

In economic theory, the demand side of the market is derived from consumer preferences. How consumers rank various goods and services dictates how much of their limited income they are willing to spend on them. If we are to view sporting contests as consumer goods, then the demand for such contests should similarly be grounded in preferences. But what determines how much a consumer is willing to pay to attend a contest? We suggested three factors above: the display of skill by the competitors, a rooting interest for a favorite team, and the suspense of the game itself—i.e., the uncertainty of outcome. The discussion in this section focuses on the latter two factors: partisanship and uncertainty of outcome. In a sense, these would seem to be competing values, but it is possibly one of the paradoxes of sports that even fans with a rooting interest enjoy a competitive contest and would lose interest if their favorite team won too easily or often. Thus, some interplay of these values likely underlies fans' attraction to sports. In this section, we offer two possible approaches for grounding these values in consumer preferences.[2]

The first approach we consider views fans as purely partisan in the sense that they root for their favorite teams regardless of the ease or frequency with which they win, but the league, acting in the collective interests of member teams, promotes competitive balance to maximize overall fan welfare. In this view, fans do not individually value competitive balance per se, but it is optimal for the league as a whole. The second approach assumes that individual fans care about competitive balance, possibly along with other values. Thus, even partisan fans derive less utility from contests in which their favorite team is too dominant. According to this approach, a desire for competitive balance (uncertainty of outcome) directly enters fans' utility functions.[3] The following sections provide simple preference-based models of both approaches, and then combine them into an integrated treatment.

Purely Partisan Fans

Regarding the desire for competitive balance, Mills and Fort (2018, p. 928) note that, "while uncertainty offers excitement, it is reasonable to expect that a preference for the home team reaching the playoffs would dominate preferences for suspense and balance for many fans." In this section, we examine the case of purely partisan fans.

Consider a fan of team i who derives utility from the success of that team. Specifically, suppose that the fan's expected utility is given by the simple linear form

$$U_i = p_i U^W + (1 - p_i) U^L \tag{6.1}$$

where p_i is the probability that team i wins, U^W is the fan's utility from winning, and U^L is the fan's utility from losing. We therefore assume that $U^W > U^L$, reflecting a preference for victory. It is possible that $U^L > 0$, meaning that the fan derives utility from the game itself apart from winning or losing; or that $U^L < 0$, meaning that the fan derives disutility from losing. For simplicity, we will assume that $U^L = 0$. Thus, equation (6.1) becomes

$$U_i = p_i U^W \tag{6.2}$$

We also assume that the utility from winning (and the disutility from losing) is the same regardless of the opponent. We thus ignore the effect of rivalries.

According to equation (6.2), fans of team *i* achieve maximum utility, and hence generate the maximum revenue for team *i*, when p_i=1. From the perspective of the league, however, the goal presumably is to maximize the aggregate revenue of all teams. In a two-team league, aggregate fan utility would therefore be given by the following Benthamite welfare function[4]

$$W = p_1 U^W + p_2 U^W \tag{6.3}$$

where the utility of fans of each team is given equal weight, reflecting, for example, equal market sizes. The goal of the league would, therefore, be to maximize equation (6.3) subject to the zero-sum constraint that $.p_1 + p_2 = 1$. Substituting the constraint into equation (6.3), however, yields $W = U^W$. It follows that the optimal combination of probabilities is indeterminate—that is, any combination of p_1 and p_2 produces the same level of welfare. This is a consequence of the linearity of fan utility in equation (6.2), which implies that any gain in utility to fans of team one from an increase in p_1 is exactly offset by a loss in utility to fans of team two (and vice versa). As a result, aggregate welfare is invariant to the p_is.[5]

As an alternative, suppose the utility function of fan *i* is given by

$$U_i = U(p_i) \tag{6.4}$$

where $U(\bullet)$ is an increasing, concave function. That is, $U' > 0$ and $U'' < 0$. This is a standard assumption in consumer theory, and in the current context reflects the intuitive idea that fans derive diminishing marginal benefits from wins as their team becomes increasingly successful. That is, wins generate increasingly smaller increments in utility. Overall league welfare now becomes

$$W = U(p_1) + U(p_2) \tag{6.5}$$

which the league maximizes subject to $p_1 + p_2 = 1$. In this case, the first-order condition defining the optimum results in the equation

$$U'(p_1) = U'(p_2) \tag{6.6}$$

which implies that $p_1 = p_2 = ½$. Thus, perfect competitive balance emerges as the optimum. In contrast to the linear utility case, equal win probabilities are optimal here because wins by weak teams (i.e., those with low p_i) are worth more to their fans at the margin than wins by strong teams (those with high

p_i) for the same reason that an extra dollar in income is worth more to a poor person than to a rich person.

This is shown graphically in Figure 6.1. Starting from a very unequal situation with $p_1 < p_2$, add a win to team 1 and take away a win from team 2, as indicated by the arrows. Clearly, the gain in utility for fans of team 1 is much larger than the loss in utility for fans of team 2. Only when all teams have equal probabilities of victory are wins equally valuable at the margin, and condition (6.6) verifies that this is the optimal outcome. When $U(p)$ was linear, no such gain from equalizing win probabilities was possible.

The optimal solution is illustrated graphically in Figure 6.2 by the tangency between the convex iso-welfare curve (labeled W) and the zero-sum constraint. The convexity of the iso-welfare curve, which is what ensures an interior solution, is a consequence of the concavity of the $U(\cdot)$ function.[6] Note that the optimum occurs at the point on the constraint where it is intersected by a 45° line through the origin, or where $p_1 = p_2 = ½$. It is important to emphasize that, although individual fans have no desire for competitive balance, that outcome emerges as a consequence of the league's goal of achieving the highest level of overall fan satisfaction, given a diminishing marginal utility of winning.

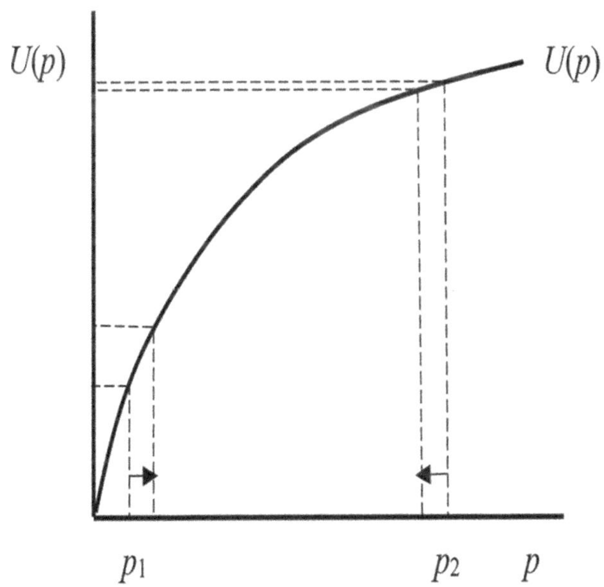

Figure 6.1 *Gain from greater competitive balance*

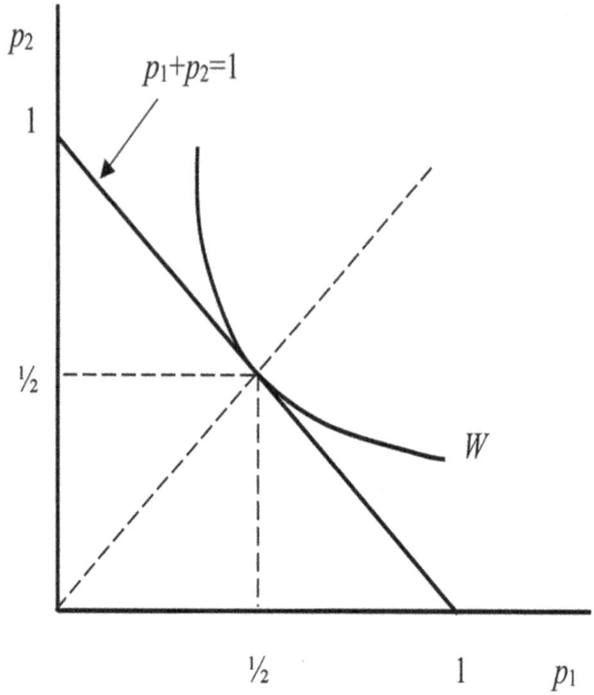

Figure 6.2 *League optimum with partisan fans*

Unequal Fan Bases

One caveat regarding the preceding analysis is that if there are unequal numbers of fans of each team, the welfare-maximizing point would reflect that asymmetry. If, for example, α is the fraction of fans who root for team 1 and $1-\alpha$ is the fraction who root for team 2, aggregate league welfare would be written as $W = \alpha U(p_1) + (1-\alpha)U(p_2)$, and the optimum condition in equation (6.6) would be

$$\alpha U'(p_1) = (1-\alpha)U'(p_2) \tag{6.6'}$$

In this case, if $\alpha > ½$, it would be optimal to set $p_1 > ½ > p_2$; that is, it would be welfare-maximizing to tilt the balance in the direction of the teams with relatively more fans. In an individual contest, this would generally suggest a bias toward home-team success since the attendance for any contest will generally consist of more fans of the home team than of the visiting team. League-wide, it suggests a bias toward teams with larger fan bases, which makes sense given the league's goal of maximizing aggregate fan happiness.

Fans Care Only About Competitive Balance

Consider now the opposite extreme where individual fans are non-partisan and care only about balanced contests. This is most descriptive of fans who have no rooting interest and therefore value suspenseful competition. It may, for example, describe the majority of fans during playoff time when all but a few teams have been eliminated.

A simple way to capture this type of non-partisan fan is with a Leontief utility function, which is most commonly used in consumer theory to describe a consumer's preferences over pairs of goods that are perfect complements. For example, think of printers and ink cartridges, which have to be used in a one-to-one correspondence, so that additional units of either good alone provide no separate value. In the current context, this implies that if one team is seen as the favorite, a fan who only cares about even contests will always root for the underdog.

In a two-team contest, this sort of preference is captured by the following form for the utility function:

$$U = \min\left[p_1, p_2\right]U^W \tag{6.7}$$

Another way to write this is[7]

$$U = \begin{cases} p_1 U^W \text{ if } p_1 \leq p_2 \\ p_2 U^W \text{ if } p_1 > p_2 \end{cases} \tag{6.8}$$

which indicates that the fan's utility depends only on the underdog's probability of victory. The indifference curves for this type of utility function are right angles, with the vertex at the point where the probabilities are equal, or $p_1 = p_2 = ½$. When this function is maximized subject to the zero-sum constraint, the optimum necessarily occurs at this vertex, as shown in Figure 6.3. Thus, each fan attains maximum utility when the league achieves perfect competitive balance.

Mixed Partisan and Non-partisan Fan Base

In reality, the overall fan base likely consists of both of the above types of fans.[8] Let us suppose in particular that a fraction α are partisan fans of team 1, a fraction β are partisan fans of team 2, and the remainder, comprising a

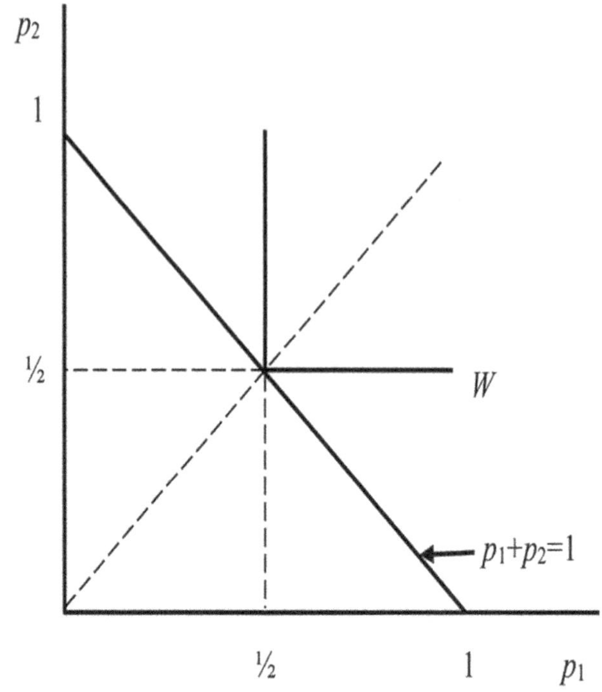

Figure 6.3 *Optimal point for non-partisan fans*

fraction 1–α – β of the total, are non-partisan in the above sense. Further, suppose that both α and β are each less than one-half, meaning that neither team's fans make up the majority of the overall fan base. This seems reasonable in a large league. In this case, let us suppose that fans of team *i* have linear utility like that in equation (6.2), while non-partisan fans have utility like that in equation (6.8). Overall league welfare would therefore be given by

$$W = \begin{cases} \left[(1-\beta)\,p_1 + \beta p_2\right]U^W \text{ if } p_1 \leq ½ \\ \left[\alpha p_1 + (1-\alpha)\,p_2\right]U^W \text{ if } p_1 > ½ \end{cases} \tag{6.9}$$

The first line says that when team 1 is the underdog, partisan fans of team 1 and non-partisan fans (together comprising a fraction 1–β of the total) root for team 1, while only partisan fans of team 2 (a fraction β of the total) root for team 2. Correspondingly, when team 2 is the underdog, partisan fans of team

2 and non-partisan fans (a fraction 1–α) root for team 2 and the remainder (a fraction α) root for team 1.

To determine the point where welfare is maximized, take the derivative of equation (6.9) with respect to p_1 to obtain

$$\frac{dW}{dp_1} = \begin{cases} (1-2\beta)U^W \text{ if } p_1 \leq ½ \\ (2\alpha-1)U^W \text{ if } p_1 > ½ \end{cases} \tag{6.10}$$

(Note that we made use of the fact that $p_2 = 1 - p_1$ in deriving these expressions.) The assumption that both α and β are strictly less than ½ implies that the first line in equation (6.10) is positive while the second line is negative. Figure 6.4 depicts the resulting welfare function, which clearly reaches its maximum point at $p_1 = p_2 = ½$. Thus, the welfare optimum for the league involves perfect competitive balance. (The same result would hold if the utility of partisan fans were concave, as in equation (6.4).) It is worth emphasizing that this conclusion holds even if the numbers of partisan fans of the two teams are not equal (that is, if $\alpha \neq \beta$). This is in contrast to the case of only partisan fans, where such an imbalance would be reflected in the welfare-maximizing

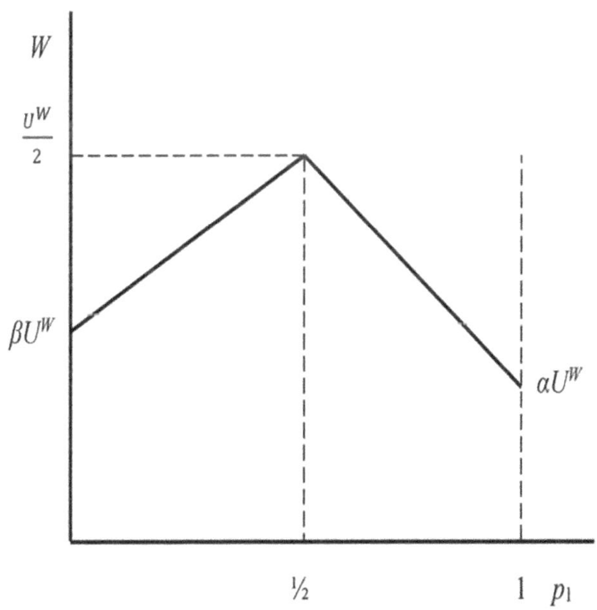

Figure 6.4 *Welfare optimum with mixed partisan and non-partisan fans*

point. Here, however, the existence of some non-partisan fans ensures that the optimum will be perfect balance because they will naturally gravitate toward the underdog, thus equalizing the effective fan bases.

The analysis in this section has shown that some reasonable characterizations of consumer preferences lead to the result that competitive balance maximizes the aggregate utility of fans. The demonstration has abstracted from various complicating factors, such as variation in the degree of fan allegiance across teams. If included, this factor, like unequal fan bases, would introduce a bias in favor of such teams that would, if considered important to league organizers, work in the direction of allowing an unbalanced league. For example, it is certainly true that leagues want teams with national fan bases to be successful.

Deriving Revenue Functions

Most existing models of professional sports leagues begin by specifying team revenue functions rather than deriving them from consumer optimization. These models generally assume, based on the UOH, that revenue functions are concave in the team's probability of winning; i.e., that revenue rises but at a decreasing rate in team performance, possibly reaching a peak at some $p > .5$.[9] In this section, we show how the consumer preference models developed above translate into team revenue functions.

First, consider the case of purely partisan fans with diminishing marginal utility. Specifically, let us rewrite the utility function in equation (6.4) more explicitly as

$$U_i = x + v(p_i) \tag{6.11}$$

where x is a composite consumption good whose price is \$1, and $v(\cdot)$ is concave in p_i. The consumer's budget constraint is $y = x + w_i$, where y is income and w_i is the consumer's willingness to pay to attend a game featuring team i. The maximum amount the consumer will pay is determined by her next best entertainment option, the value of which equals $\bar{U}$. Setting $U_i = \bar{U}$, using the budget constraint to substitute for x in equation (6.11), and solving for w_i yields the willingness to pay function for consumer i:

$$w_i = y + v(p_i) - \bar{U} \tag{6.12}$$

Willingness to pay is thus increasing in income and concave in the probability of winning.

To transform this into an aggregate revenue function for team i, allow consumers to vary in their next-best options. Specifically, suppose $\bar{U}$ is distributed uniformly on [0, G]. A consumer will attend a game if the ticket price, t_i, is less than w_i. Consumers with low enough values of $\bar{U}$ that $w_i \geq t_i$ will therefore attend a game. The resulting demand function for tickets for team i is[10]

$$D_i = m_i \frac{y + v(p_i) - t_i}{G} \tag{6.13}$$

where m_i is the total number of potential fans (the fan base) for team i. Note that D_i is downward-sloping in the ticket price, t_i. Total revenue is found by multiplying D_i by t_i to obtain

$$R_i = \frac{t_i m_i}{G}\left(y + v(p_i) - t_i\right) \tag{6.14}$$

which is increasing but concave in p_i, as is usually assumed.

For the case of purely non-partisan fans, a similar analysis would show that the associated revenue function is maximized at p_i=½ for all teams, reflecting underlying fan utility. Thus, the resulting revenue function would be maximized when the league attains perfect competitive balance.

MEASURING COMPETITIVE BALANCE

Taking as given the argument that competitive balance is an objective of sports leagues, we next ask how to assess the degree to which leagues actually achieve this goal. This is complicated by the fact that the concept is forward-looking in the sense that it prescribes an equal ex-ante probability of winning for all teams, but these probabilities are not observable. Instead, we can only observe game outcomes, which is an ex-post measure.

Given this caveat, the most common approach for measuring balance is to use a statistical measure of the dispersion of winning percentages among teams within the league (Humphreys, 2002). This is meant to reflect how closely winning percentages cluster around the league average, which is necessarily equal to .500. The usual such measure is the *standard deviation*, which is the average deviation of actual winning percentages from the league mean. The formula for standard deviation, typically denoted by the lower-case Greek letter σ, is given by

$$\sigma = \sqrt{\frac{1}{n}\sum_{i=1}^{n}(WP_i - .5)^2} \tag{6.15}$$

where WP_i is the winning percentage of team i.[11] The smaller this index, the closer the league approaches perfect competitive balance. (Note that if all teams have winning percentages of .5, then the standard deviation equals zero, representing perfect balance.)

As an illustration, consider the situation in Major League Baseball (MLB) over the ten-year period 2013–2022. The standard deviations of winning percentages for the American and National Leagues, and for the two leagues combined, are reported in Table 6.1. The results show that the overall extent of balance varies over time, with neither league being consistently more balanced than the other. Also, there is no clear time trend within each league or overall.

A problem with the index in equation (6.15) is that it is not directly comparable across leagues with different numbers of games. Humphreys (2002) therefore describes a standardization factor that allows such comparisons.[12] Using this standardized measure, Blair (2012, p. 68) provides a comparison of competitive balance across the major professional sports over the period 2005–2010. His results show that the NBA is the least balanced, while the other professional leagues (MLB, NHL, NFL) display lower but fairly similar levels of competitive balance. The relative imbalance of the NBA likely reflects the small size of teams, which means that one or two key players can allow a team to dominate the league for long stretches of time. For example, think about the dominance of the Boston Celtics, Los Angeles Lakers, and Chicago Bulls over different eras.

Evidence on Demand for Competitive Balance

What is the evidence on whether fans care about competitive balance? The answer is that it is rather weak. For example, in their review of 24 studies, Coates et al. (2014, p. 268) concluded that "no clear consensus about the relationship between expected game outcome and attendance emerges." Their own study of Major League Baseball (MLB), using attendance data from 2005 to 2010, found that attendance was positively related to home-team win probability, a result that seems more in keeping with partisan fan interests than a desire for competitive balance. Coates and Humphreys (2020) used the same data but a different empirical specification to find evidence in support of the UOH. However, several other studies have also found evidence of home-team bias in attendance data.[13] This prompted Szymanski (2003, p. 1156) to observe that "the optimal balance for the league may be greater than for the home team." This is consistent with the above approach that viewed individual fans as being purely partisan, but the league as a whole as seeking to maximize aggregate fan welfare.[14]

Table 6.1 *Standard deviation of winning percentages in Major League Baseball, 2013–2022*

MLB leagues	**2013**	**2014**	**2015**	**2016**	**2017**	**2018**	**2019**	**2020**	**2021**	**2022**
American League	.084	.061	.044	.065	.068	.113	.117	.093	.083	.082
National League	.069	.059	.081	.069	.077	.065	.078	.096	.097	.101
Overall	.075	.059	.064	.066	.071	.090	.098	.093	.083	.095

Meehan et al. (2007) extended this literature by showing that the relationship between competitive balance and game attendance in MLB depends on the point in the season when the study was done, and also whether the home or visiting team has a better record. In particular, greater balance is associated with more attendance when the home team has a better record, but there is no correlation when the visiting team has a better record.

Studies from other sports display similar conclusions. For instance, Coates and Humphreys (2012) used National Hockey League data from 2005 to 2010 to show that "fans turn out in large numbers to see games the home team is expected to win but do not turn out to see close games where the home team might lose," thus apparently contradicting the UOH (p. 365). Pawlowski (2013) likewise observed that empirical research on attendance in European professional soccer leagues has not revealed much evidence in support of the UOH; in fact, attendance in some cases has increased as a few teams have come to dominate the league. One possible explanation for this finding is that, although fans care about balance, the effect is weak relative to partisan preferences. In support of this view, Nalbantis and Pawlowski (2019) found that fans of European soccer "have a preference for games involving a favorite" (p. 798).

Pawlowski's survey of German soccer fans further reinforces this finding. He found that while the majority of fans do value UOH, the current state of imbalance in the league is not large enough to dampen fan interest. Nalbantis et al. (2017) similarly found that greater game uncertainty had a significantly positive impact on fans' willingness to pay, especially for higher-quality seats. However, once a certain level of uncertainty was achieved, fans did not value greater uncertainty. Again, it appears that fans do not desire *perfect* competitive balance.

Schreyer et al. (2018) recently examined the impact of game outcome uncertainty (GOU), as they call it, with respect to fan viewership of televised English Premier League games in Germany. They found "a significant and robust though comparatively weak relationship between GOU and transnational TV demand" (p. 633). Interestingly, they also found that male viewers were more concerned about outcome uncertainty than female viewers, though they offered no ready explanation for this difference.

Humphreys and Miceli (2020) examined the impact of travel costs on the demand for the uncertainty of outcome. Using National Basketball Association (NBA) attendance data from 1981 to 2013, they found that the attendance-maximizing odds tilted in favor of the home team in proportion to the travel distance between the home and visiting teams (a proxy for travel costs for fans of the visiting team). Mills et al. (2016) also found that demand behavior for NBA games differed for local versus out-of-market fans.

Finally, Mills and Fort (2018) used team-level attendance data for three of the four major North American professional sports leagues (baseball, basketball, and hockey) to assess the UOH. Consistent with the prior literature, they found little evidence of the impact of the UOH on attendance and only small, insignificant effects on team revenues. Rather than interpreting this as a lack of support for the UOH, however, the authors speculated that league policies aimed at promoting competitive balance have been effective enough "that imbalance does not reach extremes that would motivate fans to avoid games" (p. 926).

What all of these studies seem to show is that, while fans place some value on the uncertainty of outcome, they do not require perfect competitive balance. This is likely due to several factors, the main ones being the partisan rooting interests of hometown fans and an imbalance of fan bases across the league. It is important to emphasize, however, that in advancing the UOH, Rottenberg never claimed that it was the only factor underlying fan preferences. Thus, the mixed evidence cited here cannot be interpreted as a refutation of the hypothesis.

POLICIES AIMED AT MAINTAINING COMPETITIVE BALANCE

We finally turn to an examination of various policies leagues have put in place with the stated goal of promoting or maintaining competitive balance. We will see, however, that not all of these policies actually succeed in advancing that objective and may, in some cases, work against it.

The Reserve Clause

The first policy, alluded to earlier, is the reserve clause, which for most of the history of professional baseball tied players to their original teams, even after the expiration of any contracts between the player and the team. Under this system, teams owned the rights to a player's labor services for life and could thereby prevent him from negotiating with any other teams for the duration of his career. The reserve system was first put in place during the early years of the National League by the collective action of team owners.[15] The claimed goal was to prevent the rich teams from acquiring all the best players, which, the owners contended, would eventually ruin competitive balance.[16] However, teams retained the right to sell players, which, it turns out, actually undermines the claimed purpose of the clause.

To examine the impact of the reserve clause, it will be useful first to derive the equilibrium outcome in a league of profit-maximizing teams that potentially differ in their resources due to different market sizes, or possibly owners with different levels of generosity.[17] To keep matters simple, consider a league consisting of two teams, where revenue is an increasing function of winning percentage (or probability of victory) and also of market size, m_i. Consistent with the above formulation, the revenue of team i is given by

$$TR_i = R\left(p_i\left(x_i\right), m_i\right) \tag{6.16}$$

where $p_i\left(x_i\right)$ is the probability of victory (expected win percentage), which is assumed to be an increasing function of the team's spending on talent, x_i, as detailed in Chapter 5. Specifically, let $p_1 = x_1 / \left(x_1 + x_2\right)$ and $p_2 = x_2 / \left(x_1 + x_2\right)$ as we assumed there. To further simplify matters and make the analysis here compatible with that in Chapter 5, we assume that the revenue function in equation (6.16) has the following explicit form:

$$TR_i = p_i m_i = \left(\frac{x_i}{x_1 + x_2}\right) m_i \tag{6.17}$$

where m_i is the (fixed) revenue obtainable from an increase in team i's probability of winning, with larger values of m_i reflecting larger market sizes.

Team i will choose x_i to maximize its profit, given by $\pi_i = TR_i - x_i$. Using the formula in equation (6.17), this results in the conditions

$$\left(\frac{x_2}{(x_1 + x_2)^2}\right) m_1 = 1 \tag{6.18}$$

$$\left(\frac{x_1}{(x_1 + x_2)^2}\right) m_2 = 1 \tag{6.19}$$

for teams 1 and 2, respectively. Together, these two equations imply that, in equilibrium

$$\frac{x_1}{x_2} = \frac{m_1}{m_2} \tag{6.20}$$

Thus, the ratio of investments is equal to the ratio of potential revenues. If $m_1 = m_2$, teams will choose the same level of talent (i.e., $x_1^* = x_2^*$), and thus there will be perfect competitive balance (i.e., $p_1 = p_2 = ½$). However, if $m_1 > m_2$, team 1 will acquire more talent (i.e., $x_1^* > x_2^*$), and the league will be imbalanced (i.e., $p_1 > ½ > p_2$).

The latter outcome is the situation that owners feared when devising the reserve clause. The question is whether it is a good remedy. On the face of it, it sounded good because, in theory, it allowed small market teams to protect their best players from being poached by teams willing or able to pay more. To see why it does not necessarily achieve that outcome, consider a simple example.

Suppose there is a player whose value to his current team, team 1, is $100,000, but his value to another team, team 2, is $150,000, where the difference reflects the nature of the two markets and/or the different needs of the teams. Efficiency dictates that the player should be on team 2, and if there were full *free agency*—that is, if the player had the right to negotiate with any team—he would end up with team 2 because they would offer him the highest salary. The actual salary would depend on the bidding process across teams (as will be discussed in more detail in Chapter 9), but in any case, the result would fall somewhere between $100,000 and $150,000. Let's say it splits the difference, so the salary would be $125,000. Thus, of the $150,000 value, the player receives $125,000 and team 2 receives $25,000.

Now consider the outcome under the reserve clause where the player is tied to team 1 with a salary of $25,000. Thus, team 1 receives a surplus of $75,000 from employing the player (=$100,000–$25,000). Since the player is forbidden to negotiate with team 2, one might suppose that team 1 will hold on to him. But recall that under the reserve system, teams were able to sell players (and their contracts) to other teams, and in this example, team 2 would be willing to pay up to $125,000 for the player, which equals his value to that team ($150,000) less his current salary of $25,000. Thus, there is room for a bargain between team 1, whose surplus from the player is $75,000, and team 2, whose surplus from the player is $125,000. Assuming again that the transactors split the surplus, team 2 would pay $100,000 for the player's contract. In this case, the player's total value of $150,000 on his new team would be divided as follows: $25,000 for team 2 (=$150,000–$100,000–$25,000); $25,000 for the player (his contract salary); and $100,000 for team 1 (the sale price).

The preceding example is perfectly general and is known as the *Rottenberg Invariance Proposition*, named after the economist who first stated it (Rottenberg, 1956). It asserts that a player will end up with the team that values him the most, regardless of who initially owns the rights to that player's labor services.[18] Note that this result invalidates the core justification for the reserve system because it shows that as long as player contracts can be traded or sold, profit-maximizing owners will have an incentive to sell players to the highest bidder. The system therefore will not prevent league imbalance that might arise from different abilities to pay. The only effect of the reserve clause is on the *distribution* of the economic returns from a player's labor services. In the case of free agency, the player owns his own labor services and therefore gets the bulk of the return from those services, whereas under the reserve clause, the team that initially owned the player's services receives most of the return.

In both cases, however, the player ends up with the team that values his labor most.

Quirk and Fort (1992) offered a simple test of the Rottenberg Proposition in the form of a comparison of the standard deviation of winning percentages in Major League Baseball during the years immediately before and after repeal of the reserve system. Table 6.2 shows that the standard deviations in the American and National Leagues during the 14 years before (1963–1976) and after (1977–1990) repeal remained virtually identical, showing that competitive balance was unchanged. (In fact, both standard deviations went down slightly, indicating more balance.) We will return to the reserve system in Major League Baseball in Chapter 10, where we will offer a defense of a limited version of it, as currently exists.

Table 6.2 *Impact of the repeal of the reserve system in MLB, 1963–1990*

League	1963–1976	1977–1990
American	.071	.070
National	.066	.064

Revenue Sharing

Another policy that leagues commonly employ to equalize the ability of teams to acquire talent is revenue sharing. Under this policy, when two teams compete at each other's home arenas, they share the gate receipts according to some fixed formula. Thus, if the attendance of one team is systematically larger, revenue sharing will reduce the discrepancy, and under full revenue sharing, all teams would receive the same revenue. The logic is that this will allow teams to compete equally for talent. However, the actual outcome turns out to be just the opposite.

To see this in the context of the above model of revenue generation, suppose teams retain a fraction θ of the revenue from their home games, while visitors get the remaining fraction, $1-\theta$. For an equal number of home and away games, team 1's expected profit under this system is

$$\pi_1 = \theta\left(\frac{x_1}{x_1 + x_2}\right)m_1 + (1-\theta)\left(\frac{x_2}{x_1 + x_2}\right)m_2 - x_1 \tag{6.21}$$

Team 1's optimal choice of talent will therefore solve

$$\theta\left(\frac{x_2}{(x_1+x_2)^2}\right)m_1-(1-\theta)\left(\frac{x_2}{(x_1+x_2)^2}\right)m_2=1$$

or

$$\left(\frac{x_2}{(x_1+x_2)^2}\right)\left(\theta m_1-(1-\theta)m_2\right)=1 \tag{6.22}$$

A corresponding condition exists for team 2. Comparing equation (6.22) with equation (6.18) (the case of no revenue sharing) shows that, for $\theta<1$, team 1 has a diminished incentive to acquire talent under revenue sharing. This is true for two reasons. First, it only gets to retain a fraction θ of its home gate receipts, and second, by increasing its own strength it necessarily reduces its opponent's strength, which lowers its expected gate receipts from its opponent's home games. Thus, one effect of revenue sharing is to dilute the incentive of teams to spend on talent. The effect is similar to that created by a graduated award scheme as demonstrated in Chapter 5.

Note further that according to equation (6.21), team 1 will only spend a positive amount on talent if $\theta m_1>(1-\theta)m_2$, or if

$$\theta>\frac{m_2}{m_1+m_2} \tag{6.23}$$

The corresponding requirement for team 2 to spend a positive amount is

$$\theta>\frac{m_1}{m_1+m_2} \tag{6.24}$$

If the teams have equal market sizes, these conditions imply that $\theta>½$ for both teams. Thus, revenue sharing cannot be perfect—that is, teams must expect to retain more than half of the revenue from their home games. If this were not the case, teams would have no incentive to try to win because they would earn at least as much from away games where fans want them to lose.[19] If the teams are unequal—which is the usual motivation for revenue sharing—then conditions (6.23) and (6.24) imply that the θ must exceed the larger of the right-hand sides of the two conditions. If, for example, m_1 is twice as big as m_2, θ would have to exceed ⅔. Otherwise, the small market team would not have a sufficient incentive to try to win. Intuitively, the home-team share has to be large enough to more than offset the incentive of the small-market team to try to lose on the road.

Consider finally the effect of revenue sharing on competitive balance—i.e., on *relative* investment levels. First, if the teams are identical, there is no effect of revenue sharing on competitive balance, provided that $\theta > ½$. This is true because when $m_1 = m_2$, the share parameter θ drops out of condition (6.22) and so the teams choose identical levels of talent. Although both invest in less talent than in the absence of revenue sharing,[20] the ratio remains the same, and so $p_1 = p_2 = ½$. When $m_1 > m_2$, however, revenue sharing actually exacerbates the imbalance. Again, both teams invest less than without revenue sharing, but it turns out that the small-market team reduces its investment by more. To prove this, note that equation (6.22) and the corresponding condition for team 2 imply that, under revenue sharing, x_1/x_2 is equal to the ratio

$$\frac{\theta m_1 - (1-\theta) m_2}{\theta m_2 - (1-\theta) m_1} \tag{6.25}$$

where we assume that the numerator and the denominator are strictly positive. Note that if $\theta = 1$, this reduces to m_1 / m_2, which is the case of no revenue sharing. Now, taking the derivative of this expression with respect to θ shows that it is negative when $m_1 > m_2$. Thus, starting from $\theta=1$, as θ is lowered (i.e., as revenue sharing is introduced), the ratio in equation (6.25) increases, which causes x_1 / x_2 to rise.

Table 6.3 illustrates this result with a numerical example. In the example, $m_1 = 2$ and $m_2 = 1$. Thus, when there is no revenue sharing ($\theta=1$), $x_1^* / x_2^* = m_1 / m_2 = 2$ (the top row). However, as θ is reduced, x_1^* / x_2^* rises, meaning that there is greater imbalance. In other words, more revenue sharing increases the difference in spending levels. This, of course, is the opposite of the intended effect. Finally, as noted above, total investment in effort, $x_1^* + x_2^*$, decreases as θ falls.[21]

Table 6.3 Impact of revenue sharing

θ	x_1^*	x_2^*	x_1^*/x_2^*	$x_1^*+x_2^*$	$\pi_1+\pi_2$
1	.44	.22	2	.66	1.01
.95	.40	.18	2.18	.58	1.11
.90	.35	.14	2.43	.49	1.22
.85	.30	.11	2.82	.41	1.32
.80	.24	.07	3.50	.31	1.46
.75	.17	.03	5	.20	1.65

Note: $m_1=2$ and $m_2=1$.

If revenue sharing does not work to equalize spending, then why is it so widely used? One explanation is that it increases aggregate league profits, as shown by the final column in Table 6.3. The way it does this is by limiting spending on talent ($x_1^*+x_2^*$), which in the current formulation has the character of a wasteful "arms race." This may be the real motivation for the pervasiveness of the policy, despite its detrimental effect on competitive balance.[22]

Salary Caps

Another policy some leagues invoke to equalize team spending is a salary cap. Under this policy, individual player salaries are not capped, but overall payroll is. This often creates difficult decisions for teams regarding the make-up of the roster, such as how much of the overall budget to devote to star players. Such decision-making is where the general manager of a team earns his or her paycheck. (We discuss some of the relevant considerations in Chapter 8 in the context of the Moneyball hypothesis.) Here, however, we focus on the specific question of how a salary cap affects competitive balance.

Of course, a cap can only matter if it is a binding constraint on some teams. Under a binding cap set at B, team i's problem is to choose x_i to maximize revenue, $R\left(p_i\left(x_i\right)\right)$, subject to the constraint that $x_i \leq B$. The outcome is shown graphically in Figure 6.5, where the resulting choice of talent is $\bar{x}$, as compared with the level that would have maximized profit, $R\left(p_i\left(x_i\right)\right) - x_i$, denoted by x^* in the graph.

If the cap is binding on all teams, then the result will be perfect competitive balance, as each team's talent will be equivalent. The more likely situation, however, is that the cap will be binding for some teams and not for others. This will result in a more balanced league. Table 6.4 illustrates this point with a simple three-team example. The table shows team payrolls (in millions) without the cap and with a cap set at $100 million, which is binding on teams 1 and 2 but not on team 3. It also shows the resulting probabilities of winning a league championship, which are computed based on each team's payroll relative to the overall league payroll. Note that the cap has substantially equalized the prospects of all the all teams in the league by weakening the highest-spending teams. As was the case with revenue sharing, however, overall spending on talent is diminished.[23]

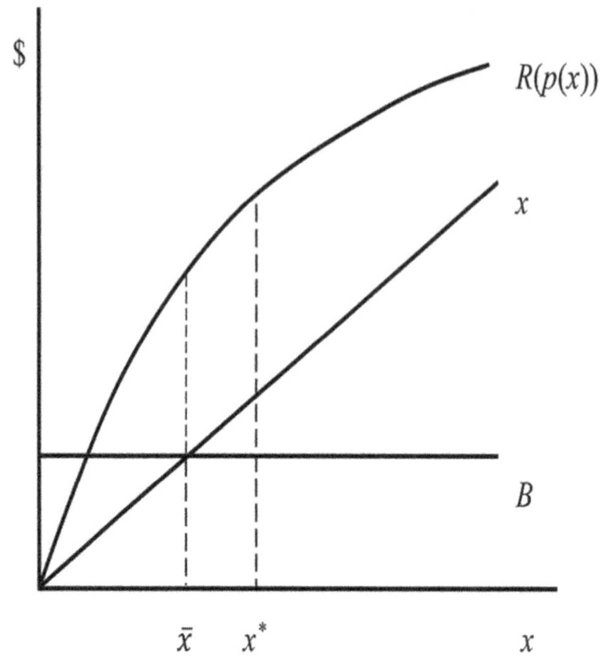

Figure 6.5 *Impact of a salary cap*

Table 6.4 *(a) Impact of a salary cap – no cap*

Team	Payroll	***p***
1	\$150	40.1
2	\$130	35.1
3	\$90	24.3

Table 6.4 *(b) Impact of a salary cap – cap*

Team	Payroll	***p***
1	\$100	34.5
2	\$100	34.5
3	\$90	31.0

Luxury Tax

Instead of a salary cap, some leagues (such as Major League Baseball) institute a *luxury tax*, which does not limit total team spending on payroll but subjects any spending above a certain limit to a tax. Suppose, for example, that a team's total payroll is \$150 million, and the limit for tax purposes is \$100 million. Then \$50 million would be subject to the tax. If the rate is 30%, the tax would be 0.30 × \$50 million = \$15 million, and the team's total payroll would be \$150 million + \$15 million = \$165 million.

The impact on competitive balance is illustrated in Figure 6.6. Consider a tax rate of t, which is imposed on any spending over the level $\bar{x}$. Thus, teams face a marginal cost of \$1 for $x \leq \bar{x}$ but \$(1+t) for $x > \bar{x}$. The relevant segments are shown by the darkened, discontinuous line in the graph. The effect of the tax is to raise the marginal cost for any spending above the threshold level. The resources of teams with different marginal revenue curves are illustrated.

First, for teams that do not reach that threshold, there will be no effect. This is the case for Team 1, whose choice of talent, x_1^*, as determined by the point where MR_1=1, falls short of the level at which the tax kicks in. At the other

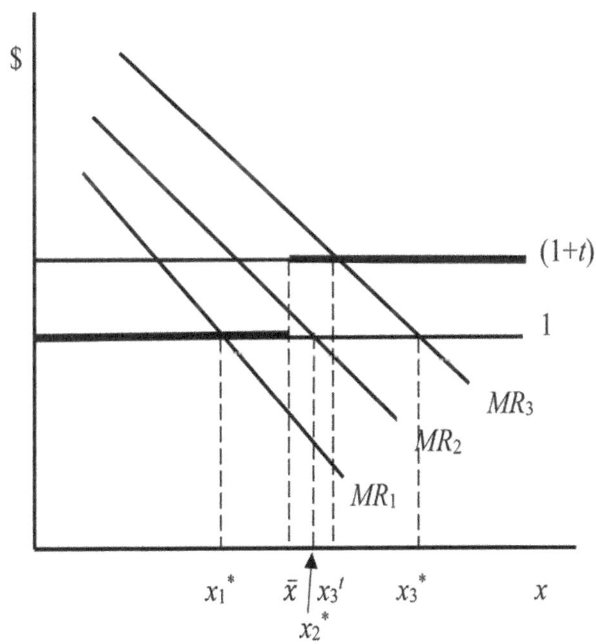

Figure 6.6 Impact of a luxury tax

end of the spectrum, Team 3, for which the tax clearly applies, lowers its talent level from x_3^*, which is what it would have chosen in the absence of the tax (i.e., at the point where MR_3=1), to x_3^t, which occurs where $MR_3 = 1 + t$.

Finally, some teams will cluster at the threshold, $\bar{x}$. Although these teams would like to spend $x > \bar{x}$, they refrain from doing so to avoid the tax.[24] This is the case for Team 2, which would choose x_2^* in the absence of the tax but chooses $\bar{x}$ in its presence. The overall effect will be to create a clustering of teams at the threshold, while some teams will remain below that level and some go above it. As the tax rate t is raised, holding $\bar{x}$ fixed, some teams that chose to exceed the cap and pay the tax will now revert to $\bar{x}$. Thus, if t gets large enough, the tax will in effect become a cap.

The key difference between hard salary caps and a luxury tax is that the latter does not impose an absolute constraint on spending. Thus, as long as t is not too high, some rich teams will spend above the threshold $\bar{x}$, which may be good for the league (if it wants large-market teams to be successful) and is certainly good for the players. Also, the tax produces revenue that can be redistributed.

Reverse-order Drafts

Most professional leagues in the United States have so-called reverse-order drafts, which allow teams that finish with the worst records to have the earliest picks in the following year's draft of amateur players.[25] The obvious objective is to help those teams acquire the highest-rated prospects so that they can become more competitive in the future. Again, this sounds good on its face, but in terms of its effect on competitive balance, it potentially falls prey to the Rottenberg Proposition in the sense that teams can always trade or sell their draft picks. As a result, top players will end up with the teams that value them the most regardless of who initially drafts them. The principal impact of reverse-order drafts is therefore to subsidize teams that finish lower in the standings, and this will increase their ability to compete with richer teams if they choose to spend the money on acquiring better players. And, if teams are win- rather than profit-maximizers, they may actually choose to retain their draft picks rather than sell them, thereby immediately becoming more competitive on the field.

An undesirable feature of reverse-order drafts is that they may encourage "tanking" by low-ranked teams toward the end of a season in order to improve their draft standing. Although there is little doubt that this happens, the reputation, competitive drive, and job security of players, coaches, and general managers tend to work against this strategy.

Relegation

Finally, we consider the practice of *relegation*, which is not used in the United States but is common in European professional sports leagues. Under relegation, the lowest-placing teams in a league are demoted to an inferior league, and the top-finishing teams in that lower league are promoted. The assumption here is that teams will have a strong incentive to avoid relegation because of the loss of revenue and prestige. This will principally affect the behavior of teams at the low end of the talent distribution and will likely cause upward compression of talent as teams in danger of relegation seek to acquire better players toward the end of the season. This is in contrast to the downward compression of talent that we saw under the salary cap and luxury tax.

An interesting effect of relegation, if it were employed in conjunction with a reverse-order draft, is that it would serve as an effective deterrent against tanking. Such a practice is never desirable in a sports league because it undermines fans' confidence in the nature of competition in the same way that betting on games can (as will be discussed in Chapter 12).

SUMMARY

This chapter examined the issue of competitive balance, which is a foundational concept in sports economics. Competitive balance represents the idea that the outcome of sporting contests ideally should be uncertain because fans value suspenseful contests. The chapter began by seeking to ground this desire for balanced competition in fan preferences using standard consumer theory. The discussion then turned to the measurement of competitive balance, which is most commonly done by calculating the standard deviation of winning percentages across a league. A lower standard deviation reflects less dispersion in team outcomes and hence signals greater competitive balance (at least in terms of outcomes).

Given the assertion that competitive balance is an objective of sports leagues, we reviewed the empirical evidence on whether actual fan behavior reflects such a desire. The results were mixed, with studies showing some desire for balanced competition, but also, not surprisingly, a bias in favor of home team success.

Finally, we examined several policies that have been employed by leagues to promote or maintain competitive balance. Our findings regarding the efficacy of these policies were also mixed. We specifically concluded that the reserve system and reverse-order drafts did not necessarily enhance competitive balance as a consequence of the Rottenberg Invariance Proposition, which asserts that players end up with the team that values them most regardless of who initially owns their labor services. We also showed that revenue sharing fails to promote balance, and indeed it may worsen it by tilting investments in talent even more toward large-market teams. On the other hand, salary caps, luxury taxes, and relegation do tend to equalize the distribution of talent. The first two accomplish this by causing the downward compression of talent (i.e., they induce less investment in talent/effort by richer teams), while the last one causes upward compression (i.e., it incentivizes greater investment in talent/effort by lower-ranked teams).

EXERCISES

6.1. Consider the following winning percentages (Table E6.1) for a ten-team league over two seasons:

Table E6.1 Winning percentages over two seasons

Team	Year 1	Year 2
A	.300	.380
B	.350	.400
C	.400	.440
D	.450	.460
E	.500	.500
F	.500	.500
G	.550	.540
H	.600	.560
I	.650	.600
J	.700	.620

Calculate the standard deviation for each year as a measure of competitive balance. (Use a spreadsheet, or the formula in equation (6.15).) Which year has greater competitive balance?

6.2. Choose one of the major sports leagues (MLB, NFL, NHL, NBA, WNBA, Premier League) and compute the standard deviation for the most recent two full seasons. How did competitive balance change? (In hockey, treat overtime losses as losses, and in football and soccer, treat ties/draws as half a win and half a loss.) Websites for each league provide yearly team standings: www.mlb.com; www.nfl.com; www.nhl.com; www.nba.com; www.wnba.com; www.premierleague.com

6.3. Suppose a team has a total revenue function given by $TR(x) = 5x - .05x^2$, where x is the team's total payroll (in millions). Its corresponding marginal revenue function is therefore $MR(x) = 5 - .1x$. Its total spending on players, by construction, is $TC = x$, which makes its marginal cost MC=1.
   (a) Derive the team's profit-maximizing level of spending in the absence of a luxury tax.
   (b) Now suppose a luxury tax of 30% is imposed on spending above 30 (i.e., MC=1.3 for x >30). Derive the optimal level of spending in this case. (Hint: equate $MR(x)$ to MC=1.3 and solve for x.) Compute the tax the team must pay at this level of spending.
   (c) Alternatively, the team could have chosen x=30 to avoid paying any tax. Show that the team's profit is higher at the employment level you computed in (b), even though the team must pay a luxury tax on the extra spending. Finally, show that if the team spends the level you computed in (a), it would also earn less profit than it would by choosing the level you computed in (b).

NOTES

1. See Zimbalist (2002) for a survey of the issue.
2. This discussion is based on Humphreys and Miceli (2019).
3. Examples of this approach are Coates, Humphreys, and Zhou (2014) and Miceli (2024a).
4. In an n-team league, $W = \sum_{i=1}^{n} p_i U^W$, where p_i is interpreted as the probability of team i winning the league championship.
5. If the U^W s vary across teams, then it would be optimal to set p=1 for the team whose fans have the highest U^W and p=0 for all other teams.
6. This is proven in the Appendix.
7. This formulation arbitrarily assumes that the fan roots for team 1 when they are evenly matched.
8. Miceli (2024a) proposes a utility function for fans that simultaneously reflects partisanship and a desire for competitive balance.
9. See, for example, El-Hodiri and Quirk (1971), Vrooman (1995), Fort and Quirk (1995), Késenne (2000), and Dietl et al. (2009).
10. In particular, the fraction of fans who attend games is given by $\Pr(w_i \geq t_i) = \Pr(\bar{u} \leq y + v(p_i) - t_i)$. For a uniform distribution with $\bar{U} \in [0,G]$, we obtain $(y+v(p_i)-t_i)/G$, which is then multiplied by the total number of potential fans for team $_i$, m_i, to get the expression in equation (6.13).
11. The difference $wP_i - .5$ is squared to ensure a positive number. Taking the square root restores the appropriate scale.
12. Specifically, he defines the standard deviation in an "idealized" league in which all teams have equal winning percentages of .500. This is given by

$.500/\sqrt{G}$, where G is the number of games. A generalized index of competitive balance is the ratio of (6.15) to this idealized standard deviation.

13. See, for example, Knowles et al. (1992), Maennig and Mueller (2023), and Mills and Fort (2023).
14. It is also in keeping with the theoretical framework in Miceli (2024a).
15. The league first formed in 1876, which is regarded as the first year of "major league" baseball. Professional leagues existed prior to that time, but are not now regarded as major leagues. See Ryczek (1999).
16. See Szymanski (2009, p. 73) and Ward and Burns (1994, p. 24).
17. See El-Hodiri and Quirk (1971), on which this analysis is based.
18. The result is closely related to (one might say it anticipated) the Coase Theorem, which says that property rights will move to their highest valuing user, regardless of their initial ownership, as long as transaction costs are low (Coase, 1960).
19. Bradbury (2007, p. 81) also makes this point.
20. This is true because with $m_1 = m_2 = m$, $\theta m_1 - (1-\theta)m_2 = (2\theta - 1)m$, which is less than one for $\theta < 1$.
21. Szymanski and Kesenne (2004) were the first to derive these results.
22. See Miceli (2024b).
23. Dietl et al. (2012) study the impact of salary caps, and Dietl et al. (2011) examine the joint impact of revenue sharing and salary restrictions.
24. In this case, $1+t > MR > 1$ at $\bar{x}$.
25. See, for example, Kahane (2006).

APPENDIX: CONVEXITY OF ISO-WELFARE CURVES

The claim in the text is that the welfare function in equation (6.5) has convex iso-welfare lines in (p_2, p_1) space as a consequence of the concavity of the $U(\cdot)$ function. To prove this, totally differentiate equation (6.5) to obtain

$$dW = U'(p_1)dp_1 + U'(p_2)dp_2 \tag{A6.1}$$

Setting this equal to zero and solving for dp_2 / dp_1 yields the slope of an iso-welfare line:

$$\frac{dp_2}{dp_1} = -\frac{U'(p_1)}{U'(p_2)} \tag{A6.2}$$

Now take the second derivative of this expression:

$$\frac{d^2 p_2}{dp_1^2} = \frac{-U'(p_2)U''(p_1) + U'(p_1)U''(p_2)\left(\frac{dp_2}{dp_1}\right)}{U'(p_2)^2} \tag{A6.3}$$

The sign of this depends on the sign of the numerator. After substituting from equation (A6.2) for dp_2 / dp_1, we obtain

$$numerator = -U'(p_2)U''(p_1) - U'(p_1)U''(p_2)\left(\frac{U'(p_1)}{U'(p_2)}\right) \tag{A6.4}$$

which is positive by virtue of the fact that $U' > 0$ and $U'' < 0$.

7. Rules and enforcement

An essential feature of a sporting event or contest of any kind is the enactment and enforcement of a set of rules designed to standardize play and ensure a fair contest. Rules define the nature of the contest, how it is won, and what types of strategies or tactics are permitted. Some rules also concern off-field issues, such as the manner in which players can be acquired and transferred, and player conduct. Compliance with off-field rules is governed by procedures put in place by the league, often as part of an agreement with a players' union (such as rules governing drug testing), while compliance with on-field rules is governed by referees or umpires who monitor play, increasingly in collaboration with video replay officials. Sanctions are generally pre-determined, though for egregious violations, ordinary penalties can be augmented later by more severe sanctions, such as fines or suspensions, following an investigation. And of course, if a player's actions off or on the field violate the laws of society, he or she will be subject to the appropriate public sanctions as well as whatever sanctions the league imposes.

Our analysis of rules and enforcement in this chapter will make use of insights gained from the economic analysis of crime and punishment (Becker, 1968). The basic concept underlying that approach is that laws are designed to guide people's behavior in certain socially desirable ways by specifying "prices" (sanctions) that reflect the social costs of potentially harmful activities. For example, fines for speeding ideally reflect the risk to oneself and others from driving at excessive speeds, and the enforcement of those fines gives rational drivers an incentive to weigh the full social costs and benefits of driving at a certain speed.

One of the central insights of the economic approach to crime is that optimal enforcement does not generally involve complete deterrence of harmful behavior. In other words, there is an optimal crime rate that is ordinarily not zero. This is true, first because the behavior in question often has an offsetting social benefit, and second because complete deterrence would often be too costly to achieve, especially when the offending activity is hard to detect. These same ideas will prove relevant to our study of the optimal enforcement of sporting rules, leading to the conclusion that some rule violation is an essential feature of sports competition.

The analysis of these issues begins by categorizing sports rules, and then turns to compliance and enforcement issues, including what the optimal penalty should be for a violation, both on and off the field, and also the impact of, and response to, errors in enforcement. The discussion then turns to the evolution of rules—how and why they change in response to changing technologies, tastes, and knowledge. Finally, the chapter discusses the unintended consequences of rule changes. The focus here is on how players rationally respond to rule changes, often producing outcomes that were not contemplated by rule makers and that, in some cases, counteract the original intent of the change.

CATEGORIZING RULE VIOLATIONS

As suggested above, we will categorize rules into two broad types: off-field rules and on-field rules, or rules of play. Most off-field violations involve actions that are intentional, such as the use of banned substances, betting on games or shaving points, altering equipment (e.g., corking bats or deflating footballs), spying on rival teams, stealing signs, and other forms of "cheating." In this sense, they are similar to crimes in ordinary law, and hence one supposes that they should be completely deterred, if that were practically possible. In other words, there are no offsetting benefits to the offending actions.

In contrast, most on-field violations are by-products of ordinary play and thus are more like accidents than crimes. Fouls in basketball and soccer, and penalties in football and hockey, are examples. Violations of this sort are therefore part of the game itself in the sense that it would not be possible to eliminate them without dramatically altering the nature of play. Think of all-star games, which are often played with the intention to avoid injury and so involve few fouls or penalties, but also possess much less of the intensity of competition that fans crave. Some rule violations are therefore an essential aspect of sports, especially when played at the highest level, where skilled athletes seek every advantage against their opponents. For instance, Walker (2017, p. 132), in his analysis of what underlies the success of great sports teams, distinguishes between what he calls "hostile" aggression that is intended to do harm and "instrumental" aggression that is done in pursuit of a competitive advantage. This dichotomy epitomizes the nature of rule violations in sports.

In this same vein, Ellickson (2016) describes how private associations, such as sports leagues, create rules aimed at controlling the behavior of their members. This is obviously true of a league's promulgation and enforcement of rules of play, but he argues that leagues also sometimes enforce rules concerning off-field behaviors that are unrelated to the sport *per se* and therefore, in effect, substitute for laws enforced by society at large. A noteworthy example is the imposition of sanctions by leagues on players accused of domestic violence. Ellickson suggests two possible reasons for this seeming pre-emption of the criminal justice system by a sports league. The first is to protect the image and integrity of the game in the eyes of fans and sponsors. This is a narrow, sports-related objective. Beyond that, however, he suggests that leagues "may have acted to limit players' domestic violence because members of the public widely perceive that the other potential controllers of domestic violence are particularly inept" (Ellickson, 2016, p. 260). In other words, sports leagues sometimes take on the larger role of controlling member behavior in those circumstances where other forms of social control are inadequate or too costly. This is a more debatable form of rule enforcement, which some would argue is inappropriate.

In view of the preceding discussion, it would seem useful to distinguish rule violations along these lines—namely, to think of violations of off-field rules as "crimes" and violations of on-field rules as "accidents." Certainly, crimes and accidents are treated very differently in ordinary law. Crimes, as intentional harms, are generally punished more harshly, potentially carrying the threat of imprisonment, whereas accidents, though still legal wrongs (torts), do not subject the injurer to the same moral opprobrium and are typically remedied by the obligation of the injurer to pay monetary compensation to victims. The economic approach to crime, as pioneered by Becker, however, reveals that intent is *not* the most important factor when thinking about optimal law enforcement. We will pursue that insight here.

The economic analysis of rule enforcement begins in the next section by examining the incentive effect of rules; that is, how they determine the behavior of individual competitors. It will become apparent in that discussion why intent is not a meaningful concept in this context either. Rather, it turns out to be more useful to think about how a particular behavior or action affects the risk of a violation, what the costs of that violation are in relation to the benefits of the action, and how easy or difficult it is to detect a violation.

COMPLIANCE WITH RULES

We suppose that athletes (and/or coaches) make decisions both on and off the field based on a comparison of the costs and benefits of those decisions, particularly as to how they contribute to the success of the team of which the decision maker is a member.[1] This follows the approach in Becker (1968), who assumes potential criminals act purely based on this sort of rational calculation.[2] Walker (2017) identified a similar motivation among elite athletes, who, he discovered, "...were not immune to pushing the rules to the breaking point. In fact, they often did so intentionally" (p. 132). This is truly the behavior of rational economic decision makers.

Following the basic set-up in Chapter 5, we consider an action or strategy, x, that affects the expected value of winning, $V(x)$. In other words, $V(x)$ is the incremental gain (e.g., the increased probability of victory) from taking an action x rather than not taking it. The action x could be a particular on-field strategy (e.g., using a zone defense versus man-to-man or pitching high and tight to an opposing team's best hitter) or a decision off the field (e.g., taking steroids or altering equipment).

Now suppose that the action could lead to a rule violation, either by its nature (taking steroids) or as an unavoidable by-product of permissible behavior (e.g., throwing pitches high and inside or playing aggressively on defense). To be specific, let $r(x)$ be the probability that action x results in a violation, where $r(x)=1$ if the chosen action x is known with certainty to be a rule violation, and $r(x)<1$ if a violation is only a possibility. In this way, the $r(\cdot)$ function reflects league policy over what constitutes a rule violation (the "rulebook") but also the judgment of officials about whether or when a particular action "crosses the line" and becomes a violation.

How are rule violations defined? This is a policy question that leagues have to confront, much like the question of what acts are deemed crimes in the larger society. Presumably, an act has to be harmful in some way, either physically or to the integrity or purpose of the game, but there's a lot of discretion here. While some acts are clear violations, others are subjective. For example, nowadays, the use of performance-enhancing drugs is a certain violation in most sports (if detected), whereas actions that meet the definition of holding in football, a foul in basketball or soccer, or intentionally throwing at a batter in baseball, involve the exercise of judgment by game officials. Likewise, when is sign stealing a legitimate form of "gamesmanship," and when does it become an unfair attempt to gain a competitive advantage?[3] Ultimately, these are questions outside the scope of economics. In any case, we can think of r as defining the *scope* of rules, whether comprising application of "black-letter" rules or judgments about allowable actions.

Even if a violation occurs, however, it may not be detected with certainty. This will be captured by the parameter q, which is defined as the probability that a violation is detected, conditional on its having occurred, where $0 \leq q \leq 1$. Generally, one supposes that q will be near one for on-field violations, where monitoring by game officials—referees or umpires—is continuous and increasingly subject to video review. In practice, however, the discretion of officials will have an impact on q based on how strictly they apply a rule. There is much debate, for example, as to how interventionist officials should be, with some fans believing they should "just let the teams play" and others insisting that they should "keep control of the game."

As for off-field violations, q may be substantially less than one because monitoring is much more difficult. The magnitude of q can be increased, however, by raising the intensity of monitoring (e.g., requiring more frequent drug testing), but the cost of doing so must be weighed against the benefits, as will be discussed below.[4] Finally, let s be the sanction, or penalty, for a detected violation. This can take the form of an on-field penalty designed to confer a competitive disadvantage to the violator—like loss of yardage in football, free throws in basketball, free kicks in soccer, or power plays in hockey—or a fine or suspension for more serious violations. We will also discuss the determination of s below.

Putting all of this together, we can now describe the compliance decision of an individual competitor. Specifically, a competitor will take action x if the expected gain exceeds the expected sanction, or if

$$V(x) > r(x)qs \tag{7.1}$$

This condition will be more likely to hold the larger the expected gains from employing the strategy (the left-hand side of equation (7.1)), and the smaller the likelihood of a violation, the probability of detection, and the sanction. As a consequence, the league can control competitor behavior both through its definition of rules and its enforcement of them. This represents the deterrence function of rules.

At this point, we can see why "intent" is not really a meaningful concept here. This is particularly true when $r < 1$ because the violation is accidental, though it can nonetheless be harmful and hence deserving of punishment. Conversely, intentional violations (those for which $r(x) = 1$) may still be committed if the competitor believes the likelihood of detection and/or sanction is low enough. This brings us to the question of enforcement.

OPTIMAL ENFORCEMENT OF RULES

Given the preceding analysis of compliance behavior, we can now turn to the optimal enforcement of rules, taking as given the set of rules as embodied by the $r(\cdot)$ function. According to equation (7.1), the compliance decision of competitors depends on the expected sanction, or the product of q and s. This idea is illustrated in Figure 7.1, where the downward-sloping line represents all those combinations of q and s which, when multiplied, yield the same product.[5] Any point on this line will therefore result in the same expected sanction and hence the same rate of violations, and so we will refer to it as an "iso-deterrence" line. The two indicated points show a low-detection, high-sanction combination (point A), and a high-detection, low-sanction combination (point B). Based on our earlier discussion, we might associate point A with off-field violations, which are typically hard to detect because they are done outside of the view of the enforcement authority (so q is small). Thus, a harsher sanction is required to achieve a given level of deterrence (or compliance). In contrast,

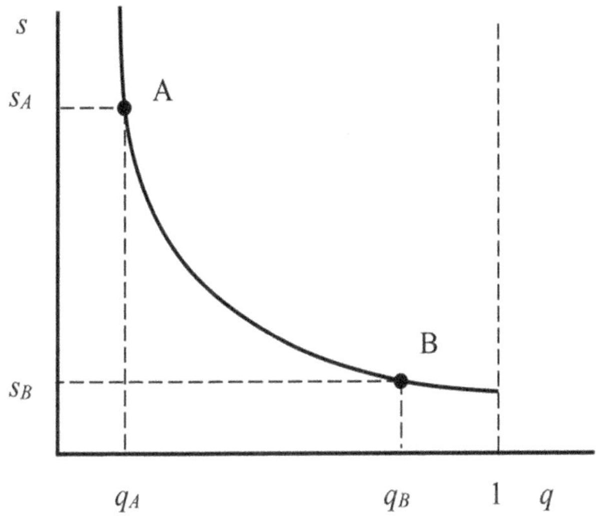

Figure 7.1 *Iso-deterrence line*

we might associate point B with most on-field violations, which are easier to detect because they are done in the plain view of game officials (so q is near 1). Thus, a milder sanction is generally satisfactory.

The preceding example has assumed that the desired rate of infractions, as depicted by points A and B, is the same, given that they lie on the same iso-deterrence line. Different infractions, however, impose different levels of harm, and so the optimal infraction rate may differ. The next step is therefore to determine the optimal infraction rate from the league's perspective. This involves determining the overall costs and benefits of an action x. One measure of benefits that we employed in Chapter 5 was the aggregate revenue, which reflects the willingness to pay of fans. Here, we will write it as a function of the total level of competitor effort, or $R(X)$, where X represents an index of the total use of strategy x across the league as a whole. (The gain to individual competitors, $V(x)$, would *not* be counted because it is offset by a corresponding loss to their opponents.)

On the cost side, we write $N(X)h$ as the total harm from violations, where N is the number of violations (which depends positively on X as determined by the $r(X)$ function), and h is the harm per violation. This could reflect physical harm (from an overly aggressive strategy, say, or from steroid use), or harm to the sport from violating the spirit or objective of the contest (for example, cheating or "dirty" play). In what follows, we will take the apprehension rate, q, as given (either high or low) and focus on the choice of the sanction, s.

The overall problem for the league is therefore to choose s to maximize net benefits, given by

$$R\left(X\left(s\right)\right)-N\left(X\left(s\right)\right)h \tag{7.2}$$

subject to the participation constraints of the competitors. The function $X\left(s\right)$ is decreasing in s based on the above compliance model. We are assuming here that there is no administrative cost to increasing the severity of the sanction itself (i.e., raising the fine or the magnitude of the on-field penalty). Assuming that the participation constraints are not binding, the optimal sanction for a particular rule violation will satisfy the first-order condition

$$\left(\frac{dR}{dX}-\frac{dN}{dX}h\right)\frac{dX}{ds}=0 \tag{7.3}$$

or simply

$$\frac{dR}{dX}=\frac{dN}{dX}h \tag{7.4}$$

The left-hand side of equation (7.4) is the marginal benefit of action X, consisting of the increment in revenue resulting from fan enjoyment from a more exciting contest (given that $dR\,/\,dX>0$), while the right-hand side is the marginal cost of an increase in X, arising from the greater number of rule violations and the consequent increased harm (given that $dN\,/\,dX>0$). An increase in the sanction, s, reduces the aggregate amount of action x as described above (i.e., $dX\,/\,ds<0$), which affects both the benefit and cost. The optimal sanction occurs at the point where the two effects are equated at the margin.

Figure 7.2 illustrates the result depicted in condition (7.4). The upper panel shows the intersection of the marginal benefit and marginal cost curves, which yields the optimal level of action, X^*, while the lower panel shows the sanction, s^*, needed to achieve that level of compliance given the negative effect of s on X. Figure 7.2 also shows what happens as the activity in question either leads to more rule violations (i.e., $dN\,/\,dX$ increases), or is more harmful (i.e., a violation entails a larger h). Both factors result in an upward shift in the marginal cost curve, as indicated by the arrow, which results in a lower optimal level of activity X, in the upper panel and a corresponding increase in the optimal sanction for a rule violation in the lower panel.

The preceding analysis treated the probability of detection as fixed, but we saw above that detection will vary according to the harm from the infraction. Figure 7.3 incorporates that consideration by showing two iso-deterrence lines, one for a low level of harm and one for a high level of harm. Recall

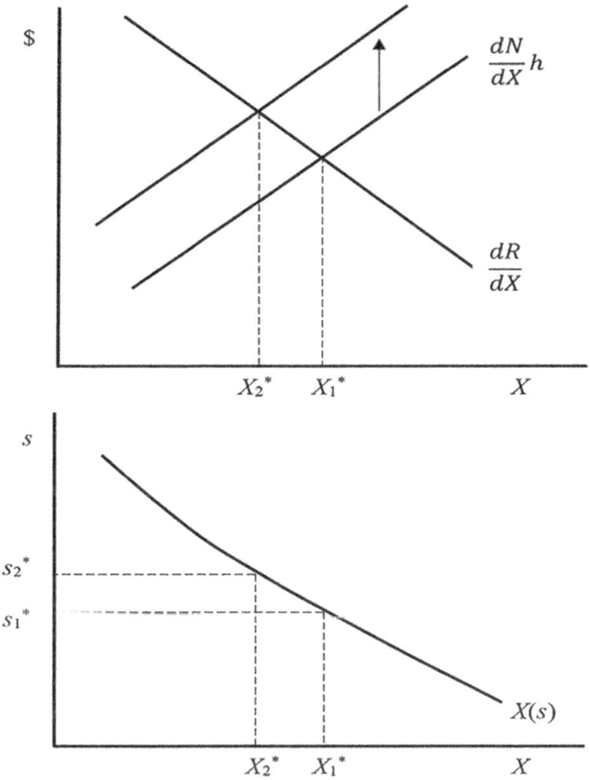

Figure 7.2 *Optimal enforcement*

that along either curve, the product qs is constant, and so the infraction rate is constant for any combination of q and s along that line. If we suppose that both curves correspond to an optimal solution to condition (7.4) but with different values of h, then the curve that is shifted further outward, representing a higher level of harm, implies a larger optimal value of the expected sanction, qs. The particular values of q and s, however, are not uniquely determined in each solution—any combination along a given curve achieves the same level of compliance.

To illustrate the above analysis of optimal enforcement, two points on each curve in Figure 7.3 are shown. These depict four possible outcomes: (i) a high level of harm and a low detection probability (point A); (ii) a low level of harm and a low detection probability (point B); (iii) a high level of harm and a high

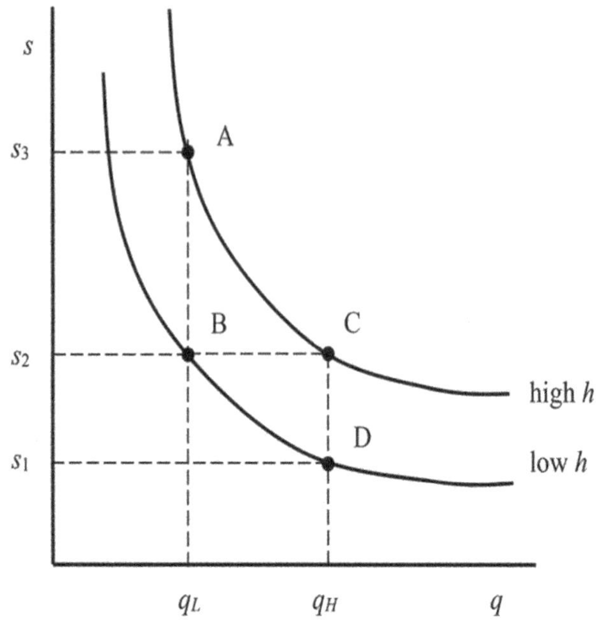

Figure 7.3 *Optimal enforcement outcomes*

detection probability (point C); and (iv) a low level of harm and a high detection probability (point D). We consider these in reverse order.

First, consider point D. This corresponds to most on-field infractions, which are both easy to detect (high q) and involve little harm (low h). The optimal sanction, s_1, is therefore small. Examples are ordinary penalties in football, for which the usual sanction is a loss of yardage, and fouls in basketball and soccer, for which the usual penalty is free throws, free kicks, or simply a change of possession. Next, consider point C, which involves a high detection rate (high q) and a high level of harm. In this case, the optimal sanction, s_2, is moderate. Sanctions for these more flagrant on-field violations involve harsher on-field penalties and/or possible expulsion from one or more games. Examples include yellow- and red-card fouls in soccer, illegal contact penalties in football and basketball, and intentionally throwing at a batter in baseball.

The other two outcomes involve a low probability of detection (low q) and, therefore, generally represent off-field violations. Point B involves a low level of harm, but because of the low detection probability, the optimal sanction must be moderate (s_2) to achieve the desired level of deterrence. An example here might include equipment tampering, such as the famous "Deflategate" controversy from the 2014–15 NFL playoff game between the New England Patriots and Indianapolis Colts. The harm from this sort of violation is probably slight, but the low detection probability makes it appropriate to impose a moderately stiff penalty. For instance, the quarterback, Tom Brady, received a four-game suspension at the start of the following season, and the Patriots received a $1 million fine and the loss of two draft picks.

Finally, point A involves high harm coupled with a low detection probability, thus necessitating a harsh sanction (s_3). Examples here include betting on games or egregious off-field behavior, both of which usually result in lengthy, if not lifetime, suspensions.[6] In this case, the very harsh sanction reflects both the difficulty of detection and the high perceived level of harm from the infraction. The Houston Astros' sign-stealing scandal during the 2017 and 2018 seasons, which was only revealed by a whistleblower, may fall into this category or the previous one, depending on how harmful to competition one thinks using electronic means to steal signs is.

ERRORS IN THE DETECTION OF VIOLATIONS

The analysis to this point has assumed that the detection of a violation, when one occurs, is uncertain, as reflected by the fact that $q<1$. That is, some violators "get away with it." In the law enforcement literature, this is often referred to as a "Type 2 error," or a false acquittal.[7] As we have seen, a greater likelihood of this type of error (i.e., a smaller value of q) will reduce the ability of rule enforcement to deter violations. However, another type of error is also possible; namely, the detection of a violation when none has occurred. This is referred to as a "Type 1 error," or a false conviction. Somewhat paradoxically, a greater likelihood of this type of error will also reduce the deterrent function of rule enforcement.

To see why, suppose that a competitor chooses not to take action x for fear of committing a violation, but a violation is nevertheless detected. This would be the case, for example, if a false positive result is obtained from a random drug test or if a player is wrongly charged with a foul. Let t be the probability of a violation being wrongfully detected when a competitor chooses *not* to take action x, resulting in an expected sanction of ts. Returning to the compliance decision in equation (7.1), the competitor will now choose to undertake action x if the net benefit of doing so exceeds the cost of not taking the action, including the risk of a wrongful penalty:

$$V(x)-r(x)qs>-ts \tag{7.5}$$

Rewriting this, we obtain the new compliance condition, which accounts for both types of errors:

$$V(x) > \left[r(x)q - t\right]s \tag{7.6}$$

It seems reasonable to assume that $r(x)q - t > 0$, or that the probability of a correct penalty exceeds that of an incorrect one—in other words, officials get it right more often than not. (If this were not the case, rule enforcement would be completely unreliable.) It nevertheless follows from equation (7.6) that an increase in both types of errors—i.e., a decrease in q (more Type 2 errors) or an increase in t (more Type 1 errors)—reduces the expected sanction from taking action x (i.e., makes the right-hand side of equation (7.6) smaller), thereby mitigating the deterrence effect of the sanction s. Intuitively, the combination of under- and over-detection reduces the differential between the returns from taking and not taking the action.

The foregoing analysis highlights the benefit of the accurate detection of rule violations and provides an economic rationale for the increasing use of video replay technology as a means of improving the accuracy of certain on-field decisions by referees and umpires. Specifically, video replay will both increase q and decrease t. As it is currently employed in most sports, video replay has not completely replaced human monitoring but is used instead as a means of error correction on disputed plays (though all plays are now reviewed in the English Premier League). In this sense, its role can be likened to that of appeals courts in ordinary legal systems.[8]

Although correcting errors is advantageous, the routine use of appeals in sports or law would be very costly. In sports, this cost consists of the delay to the game and the diminished confidence that fans and players have in human officiating. Additionally, some fans bemoan the loss of the "human element" in officiating—essentially, the possibility of bad calls—which they consider to be part of the game. This trade-off suggests that the use of video replay should be limited to situations in which the possibility or cost of an error is especially high.

But that raises the question of who gets to decide when video replay will be used. In law, appeals to a higher court are generally initiated by the losing party in a lawsuit rather than by allowing the appeals court itself to pick which cases to review. This makes sense since the loser is typically in the best position to determine if the benefits of pursuing an appeal exceed the cost. A coach's challenges similarly allow the party that stands to gain the most from a reversal—the "victim" of a bad call—the right to appeal it. Limiting the number of coach appeals, however, forces coaches to use them judiciously—i.e., only for calls that are clearly wrong, particularly harmful, or that happened at a crucial time in the game—thereby implicitly accounting for the cost of delay. In some cases, however, appeals are initiated by the officials themselves, usually during crucial times of the game (e.g., the last two minutes of each half in football) or when there is disagreement among the officials as to the correct ruling.

As a final point, the use of video replay, because of its heightened ability to discriminate between violations and non-violations, can lead to changes in the rules themselves by requiring a more refined definition of what the rule in question means. For example, the use of replay in professional football has required league officials to establish clearer guidelines as to what constitutes a legal catch.

EVOLUTION OF RULES

All organized sports provide in their "constitutions" methods for changing rules so as to respond to changing technologies, tastes, and knowledge.[9] Technological changes mostly concern innovations in equipment, but they can also reflect a better understanding of what's humanly possible, both of which can affect how a game is played. Probably the most common effect of technology in team sports concerns the balance between offense and defense. For example, baseball historians commonly divide the history of the game into the "dead ball" era (pre-1920) and the "live ball" era (post-1920), reflecting a change to a livelier ball that traveled farther when hit. The change coincided with the arrival of Babe Ruth, who took full advantage of the innovation and almost single-handedly changed the way the game was played. In response, game strategies began to switch from the prevailing approach of trying to manufacture one run at a time using tactics like bunting and base stealing (so-called "small-ball"), to one based more on power and explosive offense (Felber and Gillette, 2001). More recent innovations in this regard include the use of defensive shifts,[10] and emphasis on the "launch angle" of a batter's swing, a tactic aimed at increasing home runs.

Generally speaking, however, advances in technology tend to be neutral with regard to the balance between offense and defense. For example, new kinds of pitches and better fielding gloves were developed to offset the offensive advantage of the livelier ball. But sometimes large imbalances arise, compelling rule-makers to intervene. One such situation arose in Major League Baseball in the late 1960s, when pitching had become dominant and fans, who had developed a taste for offense, registered their dissatisfaction by staying away from ballparks (Ryczek, 2017, Chapter 2).[11] This was obviously unacceptable to owners and league officials, who quickly responded in 1969 by lowering the pitcher's mound five inches and shrinking the size of the strike zone. And in 1973, the American League created the designated hitter (as will be discussed further below). Within a few years, an acceptable balance between offense and defense had been re-established.

A similar imbalance existed in the National Hockey League during the early 2000s, when it was perceived by league officials that goal-scoring had dropped to an unacceptably low level. Rule-makers again responded in various ways. They reduced the allowable size of goalie pads and restricted the area where the goalie could handle the puck to the trapezoid behind the net. The league also tinkered with the rules governing overtime, first going to a four-on-four, and then a three-on-three format during the single overtime period of regular season games, and eventually instituting a shootout for games not resolved during that period. All of these changes were designed to increase offense and goal-scoring.

Rules can similarly be seen as promoting competitive balance *within games*. Think, for example, about rules that determine possession of the ball in team sports.[12] Generally, the team that scores has to give up possession of the ball rather than being able to retain possession. This is true in American football, soccer, and basketball. Such a rule is clearly aimed at making games closer by "punishing" success rather than by rewarding it.[13] An exception to this is hockey, where possession is determined randomly (i.e., by a face-off) after each goal. This was also the case in early basketball, where, up until the 1930s, a tip-off occurred after every basket. Why did basketball eventually adopt the current rule of changing possession after a score, while hockey did not? A possible reason is that hockey is a low-scoring game and possession changes hands frequently during play, so there is no great advantage to having possession. The same could be said of basketball (i.e., each possession is not highly valued) because it is a *high*-scoring game. However, using a tip-off to award possession after every basket can give a distinct advantage to one team if it has a very tall player (something that is not generally true of hockey face-offs). Thus, the modern rule was adopted in basketball early on.

One might then ask why a "make-it-take-it" rule (rewarding success) is prevalent as a rule of thumb in pick-up basketball games, in contrast to organized basketball. A possible reason is that in recreational games, competitive balance is not an important consideration. Rather, allocation of scarce court time among multiple competing users is the governing factor, and a make-it-take-it rule results in quicker games (Wittman, 2006, p. 84).

Finally, rule changes can reflect changes in knowledge about the harmfulness of certain strategies or actions. For example, recognition of the detrimental long-term health effects of using steroids and other performance-enhancing drugs, as well as the competitive advantage they conferred on users, has led professional and amateur leagues to institute drug testing of competitors accompanied by substantial penalties for violations. Recent discoveries of the health effects of concussions have similarly resulted in rule changes that outlaw and severely penalize certain types of contact in football and hockey. Sports fans clearly value aggressive play, and physical contact and risk of injury has always been an inherent aspect of these sports, but like the balance between offense and defense, rule-makers are sensitive to striking a proper balance between aggressiveness and safety, and new medical discoveries are crucial in determining where the tipping point resides between what is acceptable and what is not. The economic approach to rule enforcement provides a coherent way of thinking about how to weigh these offsetting factors.

THE IMPACT OF RULES ON BEHAVIOR: UNINTENDED CONSEQUENCES

The preceding discussion has emphasized how rules, like laws, can be used as incentive mechanisms for guiding the decisions of competitors in desirable directions. The effectiveness of rules in achieving their intended goals naturally varies, but what is sometimes more interesting are the unintended—and often undesirable—consequences of a rule change, which generally reflect the rational economic responses of competitors to those changes. In this section, we examine three examples of this phenomenon.

The Designated Hitter and Moral Hazard

In 1973, the American League instituted the designated hitter (DH) rule, which allowed a team to designate a tenth player who would bat in place of the pitcher. The National League, however, chose not to adopt the rule until 2022, when it finally became universal. The objective of the rule was to increase offense, given that most pitchers were weak hitters and represented easy outs. However, an apparent and unintended consequence has been that American League batters have been hit by pitches at a higher rate than National League batters. The reason is that pitchers in the American League, who no longer have to bat, face a lower cost of pitching inside, which is a tactic that pitchers often use to gain an advantage by intimidating batters and moving them off the plate. Opposing pitchers may still retaliate against a batter on the opposing team when one of their teammates has been hit, so the cost is not zero, but the argument is that, with the DH, pitchers *themselves* no longer faced the risk of being hit, resulting in a kind of moral hazard problem for pitchers.

Figure 7.4 shows the rate of hit-by-pitches (HBPs) per game in the American and National Leagues from 1947–1996. This represents the 50-year period beginning with integration and running through the season before inter-league play began in 1997. The data show that the HBP rate in the American League moved slightly higher than the National League rate, beginning in 1974, and remained higher during every subsequent year except 1994 and 1995.[14]

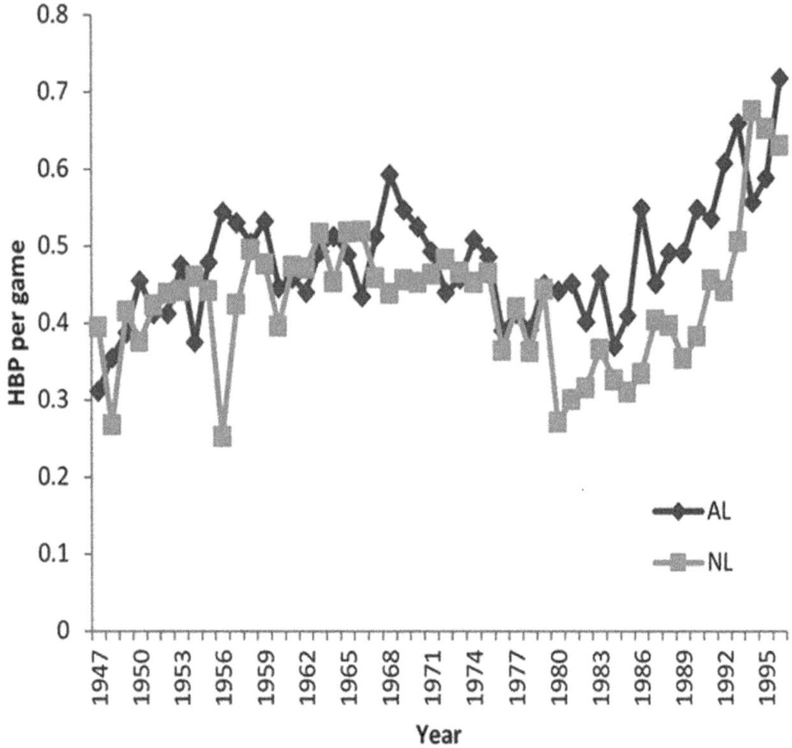

Figure 7.4 *Hit by pitch rate in the American and National Leagues, 1947–1996*

Several economists have exploited the sort of "natural experiment" that the DH rule created to conduct a more rigorous test of whether the above moral hazard argument is correct. Goff et al. (1997) provided evidence that the DH resulted in a statistically significant increase in the rate of HBPs in the American League from 1973 to 1990, the end of their sample period. While this seemed to support the moral hazard argument, other researchers pointed out an alternative explanation for the higher HBP rate in the American League; namely, that with the DH, pitchers had to face one additional good hitter whom they were more likely to intimidate, as compared with a weak-hitting pitcher. Moreover, as noted, the HBP rate in the National League exceeded that in the American League a couple of times in the 1990s.

A more recent study by Bradbury and Drinen (2006) therefore used game-level data covering the period 1973–2003 to re-examine the question. Their results confirmed the earlier finding of moral hazard by using statistical techniques to disentangle the moral hazard effect from the alternative hypothesis. The authors specifically showed that the presence of one additional good hitter in American League lineups accounts for about half of the higher incidence of HBPs in that league, with pitcher moral hazard accounting for the other half. The authors provided further confirmation of this finding by using data from inter-league games over the period 1997–2003 (another natural experiment) to show that National League pitchers also hit batters at a higher rate when facing a lineup with a DH as compared with a pitcher-batter.[15]

Safer Equipment and the Peltzman Effect

In contact sports such as football and hockey, helmets and other padding are important components of players' equipment, and it is an ongoing effort among league officials to improve the safety of that equipment, especially in light of recent medical discoveries about the long-term health effects of concussions. Safer equipment, however, is not a guarantee of fewer injuries as a consequence of the so-called "Peltzman Effect." This is the argument that when people who engage in risky activities are equipped with safer protective equipment, they will have a tendency to undertake riskier behavior, which counteracts the intended effect of the equipment (Peltzman, 1975).

Peltzman made his argument in the context of automobile safety regulations and showed that safer cars do not necessarily lead to fewer traffic deaths. The idea can be illustrated as follows. Suppose that the probability of an automobile accident is given by $p(x)$, where x is the level of precaution exercised by the driver. Thus, p is decreasing in x. In addition, suppose that the damage from an accident is $L(s)$, where s is a measure of government-mandated safety features such as seatbelts and airbags. Thus, L is decreasing in s. From the perspective of the driver, the problem is to choose the level of precaution, x, to minimize expected costs:

$$p(x)L(s)+x \tag{7.7}$$

taking s as given. (We are assuming here that the marginal cost of x is \$1.) The first-order condition defining the optimum is therefore

$$-\frac{dp(x)}{dx}L(s)=1 \tag{7.8}$$

where the left-hand side is the marginal benefit of greater precaution in the form of reduced accident losses (remember that $dp/dx<0$), while the right-hand side is the marginal cost of an additional unit of precaution. Equation

(7.8) defines the driver's optimal level of precaution, $x^*(s)$, as a function of the regulatory standard s. Figure 7.5 illustrates the result for an initial safety standard s_1, denoted by $x^*(s_1)$.

Now suppose that the government mandates an increase in safety features, to s_2, say, where $L(s_2) < L(s_1)$. How will this affect the choice of precaution by drivers? As Figure 7.5 shows, the reduction in the loss from an accident causes the negatively sloped curve, reflecting the marginal benefit from precaution, to shift down, thereby reducing the optimal level of precaution from $x^*(s_1)$ to $x^*(s_2)$. Intuitively, because they feel safer, consumers invest in less precaution, or engage in more risky behavior, resulting in an increase in the risk of an accident, or $p(x^*(s_2)) > p(x^*(s_1))$. The effect on expected accident losses is therefore ambiguous. Specifically,

$$p(x^*(s_2))L(s_2) \gtreqless p(x^*(s_1))L(s_1) \tag{7.9}$$

Peltzman (1975) showed that increased traffic safety measures did not, in fact, reduce the rate of highway deaths.

In the context of sports, safer equipment might similarly be expected to make players employ riskier strategies. For example, football players equipped with better padding and more cushioned helmets are emboldened to hit

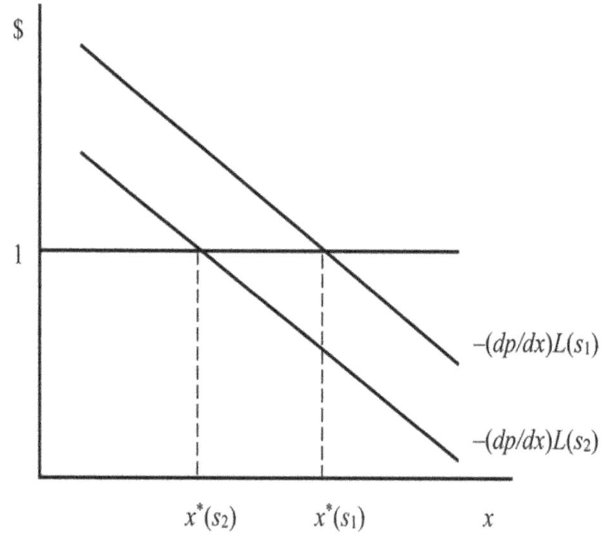

Figure 7.5 Impact of increased safety on precaution

opponents harder, resulting in a higher risk of injuries to themselves and the targeted player. A similar incentive presumably exists in hockey, where the requirement that all players must wear helmets likely increased the aggressiveness of play, and in major league baseball, where the requirement that batters must wear helmets likely increased the rate of HBPs because pitchers were less concerned about the risk of beanballs.[16]

Based on this logic, a recent study exploited the fact that hockey players in the National Hockey League (NHL) can choose whether or not to wear an additional form of protection—a partial face shield (visor)—whereas players in European and junior leagues *must* wear one, to ask if the visor requirement altered players' behavior as predicted by the Peltzman effect (Chong and Restrepo, 2017). The authors used penalty minutes as a proxy for aggressive (risky) behavior. Their finding was that the visor requirement did indeed result in a statistically significant increase in penalty minutes per game (specifically, 0.19 additional minutes per game). As shown above, this behavioral response of players, like that of automobile drivers in Peltzman's study, offsets the intended effect of visors in reducing the risk of injury to the player himself, while at the same time raising the risk of injury to other players on the ice.

Overtime Rules in Hockey and the Frequency of Overtime Games

Our final example of unintended consequences concerns the more benign impact of the rule for awarding points in overtime games in the NHL. In hockey, teams receive two points for a win, zero points for a loss, and, at the time of the change in question, they received one point for a tie. In the event of a tie in regulation time, teams play one overtime (OT) period, with a goal by either team resulting in a sudden-death victory. At the time of the change, if neither team scored in OT, the game ended in a tie. League officials, however, were concerned that fans did not like the idea of games ending in a tie. Although we have argued that fans value tight contests, they view ties as incomplete results. Following the 1998–1999 season, league officials therefore responded to the perception that too many games ended in ties by changing the overtime rules in two ways. First, one point was awarded to each team in OT games regardless of the final outcome, and second, teams in OT had to skate with four players on a side (plus the goalie) rather than the usual five on a side. (Playoff games continued to be decided by additional OT periods until a team scored.)

The goal of both rules was to increase the aggressiveness of play in OT, thereby making it less likely that a game would end in a tie. The specific idea of the point change was to remove the risk of losing in OT, which would have resulted in no points under the old rules. Teams could therefore play aggressively in pursuit of the second point rather than sitting back and playing cautiously to preserve the first point. The idea behind the four-on-four rule was to open up the ice and promote more scoring chances.

A study by Abrevaya (2004) showed that the changes had the intended effects.[17] During the three-year period prior to the rule change (the 1995–1996 through 1998–1999 seasons), 71.1 percent of OT games ended in a tie, whereas during the three years after the rule change (the 1999–2000 through 2001–2002 seasons), only 55.5 percent of OT games ended in ties. The author also found that shots on goal increased after the change, reflecting the desired increase in offensive play. An unintended effect of the change, however, was that more games *went* to OT: 22.2 percent after the change as compared with 19.8 percent before the change. Thus, the conservative play in OT before the change, which had been aimed at preserving the single point awarded for an OT tie under the old rule, had now shifted into regulation time to ensure that a team did not lose a game late, thereby sacrificing the one point awarded for *reaching* OT under the new rule.

Ties still existed under the new rules, and so beginning with the 2005–2006 season, the NHL instituted a shootout to resolve games that remained tied after OT, thereby ensuring that a winner was determined in all games. Teams that lost in OT continued to receive one point. However, fan dissatisfaction with the seeming "arbitrariness" of shootouts as the means of resolving ties led the NHL to introduce a three-on-three format during OT prior to the 2015–2016 season as a way to further promote aggressive OT play and thus reduce the number of games that required a shootout. To date, no study has evaluated the results of this change.

The examples in this section have shown that rule-making in sports, as in law, involves a constant process of adjustment, beginning with the introduction of new rules to achieve desired goals, often followed by re-adjustment to counter the unintended consequences of the initial change.

SUMMARY

This chapter examined issues relating to the rules governing sporting events using the conceptual framework developed to study the economics of law enforcement. We began by suggesting a categorization of rules into those prohibiting actions that are clearly detrimental to sporting events, such as physically harmful actions and cheating, and those that penalize actions that are necessary by-products of acceptable play, such as fouls and penalties. The former can be likened to crimes, and the latter to accidents, both of which cause harm but are treated very differently by the legal system. We then developed a model of compliance with rules as enforced by the threat of punishment, whether in the form of on-field penalties, monetary sanctions, or risk of suspension.

The economic approach to law enforcement views would-be offenders as rational decision-makers who account for the threat of punishment when making their choices, and we used the same logic with respect to sporting rules. Given compliance behavior, we examined the optimal structure of enforcement, which prescribed that punishments should generally increase with the harm from a violation and the difficulty of detection, holding other factors constant. We also asked how errors in the detection of rule violations—both over-detection and under-detection—affected the behavior of competitors. Our conclusion was that both types of errors mitigate deterrence, thereby providing a justification for the use of video replay as a means of error correction.

The next issue we addressed was the evolution of rules in response to changing technologies, tastes, and knowledge. Rules are also adjusted to maintain competitive balance in leagues where technological changes are not neutral in this respect. If, for example, an innovation gives a decided advantage to the offense, officials will often seek to make the necessary adjustments in an effort to restore the balance. We noted, however, that some changes carry with them unintended consequences as a result of the rational reactions of players, and these consequences can sometimes counteract the original intent of the change. We chronicled several examples of this effect.

EXERCISES

7.1. A particular strategy increases a team's chances of winning by .10. Let the value of winning = 100, and the cost of using the strategy = 5.
   (a) Show that the strategy provides the team a net benefit.
   (b) Now, suppose it is determined that the strategy causes harm to those players who employ it as well as their opponents. Thus, the league makes its use a violation of the rules. Assuming that the use of the strategy is detected with certainty, what is the minimal dollar value of the sanction that will just deter it? (Assume that, when indifferent, the team does not use the strategy.)
   (c) What is the minimum sanction that deters the strategy if it is detected one-quarter of the time it is used?
   (d) Show how your answers in (b) and (c) change if the value of winning increases to 150.

NOTES

1. We, therefore, ignore actions or decisions that are unrelated to sports.
2. A similar perspective was taken by Oliver Wendell Holmes (1897) in describing his "prediction theory" of law, according to which, the law is merely the

prediction by would-be lawbreakers (so-called "bad men") of what the consequences of their actions will be.

3. The now-infamous Houston Astros cheating scandal consisted of the stealing of opposing teams' signs during the 2017–2018 MLB seasons. This raised the question of when certain actions cross the line between legitimate efforts to gain a competitive edge and cheating. The consensus in this case seems to be that the use of technology to steal signs definitely crossed the line.
4. In some cases, violations may never be discovered unless a whistleblower comes forward, as happened in the Houston Astros sign-stealing scandal when a former player came forward with the accusation.
5. The line is a rectangular hyperbola, which is defined by the equation $qs = k$, or $s = k / q$ for some constant k.
6. See the further discussion of betting on sports and why it is potentially so harmful in Chapter 12.
7. See, for example, Png (1986).
8. See, for example, Shavell (1995).
9. Hart (1961), in his classic treatise *The Concept of Law*, observed that most legal systems have primary and secondary rules. Primary rules concern obligations that those subject to the laws must obey, whereas secondary rules provide the means whereby new primary rules may be created or existing ones altered.
10. However, defensive shifts are not a modern invention. In the 1940s, Lou Boudreau, player-manager of the Cleveland Indians, famously used a shift against Ted Williams.
11. The year 1968 represented the nadir of offense, when the American League batting champion, Carl Yastrzemski, was the only hitter to top the .300 mark, batting a mere .301, while Bob Gibson led the National League with an ERA of 1.12, but still managed to lose nine games (he won 22)!
12. This paragraph is based on Wittman (2006, pp. 82–84)
13. Note that this explains why teams with a lead don't always try to score. The shot clock in basketball was obviously a response to this sort of "run-out-the-clock" strategy.
14. In 1994, Major League Baseball enacted the "double-warning" rule for hit-by-pitches, under which any HBP that, in the umpire's judgment, was intentional immediately results in a warning to both benches that any subsequent hit batters will result in the ejection of the pitcher and his manager. This change is aimed at protecting pitchers from retaliation, and so lowers the cost of the first HBP and, as a result, mitigates the effect of the DH in the American League. In this light, the convergence in the HBP rate in the two leagues in 1994–95 makes economic sense (Bradbury, 2007, p. 11).
15. In inter-league games, the rule of the home team prevails. Thus, in American League parks, both teams use a DH, whereas in National League parks, both pitchers must bat. The same rule applies in the World Series.

16. The NHL helmet rule allowed players signed before June 1, 1979, to continue playing without a helmet. The MLB helmet rule required all players to wear helmets beginning in 1971.
17. Also see Brocas and Carrillo (2004), who developed a game-theoretic model of team strategy choice in response to different rules for valuing wins versus ties and for deciding the outcome of OT games. The model's predictions, though made in the context of soccer, are in accordance with the findings of Abrevaya (2004).

PART III

The Players' Labor Market

8. Player salary determination

The next several chapters examine the labor market for professional athletes. This chapter considers the manner in which player salaries are determined in professional sports leagues. Nowadays, professional athletes are very well paid, but that has not always been the case. Historically, team owners exercised considerable power in the market for players, and, even today, in the presence of strong players' unions in most sports, owners still have some control over player mobility and salaries. In other words, the market for players in most sports is not one in which players are free to negotiate with whomever they wish. Although players can generally become "free agents" after a certain amount of time spent at the major league level, they are tied to their teams before that. Even when they attain free agency, players often voluntarily sign long-term contracts that fix their salary and commit them to their current teams. The objective of this chapter is to use standard economic theory to understand how the market for players' services works—in what ways it is similar to other labor markets and in what ways it differs.

We begin with a simple model of a competitive labor market in which workers are freely mobile. This will serve as a benchmark for examining the actual situation in the players' labor market, both historically and today. The simplest model of that market is the monopsony model, which represents a market with a single *buyer*. Although overly simple because it treats labor as a homogeneous good, the model does provide insights into the sort of market power that teams exercise over players who are bound to them.

The discussion then turns to the estimation of player salaries as a function of their performance on the field. This line of literature culminated in the Moneyball hypothesis of the 1990s, which changed the way that Major League Baseball players, and eventually players in all sports, are evaluated. That hypothesis is examined in detail, and some evidence is presented on the link between spending on players and team performance on the field. The argument is then used as a point of departure for a discussion of innovation in sports and how that differs from innovation in ordinary markets.

COMPETITIVE LABOR MARKET

As a benchmark, this section describes the determination of equilibrium in a competitive labor market, meaning that neither employers (teams) nor employees (players) can control the wage rate. The demand side of the market is based on the profit-maximizing choice of labor inputs by teams, while the supply side is based on the utility-maximizing labor supply decisions of players. Consider first the behavior of teams.

Labor demand begins with the firm's production function, given by

$$Q = f(K, L) \tag{8.1}$$

where Q is the quantity of output, K is capital, and L is labor. The function $f(\cdot)$ specifies how the firm transforms inputs of capital and labor into output. Economists typically don't inquire into the details of how that is done, as it depends on the state of technology in the relevant industry, though in our discussion of the Moneyball hypothesis at the end of this chapter, we will examine some aspects of how clubs try to put a winning team on the field. At this point, however, we simply take the production technology as given. We will also take as fixed the capital input, representing, for example, the team's facilities, equipment, etc.

The firm's choice of its variable input, labor, will be made to maximize its profits.

$$\pi = P(Q)Q - wL - P_K K \tag{8.2}$$

where $P(Q)$ is the price of the firm's output (its inverse demand curve), w is the wage rate, and P_K is the price of capital. Although we will continue to assume that the firm has market power with respect to the sale of its output, we will assume for now that it is a competitor in the labor market and therefore takes the wage rate as given. It also takes the price of capital as given, and so the total cost of capital is a fixed cost.

The firm's demand for labor is found by maximizing equation (8.2) with respect to L. The condition that defines this demand is as follows:

$$\left(P + \frac{dP}{dQ}Q\right)\frac{df}{dL} = w \tag{8.3}$$

The left-hand side of this equation is called the *marginal revenue product*, or *MRP*. It measures how much an additional unit of labor increases the firm's revenue. Note that it is equal to the firm's marginal revenue (the term in parentheses) multiplied by the marginal product of labor, df / dL. In what follows, we will use the notation *MRP* to denote this quantity.

According to equation (8.3), the firm's profit-maximizing labor demand satisfies the equation

$$MRP = w \tag{8.4}$$

That is, the firm hires labor up to the point where the last unit contributes as much to revenue as it costs. This is shown graphically in panel (a) of Figure 8.1, where the *MRP* is drawn as a downward sloping curve, reflecting the diminishing marginal productivity of labor. This curve represents the firm's labor demand curve. Firm *i*'s optimal labor input, L_i^*, therefore occurs where its demand curve equals the equilibrium wage rate, w^*, which the firm takes as given.

The aggregate demand for labor in the market is the total demanded by all firms that use that particular type of labor. The market demand curve is therefore the horizontal summation of the individual firm *MRP* curves. That is, at each wage rate, it adds up all of the individual firm demands. The result is the downward-sloping curve labeled *D* in panel (b) of Figure 8.1. Equilibrium employment, L^*, and the market wage, w^*, are determined by the intersection of the demand curve with the upward-sloping labor supply curve, labeled *S*.[1]

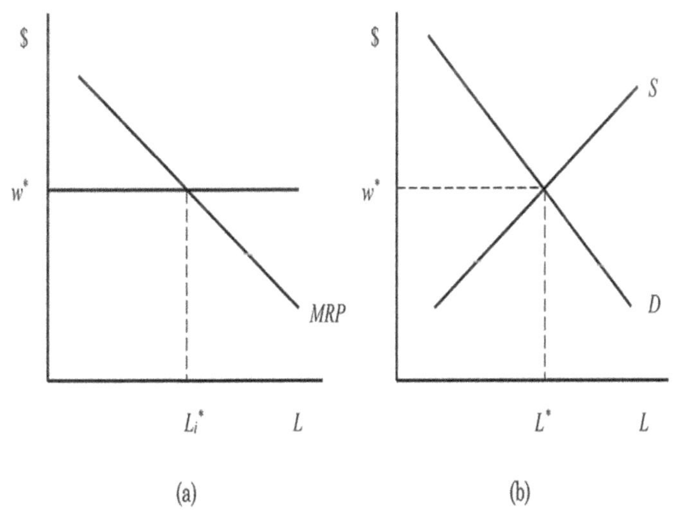

Figure 8.1 The competitive labor market at the firm (a) and market (b) level

The labor supply curve in Figure 8.1 (b) represents the next best employment opportunities for potential workers. In other words, it is the lowest wage that will just induce a worker to accept a job in this particular occupation. The upward slope reflects the idea that as the wage increases, more workers are induced to leave their current occupations (other jobs or leisure) and enter the job market.[2] We will see that it is the positive slope of the labor supply curve that creates the ability for firms to underpay workers relative to their marginal revenue products in a market characterized by monopsony power. We turn to this case now.

MONOPSONY

Monopsony power in the labor market is the counterpart to monopoly power in the output market. Whereas monopoly arises when there is one *seller* of a good, monopsony arises when there is one *buyer* of a good. In this case, the buyer is the firm, and the good is the labor input of workers. This case is of interest in sports economics because the labor market for players provides one of the best examples of monopsony in actual labor markets. There are several possible sources of this monopsony power.

The first and most important is the *reserve clause*, which was a provision of all player contracts in Major League Baseball from nearly its inception until it was struck down in 1975. The reserve clause prohibited a player from bargaining with any team other than his present one, even after his contract had run out. The player's only alternative was to leave professional baseball. As we noted in Chapter 5, teams could trade or sell players, but players were bound to their current teams. This situation clearly gave owners substantial bargaining ability when it came to salary negotiations, especially since most players, at least during the early history of the game, did not have very good outside options. As we will see, this resulted in their being paid wages well below their *MRP*'s. Another source of monopsony is amateur drafts, which give teams exclusive rights to players, at least for a set period of time. Thus, amateur players are not free to negotiate with the highest bidder. Finally, tacit collusion among teams acting in a cartel-like manner also potentially inhibits bargaining for players. Indeed, players' unions frequently allege such collusion by owners in an effort to keep free agent salaries from becoming too high.

As noted, the key to exercising monopsony power by firms is the upward-sloping labor supply curve. This implies that, starting from some initial wage rate, if the firm wants to hire an additional worker, it must raise the wage to induce that worker to accept employment. However, assuming wage discrimination is not possible (or legal), *it must also raise the wage of all previous workers*. Thus, the overall cost of hiring an additional worker is more than the last worker's wage. This is reflected by the marginal factor cost, or MFC, curve, which is defined to be the cost of hiring an additional worker.

To be more specific, note that the total labor cost of a firm facing an upward-sloping supply curve is $TC = w(L) \cdot L$, where $w(L)$ is the supply curve. The marginal factor cost curve is defined to be the change in TC as L is incrementally raised:

$$MFC = \frac{dTC}{dL} = w + \frac{dw}{dL} \cdot L \qquad (8.5)$$

Since $dw / dL > 0$, $MFC > w$. The MFC curve and the associated supply curve are shown graphically in Figure 8.2, where the vertical distance between the curves is given by the $(dw / dL)L$ term in equation (8.5).

Equilibrium in a monopsonistic market occurs at the point where the firm's marginal revenue product, the value of the last worker hired, equals the marginal factor cost, or where $MRP = MFC$. This occurs at L_M in Figure 8.2.

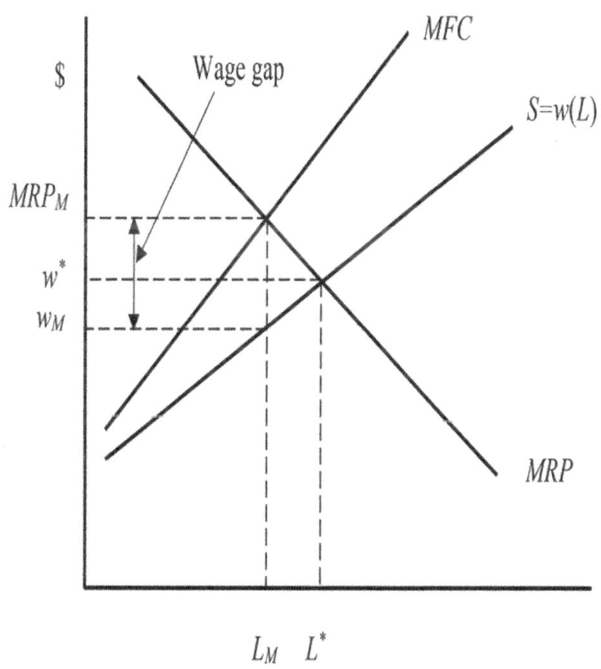

Figure 8.2 Wage (w_M) and employment (L_M) in a monopsonistic labor market

Thus, employment is below the level at which $MRP = w$, or L^*, which we saw is the outcome that would obtain in a competitive labor market. As for the wage, it is determined by the point on the *supply curve* associated with the employment level L_M. This is indicated by w_M in the graph, and it represents the lowest wage that will just induce L_M workers to accept employment. Note that this wage is both below the wage that would arise in a competitive market (w^*), and below the *MRP* of the firm at that employment level, denoted MRP_M. It therefore "undercompensates" workers relative to their value to the firm. In other words, at L_M,

$$MRP_M > w_M \tag{8.6}$$

This "wage gap" is a defining feature of equilibrium in a monopsonistic labor market.

The standard monopsony model, as just presented, is clearly an overly simplified description of the sports labor market, principally in its treatment of labor as a homogeneous input. In reality, of course, all players are different, both in terms of their positions and their skill levels. Nonetheless, the model's key insight remains relevant—namely, that in the absence of full free agency, players are underpaid relative to their marginal revenue products. We will see other reasons, besides market power, for the gap between *MRP* and *w* later in this chapter and in Chapter 10. The next topic, however, is measuring the wage gap.

MEASURING THE WAGE GAP: SCULLY'S RESEARCH

In a seminal study in the field of sports economics, Gerald Scully (1974) set out to estimate the *MRP* of major league baseball players using player performance statistics and team revenues.[3] In conducting his analysis, Scully used data from the 1968–1969 seasons, a time when the reserve clause was firmly in place. Recall from above that the *MRP* is a product of the team's marginal revenue and the marginal product of labor. Marginal revenue reflects how "wins" translate into revenue, and marginal product measures how a player's performance produces wins. Scully used a two-step procedure to determine these magnitudes.

He first estimated how a hitter's offensive production (measured by his slugging percentage[4]) and a pitcher's success on the mound (measured by his strikeout-to-walk ratio) contributed to his team's winning percentage. He found that both had positive and statistically significant effects. The second step was to estimate the effect of wins on a team's total revenue, while controlling for a team's market size. Again, he found a positive and significant effect.

Scully then used the two estimates to calculate the *MRP* of hitters and pitchers. He specifically found that a one-point increase in slugging percentage resulted in an increase in revenue of $9,504, while a 1/100 point increase in the strikeout-to-walk ratio increased revenue by $9,297. These numbers are aggregates for each team. To obtain individual player estimates, Scully assumed that each team consisted of eight regular starting or relief pitchers and 12 regular position players. Thus, each pitcher contributed 1/8 of the team's strikeout-to-walk ratio, and each position player contributed 1/12 of the team's slugging percentage. In other words, he assumed that team totals were simply aggregations of individual player contributions.[5] This led to estimates of pitcher and hitter *MRP*s as follows. In 1968, the average slugging percentage was .340, of which each hitter contributed 1/12, or 28.3.[6] Multiplying this by the estimated revenue per point of slugging percentage yielded the *MRP* for hitters:

$$MRP_H = 28.3 \times \$9504 = \$269{,}280$$

Similarly, for pitchers, the average strikeout-to-walk ratio in 1968 was about 2, to which each pitcher contributed 1/8, or .25. Combining this with the estimated revenue for pitchers (which, recall, was based on a 1/100th of a point increase in the strikeout-to-walk ratio) yielded the *MRP* for pitchers:

$$MRP_P = .25 \times 100 \times \$9297 = \$237{,}600$$

Scully also estimated player salaries as a function of performance measures and size of the market, and then compared these estimates to the computed *MRP*s. His results indicated that star players were paid only about 15 percent of their *MRP*s, while average players were paid about 20 percent of their *MRP*s. This reflects considerable market power on the part of owners.

Subsequent studies have examined player salaries in more recent times when MLB players are able to become free agents after six years of major league service. In this environment, one supposes that players are underpaid relative to their *MRP*s prior to free agency (and for a good reason, as we will argue in Chapter 10), but that free agents are paid salaries approximately equal to their *MRP*, as would happen in a competitive labor market.[7] Krautmann (1999) exploited this bifurcation in the labor market to derive estimates of the "free-market value" of players based on the salaries negotiated by free agents, which he treated as the player's true market value. He then used those estimates to impute the value of players still bound to their teams, and compared the results with their actual salaries. His conclusions were that players with less than three years of major league experience were paid only about 27 percent of their market value, while players with between three and six years of experience, who under the collective bargaining agreement have a right to salary arbitration by a neutral third party, were paid about 85 percent of their full value. Thus, considerable progress has been made by players since the era studied by Scully.

SALARY DETERMINATION IN THE FREE AGENT MARKET

This section turns to the determination of salaries in the free-agent market. This is what economists would call a "thin" market because there are very few participants, and each player is unique. In truth, there is a separate market for each player. Thus, it is hard to say what "market value" means here, as the usual techniques of supply and demand don't really apply. Rather, there is the amount that the highest-valuing team would be willing to pay to a player, which we define to be his *MRP*, and the player's opportunity cost, representing his next best option (which is probably the highest offer from another team). His actual salary—by definition, his market value—will most likely fall somewhere between these two values.

To illustrate, consider a player whose attachment to his current team is ending—either he is just entering the free-agency phase of his career, or his current contract is running out. Suppose that the value of the player to the various teams in the league, including his current team, can be ranked from highest to lowest as follows: $MRP_1 > MRP_2 > \ldots > MRP_n$. The player's value varies from team to team based on differences in the on-field needs of each team, as well as differences in the markets of teams, which affect their ability to pay high salaries. The free agent market functions much like an auction in the sense that the player will end up with the highest bidder, assuming (for now) that players only care about money. Thus, the player will end up with team one, whose *MRP* is by definition the highest. (This may or may not be the player's current team.) However, the player's salary will *not* generally be equal to MRP_1, the winning bidder's valuation. In an open marketplace, the winning team will never bid its full value, but only enough to outbid the second-highest bidder. Thus, we would expect the player's salary to be closer to MRP_2 than to MRP_1. Thus, even in a pure free-agent setting, players will be "underpaid" relative to their value to the team that acquires them.

What if a player has preferences besides money? Some players, for example, want to remain loyal to their fan base, to be in a certain geographic region, or to play for a winning franchise, and so are willing to accept a salary below the maximum they could obtain as a free agent. The explanation for this is that some players maximize *utility* rather than *income*. To capture this, we write the utility of a player with team i as $U_i(w_i)$, which is an increasing function of w_i, his wage with that team. This reflects the idea that a player's utility function, his measure of satisfaction, is unique to the team he plays for. Thus, if he has an attachment or attraction to a particular team, he will receive greater enjoyment from playing for that team for any given wage rate.

This situation is shown graphically in Figure 8.3, which depicts a player's utility with two different teams, A and B, for the case where the player has an inherent attraction to team A. Thus, $U_A(w) > U_B(w)$ for any w.[8] Now suppose that team B makes a higher wage offer to the player—that is, $w_B > w_A$, as shown in the graph. As drawn, the player nevertheless prefers to play for team A because

$$U_A(w_A) > U_B(w_B) \tag{8.7}$$

This does not mean that the player will choose team A no matter what salary team B offers. If team B offers a sufficiently large wage premium above team A's best offer, the player will accept it. The point is that some players will accept wage discounts to play for certain teams. The "winning bid" for such a player will therefore not necessarily be equal to the highest *MRP* for that player among all teams in the league. Although the winning team may end up paying him close to his *MRP* for *that team*, the player will still be receiving a wage below his maximum worth overall.

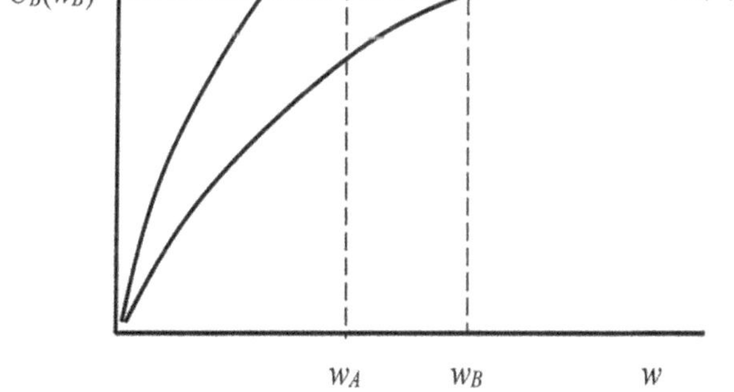

Figure 8.3 *Player preferences over two teams*

SALARY RENEGOTIATION AND HOLDOUTS

As discussed above, during the reserve clause era, players were attached to the team that originally signed them until they retired or were traded to another team. Even in the free agent era, players generally sign long-term contracts for reasons that we will explore in the next chapter. Often, however, when a player is locked into such an arrangement, he will find that his value to the team rises above his salary, possibly by a large amount. When that happens, the player would ideally like to renegotiate the contract at a salary more in line with his updated value rather than waiting for the contract to expire. Because of the contractual obligation, however, his only recourse may be to threaten a hold-out—that is, threaten to withhold his services from the team. The question is whether this can ever be an effective bargaining tool.

To examine this question, consider a player who is locked into a contract at a salary of $1 million but whose value to his team has risen to $5 million. The net value to the team is therefore $4 million if the player honors the contract. Suppose, however, that he requests a raise to $3 million and threatens to hold out if the team does not relent. If the team does relent, its net payoff would fall to $2 million (= $5–$3), whereas if it holds firm and the player makes good on his threat, each party would receive a payoff of zero.

The likely outcome of this negotiation can best be studied by using a *sequential move game* like that depicted by the game tree in Figure 8.4. Each branch of the tree represents a possible choice by the relevant decision maker.

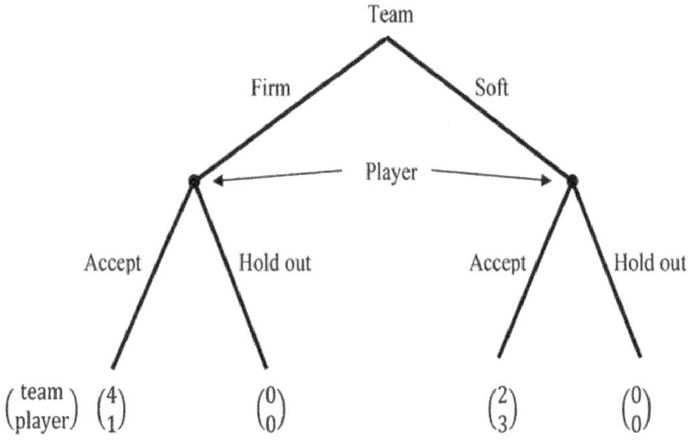

Figure 8.4 Game tree for the negotiations between a team and a player under contract

As shown, the team moves first and makes an offer to the player, and then the player decides whether to accept the offer or to hold out (refuse to play). Based on the above example, let the team's two choices either be to adopt a *firm strategy*—that is, seek to enforce the player's original salary of $1 million; or to adopt a *soft strategy*—that is, relent to the player's demand of $3 million. The player then either *accepts* the offer or *holds out.* The resulting payoffs are shown at each of the four terminal points of the game tree, with the team's payoff on top and the player's payoff on the bottom.

The equilibrium of this game is found by considering the parties' optimal choices in reverse sequence of time.[9] Thus, consider first the player's behavior, taking as given the prior choice of the team. Based on a comparison of the payoffs, it should be apparent that it is in the player's interest *to accept either offer from the team rather than to hold out.* That is, the player is better off accepting a positive salary offer of either $1 million or $3 million rather than refusing to play and getting a payoff of zero.

Now move back to the team's choice. Anticipating the player's response, the team will obviously find it optimal to adopt the firm stance and offer only $1 million because, by doing so, it will ensure itself a payoff of $4 million rather than $2 million. The unique equilibrium of the game is, therefore, the leftmost outcome, where the team gets $4 million, and the player gets $1 million.[10] In other words, the original contract remains in place. Evidently, therefore, the player's threat to hold out is ineffectual in creating an incentive for the team to give in to the player's demand. Let us examine in more detail why this is the case.

Suppose that at the outset of negotiations, the player threatens to hold out if the team doesn't offer him a salary of $3 million, and *the team actually believes the threat.* In the above game tree, this belief implies that if the team adopts a firm bargaining stance, the player will, in fact, hold out, resulting in a payoff of zero for the team. Fearing this outcome, the team will therefore rationally choose the soft stance, thereby ensuring itself a payoff of $2 million rather than zero. At least, this is the line of reasoning by the team that the player *hopes* his threat to hold out will induce. In particular, he hopes that it will deter the team from adopting the firm bargaining stance to begin with.

The problem with this logic, however, is that the player's threat to hold out is *not credible* in the sense that if the team "calls his bluff" and chooses to adopt the firm stance anyway (i.e., to offer only $1 million), the player will rationally accept that offer; otherwise, he would get a payoff of zero. In other words, once we reach this point in the game tree, the player will not find it optimal to carry out his threat. Knowing this, the team will rationally adopt the firm stance, resulting in the equilibrium described above. The sequential nature of the game and the player's incentive to accept something rather than nothing once the team makes its offer thus combine to render the player's holdout threat ineffectual.

As an illustration of the foregoing analysis, consider one of the most notorious examples of a threatened holdout in baseball history. This occurred when the great Joe DiMaggio refused to report to spring training following the 1937 season. Although the Yankee Clipper had only played in the majors for two years, he had already established himself as one of the best players in the game, batting well over .300 and driving in more than 100 runs in each of his first two seasons, and leading the majors in home runs in 1937. Indeed, one biographer observed that "No one in the history of big-league baseball had broken in with two years like DiMaggio's" (Cramer, 2000, p. 114). The Yankee owner in those days was the beer magnate Jacob Ruppert, who was also a notoriously stingy negotiator. Ruppert offered DiMaggio a salary of $25,000 for 1938, but Joe demanded $40,000, which was more than even Lou Gehrig, then at the tail end of his legendary career, was making. Neither side budged, and so Joe refused to report to spring training. However, when the press started calling him greedy, he relented and joined the Yankees on the third day of the regular season—at a salary of $25,000.

This outcome reflects the logic of the above sequential-move game in which the owner has a first-mover advantage, and the player has no alternative but to negotiate with the team to which he is currently bound. Such a scenario was typical of player–owner negotiations during the reserve-clause era, when players generally had much more to lose than owners. The threat of a holdout was, therefore, a rather weak bargaining tool, and players usually ended up accepting the owner's offer. The same is true today of negotiations between a team and a player under contract, which also occasionally result in holdout threats.

FINAL OFFER ARBITRATION IN MAJOR LEAGUE BASEBALL

We have noted that major league baseball players with at least six years of big-league experience can become free agents, whereas players with less than six years' experience remain tied to their teams. However, those with at least three years' experience are eligible for salary arbitration if they cannot reach an agreement with ownership. In the event of such a bargaining failure, the player and team would each submit their salary proposals to a neutral arbitrator who would then choose one of the proposals based on his or her assessment of which one more nearly reflects the player's worth. Notably, the arbitrator is *not* allowed to substitute his or her own estimate of the player's worth (for example, by averaging the two proposals). This procedure is referred to as final offer arbitration (FOA).

We begin our analysis of this method of dispute resolution by asking what proposals each side would rationally make in anticipation of the arbitrator's decision.[11] The key for each side is therefore to predict what proposal the other side will make, and how the arbitrator will evaluate each proposal. To proceed, let b_p be the player's proposal, and let b_o be the owner's proposal, where we can reasonably assume that $b_p > b_o$. (If this were not the case, the parties presumably would have been able to agree to terms.) Also, let w be the arbitrator's independent assessment of the player's worth, which is obviously unknown to the parties at the time they submit their proposals. Under the provisions of FOA, whichever proposal, b_p or b_o is closer to w will presumably be chosen. Thus, at the initial offer stage, there are three possibilities: (i) $b_p > b_o > w$; (ii) $b_p > w > b_o$; and (iii) $w > b_p > b_o$. In case (i), the arbitrator's choice will clearly be b_o, and in case (iii) it will clearly be b_p. In case (ii), however, it may be either proposal. It will be b_o if

$$b_p - w > w - b_o \tag{8.8}$$

and b_p if the reverse is true. It follows from equation (8.8) that b_o will be chosen if

$$w < \frac{b_p + b_o}{2} \tag{8.9}$$

or if the average of the two proposals exceeds the arbitrator's assessment. Conversely, b_p will be chosen if the average of the proposals is less than the arbitrator's assessment. It turns out that condition (8.9) and its converse subsume cases (i) and (iii), and so it is the general condition.[12]

Now let us suppose that, although the two parties are ignorant of the arbitrator's assessment w when they submit their proposals, they know the distribution from which it is drawn (perhaps based on evidence from past arbitration cases). Thus, for any pair of proposals, they can compute the probability that equation (8.9) will be satisfied, which then represents the probability that b_o will be chosen:

$$p = \Pr\left(b_o \text{ chosen}\right) = \Pr\left(w < \frac{b_p + b_o}{2}\right) \tag{8.10}$$

Correspondingly, the probability that b_p will be chosen is $1 - p$. As a result, the expected salary of the player is

$$E\left(S\right) = pb_o + \left(1 - p\right)b_p \tag{8.11}$$

The player will choose b_p to maximize this expression, taking b_o as given, while the owner will choose b_o to minimize this expression, taking b_p as given. Both parties, however, will account for the dependence of p on their proposals through equation (8.10). Specifically, both will recognize that increasing their proposals will raise p, the likelihood that the owner's proposal will be chosen. Note that this will tend to put an upward limit on the player's proposal and a downward limit on the owner's proposal.

We now characterize the likely outcome of this interaction between the player and owner by deriving the Nash equilibrium. (The arbitrator's behavior is already subsumed in the derivation of p.) For the case where w is uniformly distributed on the interval $\left[\underline{w}, \overline{w}\right]$ where $\overline{w} > \underline{w} > 0$, we obtain the equilibrium values[13]

$$b_p^* = \overline{w} \tag{8.12}$$

$$b_o^* = \underline{w} \tag{8.13}$$

Thus, the player proposes the highest value that the arbitrator would accept, and the owner proposes the lowest value. After substituting these values into equation (8.11), we obtain the player's expected salary:

$$E(S) = \frac{\overline{w} - \underline{w}}{2} \tag{8.14}$$

which is just the expected value of the arbitrator's assessment of the player's worth. Not surprisingly, when neither side has superior knowledge about the arbitrator's beliefs, neither expects to derive an advantage from proceeding to arbitration.

This conclusion raises an important question—if the outcome of arbitration is entirely predictable in this way, why would the parties ever incur the cost of resorting to it? It is, in fact, the case that the majority of contract disputes *are* settled before reaching arbitration, yet between ten and twenty percent of cases fail to settle. Several explanations have been offered for this result.[14] To examine these, let c be the extra costs that each party must incur by going to arbitration. These may include both time costs and legal expenses. The expected net gain from arbitration for the player is therefore $E(S) - c$, while the expected cost to the owner is $E(S) + c$. A settlement is possible if the two parties can agree on a salary, s, that makes both of them better off than proceeding to arbitration. This pair of requirements is

$$E(S)+c>s>E(S)-c \tag{8.15}$$

It should be clear that such an s always exists given their agreement over $E(S)$ —for example, $s = E(S)$ would do the trick. Intuitively, by settling, the parties can always implement the expected outcome of arbitration, which we have assumed they agree on, while avoiding the additional costs. As an example, if each party's expectation of the outcome of arbitration is a salary for the player of \$1.5 million, and each would incur a cost of \$200,000 to undergo arbitration, then the owner will offer up to \$1.7 million to avoid arbitration, and the player will accept any amount above \$1.3 million, which leaves a "bargaining range" of \$400,000, the exact amount of their combined costs.

One explanation for the failure of the parties to reach a settlement is "mutual optimism." We have assumed that they agree on the expected value of the arbitrator's assessment, but this may not be true. If both sides are optimistic about how the arbitrator will view their case, then the bargaining range implied by equation (8.15) may evaporate. Suppose, in the preceding example, that the player expects the arbitrator to judge his worth to be \$1.75 million while the owner expects the arbitrator to judge the player's worth to be \$1.25 million. In that case, the owner would offer at most \$1.45 million to settle, while the player would demand at least \$1.55 million, and so no settlement would be possible.

A second explanation for failure to settle is that one side has private information about some material fact, either about the player's true value or the arbitrator's assessment (for example, whether he or she is pro-owner or pro-player). This situation can also prevent settlement by causing the parties' predictions about the outcome of arbitration to diverge, thereby eliminating any settlement range.

Farmer, Pecorino, and Stango (2004) used data on filings for arbitration by major league players over the period 1990 to 1993 to try to distinguish between these two explanations. In their sample period, 527 players filed for arbitration, but only 71 (13 percent) actually proceeded to a judgment (i.e., failed to settle). Their analysis of these cases supported the mutual optimism argument. This makes sense because most of the information pertaining to the arbitration process—such as player performance statistics and the past actions of arbitrators—is public, so it is hard to imagine one side having private knowledge about relevant facts.

A third possible explanation for bargaining failure is that owners want to establish a reputation for toughness to discourage future players from filing for arbitration. This argument reflects the asymmetric position of players and owners in the salary determination process. Whereas owners are repeat participants, individual players are only eligible for a short window in their careers and will participate only once or twice.[15] Thus, in a given negotiation, owners may feel they have more at stake than the salary of the particular player at hand, and even if proceeding to arbitration is costlier in this case, the long-run costs may be lower if future players are discouraged from filing.[16]

PURCHASING WINS

We now shift from the discussion of the determination of player salaries to the question of how team spending on players translates into wins. As noted in the above analysis, this is a key relationship in the determination of player worth, and so it is important to examine it in further detail. As a first pass, we would suppose that, because players are the team's crucial input, spending more on player salaries should increase the team's chances of winning according to the following production function:

$$WP = g\left(S\right) \tag{8.16}$$

where $g\left(\cdot\right)$ is an increasing function relating a team's total spending on players, S, to its winning percentage, WP. Both of these variables are readily observable. Figure 8.5, therefore, plots winning percentage against total team payroll for the 2022 Major League Baseball season. The graph also shows the "best-fit" line from a simple linear regression of WP on S. The equation for that line is

$$WP = .374 + .00084 \cdot S \tag{8.17}$$

This says that for each additional million dollars spent on players' salaries, the average winning percentage increased by .00084. In a 162-game schedule, this means that each additional million dollars spent on payroll translates into .136 wins (=162×.00084). Stated differently, each win costs the average team about \$7.35 (=1/.136) million in labor costs.

Inspection of the raw data, however, shows that the relationship, while clearly positive, is fairly weak. One obvious explanation is that factors besides player salaries affect a team's performance on the field. One such factor is random events, such as injuries and poor performances. Another is poor management, by which we mean the inefficient use of inputs. This could involve mistakes in player evaluation or misuse of existing players. Certainly, some of this happens in professional sports because it is not an exact science, and teams that are better at managing their rosters will be more successful, all else equal.[17]

A useful way to introduce the idea of mismanagement is to think of the production function in equation (8.16) as reflecting the most efficient use of player inputs, in the sense that $g\left(S\right)$ represents the maximum number of wins

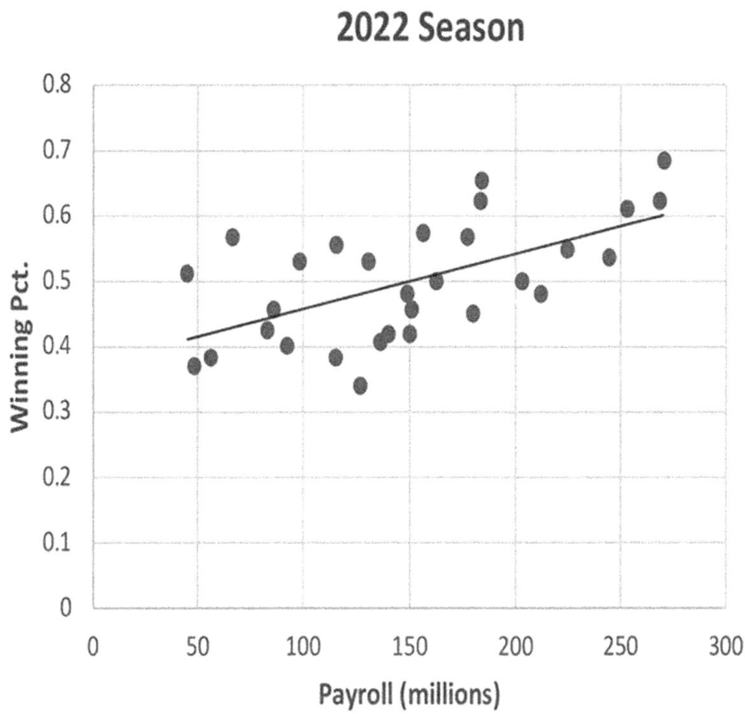

Figure 8.5 *Winning percentage as a function of total team payroll in Major League Baseball, 2022*

that can be achieved for any level of spending. The best-fit line in Figure 8.5, by contrast, weighs points above and below the line (over- and under-achievers) equally. An approach that better captures the information contained in the production function is shown graphically in Figure 8.6, where the concave shape of the $g(S)$ function reflects the usual assumption of diminishing marginal productivity. However, for the reasons noted, not all teams will be on the production frontier. For example, Figure 8.6 shows two points, A and B, representing two teams with the same payroll, S', but with different winning percentages. Team B is on the frontier, meaning that it produces the maximum number of wins from its payroll, while team A is inside the frontier, and so produces fewer wins with the same level of spending. In this sense, we say that team B is managed more efficiently than team A. Further, team B is achieving the maximum level of efficiency because it lies on the production frontier—i.e., a higher winning percentage is not possible for a spending level of S'.

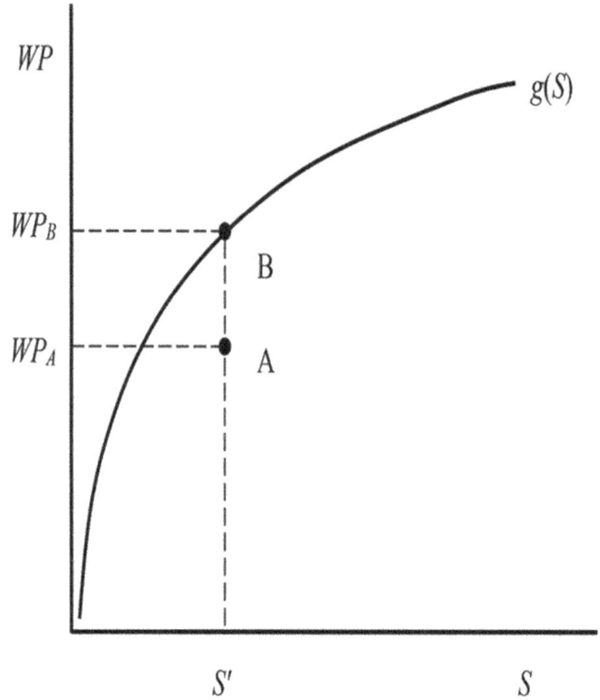

Figure 8.6 *Production function demonstrating the efficient (B) and inefficient (A) production of wins*

Using this approach, let's look again at the actual performance of MLB teams during the 2022 season. Figure 8.7 shows the same scatterplot as presented in Figure 8.5, but this time with a production frontier superimposed on it. Most teams lie well below the frontier, suggesting that they are not achieving the maximum number of possible wins for their payrolls. Only the most efficient teams lie on the frontier.[18] Note that these "efficiently-managed" teams span the range of payrolls from very low to very high.

THE MONEYBALL HYPOTHESIS

Inefficient management of economic enterprises results in forgone profits, which is often the basis for mergers and takeovers of underperforming firms. In sports, owners fire coaches and managers of losing teams, especially when they have spent a lot of money to acquire top players. But as Figure 8.7 reveals, lavish spending is no guarantee of success—many teams with low payrolls

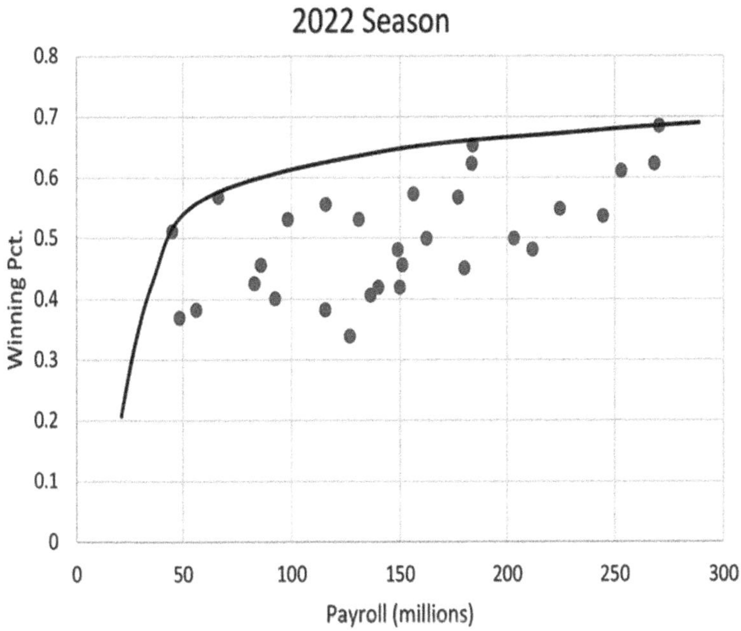

Figure 8.7 *Performance of teams compared to the production frontier, 2022 MLB season.*

find ways to compete against teams with much higher payrolls. One way they can do that is by employing innovative management techniques. The most celebrated example of this approach in recent times is the so-called *Moneyball Hypothesis*, which describes a strategy employed by the Oakland Athletics during the early 2000s to exploit an inefficiency in the way certain offensive skills were being valued by major league baseball teams (Lewis, 2003).

The specific insight of the Athletics and their management team, led by general manager Billy Beane, was that teams were apparently overpaying power hitters and underpaying players who had high on-base percentages (OBPs).[19] By exploiting this fact, the Athletics were able to assemble a team of players with high OBPs at bargain prices and thereby purchase wins more cheaply than other teams. As a result, they made the playoffs each year from 2000 to 2003 and ripped off a 20-game winning streak in 2002, the fourth-longest such streak in MLB history.

The economists Hakes and Sauer (2006) formally tested the validity of this hypothesis using data on player salaries and performance statistics for the five-year period 1999–2003. They did this by first regressing winning percentage on slugging percentage (*SLG*) (the same measure Scully used) and *OBP* to determine which statistic is the more important contributor to wins. They included a team's own measures and those of their opponents (*OPP*) to obtain the following equation:

$$WP = .502 + 2.141OBP - 1.892OPPOBP + .802SLG - 1.005OPPSLG \tag{8.18}$$

The coefficients represent the marginal contributions of the relevant variables to the team's winning percentage. Note that, while both *OBP* and *SLG* have positive coefficients, *OBP* has more than twice the effect on winning percentage compared with *SLG*.

The authors next considered the determinants of player salaries, first over the period 2000–2003. Using the approach pioneered by Scully, they regressed player salaries (excluding pitchers) on *OBP* and *SLG* plus several other control variables. The resulting equation is

$$SAL = 10.429 + .842OBP + 2.453SLG + \text{other factors} \tag{8.19}$$

Note that the coefficient for *SLG* is roughly three times that for *OBP*, showing that teams paid a significant premium for sluggers, even though equation (8.18) shows that *OBP* was the more important factor in producing wins. The Oakland Athletics were able to exploit this "error" to outperform their competition despite having a substantially lower payroll than most teams in the league during that time.

Interestingly, the undervaluation of *OBP* relative to *SLG* was at least partially corrected by the 2004 season, as evidenced by the following salary equation:

$$SAL = 9.782 + 3.681OBP + 2.175SLG + \text{other factors} \tag{8.20}$$

Here, *OBP* has surpassed *SLG* as the more important determinant of salary, though not quite to the extent warranted by its relative impact on winning percentage.[20] Still, something happened in 2004 to bring salaries more in line with relevant measures of offensive success. That "something" was probably that other teams caught on to what the Athletics were doing and began to correct their own miscalculations of what constituted an "efficient" team. The change in salaries in 2004 is evidence of this adjustment.

Ten years later, another study revisited the determination of player salaries in MLB to see if the insights from Moneyball had a lasting impact (Brown et al., 2017). The study used data from 1996 through 2011 and distinguished between free agents and players still under the reserve system, as salaries in those markets are obviously determined very differently. The results showed that in the free agent market, player compensation did reflect actual measures of statistical performance, as prescribed by the Moneyball hypothesis, whereas reserve-clause player salaries did not. Further, the compensation of reserve-clause players was below their *MRP*s, which we have seen is a defining characteristic of monopsonistic labor markets.

Congdon-Hohman and Lanning (2018) further corroborated these results. They specifically found that player compensation in the post-Moneyball era has increasingly rewarded on-base percentage and walks, reflecting the previously overlooked value of these measures of performance. It appears that when the market operates competitively, salaries in the MLB accurately reflect performance.

MONEYBALL AS TECHNOLOGICAL PROGRESS: STATISTICS VERSUS SCOUTING

From an economic perspective, the use of statistical analysis of performance measures to evaluate players (now called sports analytics), in baseball or any other sport, is an example of a technological innovation, the impact of which can be studied using the standard approach of cost-minimization. To be specific, let a team's production function for wins (q) be given by $q = f(x, y)$, where x and y are two inputs (to be defined shortly) whose unit costs are w_x and w_y, respectively. The team's total cost of assembling a roster is therefore $TC = w_x x + w_y y$. The team's problem is to choose x and y to minimize this cost, subject to the targeted number of wins, q_0.

This is a standard problem in the theory of the firm, the solution of which is defined by the equation

$$\frac{f_x}{f_y} = \frac{w_x}{w_y} \tag{8.21}$$

where f_x and f_y are the marginal productivities of inputs x and y. According to this condition, the optimal input mix is determined by the point where the ratio of the marginal productivities (called the Rate of Technical Substitution) equals the ratio of the prices of the inputs. This optimality condition is shown graphically in Figure 8.8 by the tangency between the convex-shaped "isoquant" associated with the quantity q_0, and the straight line that represents the ratio of the prices. The isoquant describes the rate at which the two inputs can be substituted for one another technologically, holding output fixed, while the cost line shows the rate at which the inputs can be substituted for each other in the market. The resulting optimal input mix is denoted (x_0^*, y_0^*).[21]

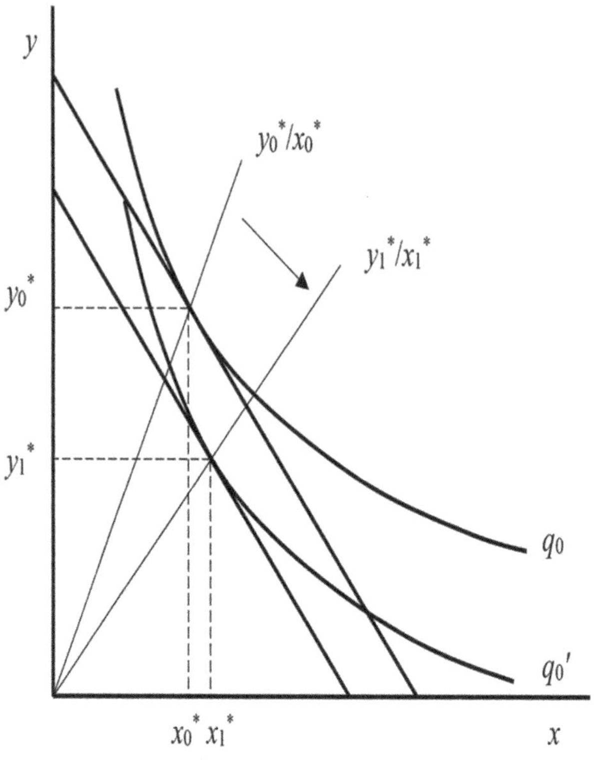

Figure 8.8 *Impact of a technological innovation on the optimal mix of inputs*

The impact of technological innovation on this problem is twofold. First, the isoquant associated with the target level of output shifts inward, meaning that the same number of wins can be produced with fewer inputs. The resulting isoquant is labeled q_0' in Figure 8.8. Second, if the innovation favors one of the inputs, the slope of the isoquant will also change. Suppose, for example, that the change causes f_x / f_y to steepen, meaning that the innovation favors input x (i.e., f_x rises relative to f_y). The result will be a shift toward the relatively more productive input. This is shown in the graph by the fact that the use of y decreases to y_1^* while the use of x increases to x_1^*. The two rays through the origin, which represent constant y / x ratios, show that the innovation causes this ratio to decrease.

Now apply this logic to the Moneyball revolution. An interesting question in this respect is whether the advent of Moneyball has made traditional scouting of players obsolete.[22] The logic of this argument is that the ability to reduce nearly every aspect of a player's performance to statistical measurement offers a purely objective means of determining that player's worth, whereas traditional scouting relies on subjective judgment and hence is prone to error. In the context of the above model, suppose that input x represents the use of statistical analysis for evaluating players, and input y represents traditional scouting. The improvement in statistical methods as a result of Moneyball, as embodied by the inward shift and steepening of the isoquant, prescribes a move away from traditional scouting and toward statistical analysis. However, the result will generally not be a total elimination of scouting, provided that it still has positive marginal productivity. For example, there almost certainly exist some aspects of player performance that defy quantification—the so-called "intangibles"—and scouting by seasoned professionals with long experience in the game probably remains the best (or only) way to assess these factors.[23] In the era of Moneyball, analytics may have become the principal means of evaluating talent, but traditional scouting will probably always have a role to play.

THE DIFFUSION OF INNOVATIONS

The preceding discussion of innovation in sports as exemplified by the Moneyball revolution illustrates something important about markets in general—namely, that when they are allowed to function freely, the resulting competition quickly eliminates any inefficiencies. The process by which this happens is that successful innovations are copied by everyone, thereby eliminating any short-term gains for innovators. This, in turn, confers benefits on consumers in the form of lower costs and higher quality products. The same is true in sports—innovative techniques such as Moneyball improve the overall quality of play, while the diffusion of the idea maintains competitive balance in the league. As a result, no team dominates in the long term from exclusive access to the innovation.

The use of statistical analysis to evaluate players, as presented above, is only one of the recent innovations in the management of sports teams. Previous innovations in major league baseball include the creation of a farm system for developing young players (more about which in Chapter 10); the use of scouts to identify promising players; expanded recruitment of Latin American players and, more recently, players from other countries, most notably Asia. A similar list could be assembled for any professional sport. By the way, not all innovations are desirable—for example, the spitball, performance-enhancing drugs, the use of video technology to steal signs or spy on rival teams, and extreme defensive shifts are all techniques that have been used but are now forbidden in modern baseball.

The paradox of innovation in sports or any context is that, while rapid diffusion is socially beneficial, it may have the detrimental effect of discouraging innovators from investing in the discovery of new techniques and inventions in the first place. The reason is that once a discovery is made public, it is difficult or impossible for the discoverer to prevent others from using it because of the public good nature of knowledge. Economists refer to this as the *appropriability problem.* The situation is therefore something of a Catch-22: innovations are most valuable when made widely available, but such availability may reduce the incentives to develop the innovation.

The government remedies this problem in ordinary markets by issuing patents, which protect the property rights to an invention for a limited period of time (20 years), during which time the patent holder has exclusive rights to market the invention. While this creates a temporary monopoly, thereby limiting the market for the invention and hence its widespread use, the logic is that the resulting profit stream for the inventor is essential to provide a return on the initial investment in research and development. A limited patent life, it is argued, balances these offsetting factors.

In principle, the same logic would apply to innovations in sports. As Bradbury (2007, pp. 128–129) observes, "By finding cheaper methods for acquiring the things that lead to wins—an undervalued player, a coach who motivates his players, or a new training regimen—a team can purchase more wins on the same budget." Never mentioned in connection with this sort of inventive activity, however, is the possibility of granting teams exclusive rights to employ a new technique or strategy—something like a patent. The question is, why not, given that the logic is identical to that underlying a patent for product innovations? Why, for example, couldn't Branch Rickey, then general manager of the St. Louis Cardinals, have claimed exclusive rights to develop a farm system for training players? Likewise, why couldn't the inventor of the forward pass in football, the jump shot in basketball, or the two-handed backhand in tennis have claimed exclusive rights, at least temporarily, to use those techniques, which clearly would have given that athlete a decisive advantage? These questions may seem silly, but only because we have not thought of these sorts of innovations from an economic perspective in light of the trade-off between incentives to invest in an invention and allowing its widespread use. Surely the inventors of these ideas would have liked to have retained exclusive rights to their use—just like other inventors—thereby gaining a competitive advantage. But that has never happened and never will in sports. Is there a good reason for this difference?

One obvious reason would be the difficulty of enforcing such rights, but that is not a problem unique to sports. There is, however, a deeper reason that hinges on the difference between what competition means in markets versus what it means in sports. Competition in markets, both over price and through the introduction of new and better products, is, of course, motivated at the firm level by the desire for profits, but its principal social benefit is consumer welfare in the form of lower costs and better products. In this sense, economic competition is a *means to an end*; that is, innovation ultimately improves consumer welfare.

The same is true in sports to the extent that competition among teams improves the overall quality of play, but what is different is that in sports, competition is not just a means *but is also an end in itself.* This is embodied in the desire for competitive balance, which, as discussed at length in Chapter 6, is a core principle of sports economics. Although fans undoubtedly value the refinements in play that arise out of innovative techniques and strategies, they would appreciate it much less if the innovators gained an enduring competitive advantage from their exclusive use of those techniques. Thus, while the same trade-off between incentives to innovate and the gains from widespread use of those innovations is surely present in sports, on balance the benefits of widespread use are greater in sports than in ordinary markets, a situation that works in the direction of not granting exclusive rights, even if they could be enforced.[24]

Think, for example, of an innovation in baseball as opposed to, say, medicine or communications. If a person could be magically transported back to the 1920s, for example, he or she would easily recognize the game of baseball as basically the same as the modern version. However, that would clearly not be true of the other two industries, where technological advances have dramatically improved the product. Indeed, it is hard to think of life before the invention of the cell phone, not to mention penicillin.

It is, of course, an empirical question as to whether a policy of not granting exclusive rights has suppressed the rate of innovations in sports.[25] However, it seems clear that most sports have nevertheless evolved substantially throughout their history, suggesting that the benefits of innovation, even if only short-lived (as was apparently true of the Moneyball strategy), are more than adequate both to encourage innovation and to keep up fans' interest. This is true because players and teams will always seek an advantage, even a temporary one, over an opponent. To be sure, successful ideas will then be quickly copied to the extent that is possible (though teams may strive to keep secret some knowledge that they believe gives them an enduring advantage),[26] but efforts to innovate will nevertheless continue. Bradbury (2007, p. 130) therefore concludes that "The great lesson … is that inefficiencies in markets don't persist for long. To win by innovation, one must be adept at finding inefficiencies and swift at acting on them once they are found."

In light of the foregoing discussion, it is perhaps paradoxical to note that an important source of competition in markets—namely, free entry—is definitely *not* allowed in professional sports. This raises the question as to why one source of monopoly—patents—is not allowed in the service of protecting competitive balance, whereas another source—barriers to entry—is maintained. One answer, discussed in Chapter 4, is that leagues want to maintain a cartel. While this may be true, there is another, more benign (i.e., fan-friendly) reason—namely, that unrestricted entry will dilute the quality of play by spreading the limited supply of talented players more thinly. For this reason, leagues are wary of allowing expansion, even when profit opportunities exist. The same problem arises in ordinary markets to the extent that a key input is in scarce supply, so that it cannot be replicated by new entrants. Professional services such as medicine, law, and financial planning might be the best examples of this sort of market, and the government and/or professional organizations do, in fact, limit entry by enacting licensing requirements for these practitioners (Leland, 1979). We pursue this point further in Chapter 10 in the context of the screening function of the minor leagues.

Another source of monopoly power in sports is the manner in which amateur players are first acquired by teams. As has been noted, most professional leagues use a highly structured draft system to acquire players, and those players are then tied to that team for a fixed time period before they can attain free-agent status. It is somewhat puzzling that such a system has remained in place even in the presence of a strong players' union in most sports. We will provide an economic rationale for this situation in Chapter 10.

SUMMARY

This chapter began the analysis of the players' labor market by examining the determination of player salaries. We first explored employment and wages in a monopsonistic labor market, where teams have sole rights to their players under the reserve system. The result is that wages are set below a player's marginal revenue product, and employment falls short of what would exist in a competitive labor market. Although the monopsony model is a simplified description of actual labor markets in that it treats labor as a homogeneous input, it provides a stylized picture of how teams exploit their market power over players. Empirical studies of actual salary determination, pioneered by Gerald Scully's analysis of the market for major league baseball players, verified that, prior to the free-agent era, players were substantially underpaid relative to their values to their teams. More recent studies have shown that salaries more closely approach the full value of players, particularly as players approach eligibility for free agency.

The analysis of salary determination in a free-agent market showed that even when teams have to bid for players, the winning team will only have to pay the value of the player to the second-highest bidder. And if a player has a non-monetary attachment to some particular team, he may accept a salary below the highest bid in the market. The chapter also discussed salary negotiations between a team and a player bound to that team, either by contract or by the reserve system. In those cases, the only strategy available to the player is to threaten to hold out, but simple game theory showed that this strategy is unlikely to result in a substantial pay increase.

The chapter then turned to the manner in which team spending on players translates into wins. Although more spending should increase a team's prospects on the field, evidence suggests that the correlation is very weak. This reflects random factors that influence game outcomes, but also the existence of inefficiencies in personnel management. The latter point led us to a discussion of the Moneyball hypothesis, which is the argument that statistical analysis of the factors that contribute to success on the field can improve the efficiency of salary determination and can also allow small-market teams to compete with large-market teams. The Oakland A's of the early 2000s were a case in point. As other teams copied the A's strategy, however, the advantage was eliminated. This conclusion provided a point of departure for a discussion of the nature of innovation in sports, and the desirability, in that context at least, of rapid diffusion of new ideas in a competitive market setting.

EXERCISES

8.1. Suppose the supply curve for backup catchers is given by $w = 200{,}000+10{,}000q$, where w is the wage rate and L is the number of catchers. The corresponding marginal factor cost is $MFC=200{,}000+20{,}000q$. Also, let the marginal revenue product of catchers be $MRP=800{,}000-10{,}000q$.
   (a) Find the competitive wage and employment level.
   (b) Find the wage and employment level under monopsony.
   (c) Compute the wage gap under monopsony.
   (d) Illustrate the above results in a graph.

8.2. Consider table E8.1's data on team salaries and winning percentage for a particular year:

Table E8.1 *Team salaries and winning percentage*

Table	Salary (mil $)	Winning pct.
1	230	.530
2	220	.600
3	165	.450
4	150	.590
5	145	.560
6	140	.470
7	120	.390
8	115	.580
9	75	.400
10	70	.450

Plot these points on a graph with winning percentage on the vertical axis and salary on the horizontal axis. Which teams are on the Production Possibility Frontier?

NOTES

1. Obviously, the two graphs in Figure 8.1 are not drawn to scale. In equilibrium, total employment, L, in panel (b) must be equal to the sum of the L_i across all firms.
2. The market supply curve, like the market demand curve, is the horizontal summation of individual labor supply curves, which are the product of the optimal time allocation decisions of individuals when choosing between labor and leisure.
3. Also see Bradbury (2007, Ch. 13).
4. A player's slugging percentage is computed as the total bases from hits divided by the total number of at-bats.
5. This approach thus ignores the team production problem, which involves disentangling the individual contributions of players. See Chapter 9.
6. As noted in Chapter 7, the year 1968 was a low-water mark for offense in baseball, and so a slugging percentage of 340 (actually, .340) was well below the norm. As a basis for comparison, the league-wide slugging percentage in 2022 was .395.
7. In the next section, however, we will argue that even in a true free agent market, players probably will not receive their full *MRP*.
8. The curves are drawn as concave, reflecting a diminishing marginal utility of income. This assumption is conventional but is not essential to the current discussion.

9. This approach to determining the equilibrium of a sequential move game is called "backward induction."
10. Formally, we say that this outcome is the unique subgame perfect Nash equilibrium of the sequential-move game.
11. The following analysis is based on Farber (1980). .
12. To see why, note that in case (i) $w < (b_p + b_o) / 2$ and so b_o is chosen, whereas in case (iii) $w > (b_p + b_o) / 2$ and so b_p is chosen.
13. The details of the derivation are contained in the Appendix to this chapter.
14. The arguments are based on economic models of why some legal disputes end up going to trial rather than settling out of court. See, for example, Cooter and Rubinfeld (1989).
15. A countervailing factor is that players may employ agents who are repeat participants and who, like owners, may wish to establish a reputation for tough bargaining. The question is whether players would allow themselves to be "used" by agents in this way.
16. A similar argument may explain why some legal disputes involving repeat defendants, such as insurance companies or large corporations, proceed to trial despite the high cost.
17. On this point, see Bradbury (2007, Ch. 7).
18. In fact, these teams *define* the frontier since there is no way to know whether they could have produced more wins.
19. On-base percentage is computed as the sum of hits, walks, and hit by pitches, divided by total plate appearances.
20. This could be partially due to the existence of long-term contracts, which limit the ability of teams to fully adjust salaries from year to year.
21. Varying the output level traces out the team's cost-of-wins function.
22. There is an interesting scene in the movie *Moneyball* in which a group of scouts spar with the general manager over the value of using statistics compared with traditional scouting techniques for evaluating players.
23. See the discussion in Phillips (2019).
24. Bradbury (2007, p. 134) makes a similar argument.
25. There are, in fact, some economists who argue that the incentive benefits of patents are overstated, and hence that they should be eliminated in the interest of wider and faster availability of inventions (Boldrin and Levine, 2008).
26. Of course, the movement of players and coaches limits the ability of teams to protect such "trade secrets."
27. It is easily verified that the second-order condition for a maximum is satisfied.
28. Again, the second-order condition is satisfied.

APPENDIX

This appendix provides the mathematical details of the derivation of the Nash equilibrium of the FOA game described in the text. The analysis will assume a uniform distribution of the arbitrator's valuation of the player—specifically, that $w \in \left[\underline{w}, \overline{w}\right]$—though the qualitative results hold more generally. Given that assumption, equation (8.10) in the text becomes

$$p = \frac{\frac{b_p + b_o}{2} - \underline{w}}{\overline{w} - \underline{w}} \tag{A8.1}$$

We said that the player's strategy involves maximizing equation (8.11) with respect to his choice of b_{p}, given equation (A8.1) and b_{o}. This problem yields the first-order condition

$$\frac{b_{\mathrm{o}} - b_{\mathrm{p}}}{2\left(\overline{w} - \underline{w}\right)} + \left[1 - \frac{\frac{b_{\mathrm{p}} + b_{\mathrm{o}}}{2} - \underline{w}}{\overline{w} - \underline{w}}\right] = 0 \tag{A8.2}$$

The solution is $b_p^* = \overline{w}$ regardless of the owner's choice of b_o.[27] Thus, the player has a *dominant strategy* of proposing the highest valuation that is acceptable to the arbitrator, no matter what the owner proposes.

In like manner, the owner will choose b_{o} to minimize equation (8.11), given equation (A8.1) and b_{p}. The resulting first-order condition in this case is[28]

$$\frac{b_{\mathrm{o}} - b_{\mathrm{p}}}{2\left(\overline{w} - \underline{w}\right)} + \frac{\frac{b_{\mathrm{p}} + b_{\mathrm{o}}}{2} - \underline{w}}{\overline{w} - \underline{w}} = 0 \tag{A8.3}$$

Solving this equation yields $b_{\mathrm{o}}^* = \underline{w}$ regardless of the player's choice of b_{p}. Thus, the owner has a dominant strategy of proposing the lowest valuation that is acceptable to the arbitrator.

9. Player contracts: risk sharing and incentives

In the modern era of professional sports, where players stand on a fairly equal footing with ownership owing to strong players' unions, long-term (multi-year) contracts are nevertheless the norm. This chapter undertakes an economic analysis of these contracts with a focus on two factors: risk-sharing and incentives. Risks in sports arise from inherent uncertainties associated with the nature of sporting competition ("how the ball bounces"), as well as from the possibility of injury that can shorten a player's season or career, and in some cases can even pose long-term health hazards. Long-term and guaranteed-salary contracts are clearly an effort to protect players from the income variability that such risks pose. The downside of such contracts, however, is that guaranteed contracts sever the link between player performance and income, which can blunt incentives for players to exert effort, especially when it is difficult or impossible to accurately monitor a player's effort. This concern is obviously the basis for incentive clauses included in many players' contracts, which link pay to certain measurable achievements, such as making the all-star team or earning post-season awards.

This chapter uses the economic theory of contracts, sometimes referred to as principal–agent theory, to study the inherent trade-off between risk-sharing and incentives in the structure of player contracts. After laying out the principal–agent model in general, we first examine optimal risk-sharing contracts, which prescribe a fixed wage for a risk-averse employee working for a risk-neutral employer. At the other extreme are pure incentive contracts, which prescribe imposing all of the risk on employees as a means of creating powerful incentives for them to exert effort. When both factors are present, optimal contracts combine a fixed salary with incentive clauses that condition payment on performance. Actual player contracts closely resemble this structure.

The chapter concludes by addressing the issue of "team production," which complicates the problem of disentangling the inputs of individual members to a team's overall success. We argue that holding the coach/manager responsible for a team's performance is a rational response to this problem.

THE PRINCIPAL–AGENT MODEL

Economists study the relationship between an employer and an employee using the *principal–agent model*. In this paradigm, the employer (the principal) hires an employee (the agent) to carry out some task or job in return for compensation, the terms of which are spelt out in a contract. It is usually assumed that the principal cannot accurately observe the effort of the agent in completing the assigned task, and so compensation cannot be conditioned on the agent's effort (an input), but rather must depend on some observable measure of output, which is assumed to be an increasing function of the agent's effort but also depends on random factors that prevent the principal from perfectly inferring the agent's effort from output.

To be a bit more formal, let the production function that determines output be given by

$$q = f(e,\theta) \tag{9.1}$$

where q is the observed quantity of output, e is the agent's effort, and θ is a random variable. We assume that output is increasing in the agent's effort at a decreasing rate, reflecting the usual assumption of diminishing marginal productivity.

As a benchmark for examining the performance of the various contracts below, we first consider the socially optimal effort level, which is defined to be the effort level that the principal would instruct the agent to undertake if that were possible. Alternatively stated, it is the effort the principal herself would choose if she were acting as her own agent (i.e., if she were self-employed). This is defined to be the level of e that maximizes the expected net value of output, given by:

$$P{\cdot}E\left[f(e,\theta)\right] - ce \tag{9.2}$$

where P is the market price of output (which is taken as given), $E\left[\cdot\right]$ is the expectations operator taken over the random variable θ, and c is the marginal cost of the agent's effort. It is important to remember that effort must be chosen before the realization of the random factor, so the best the principal can do is maximize *expected* net output. As a result, effort cannot be conditional on the realization of θ. Under these circumstances, the optimal effort, e^*, is determined by the first-order condition

$$P{\cdot}E\left[f_e\right] = c \tag{9.3}$$

which says that the expected marginal benefit of effort (i.e., price multiplied by the expected marginal productivity) should be equated to the marginal cost of effort.

To provide a context for the analysis of sports contracts, we will examine a prototypical example of the principal–agent relationship; namely, a contract between a landowner and a tenant-farmer who has been hired to cultivate the owner's land. Output, in this case, is the crop yield, which is increasing with the farmer's effort but also depends unpredictably on weather. A type of contract that has commonly been used in the history of agriculture and which has been studied extensively by economists (see, for example, Cheung, 1969), is the *sharecropping contract*, which provides for the crop to be divided in some pre-arranged way (say 50–50) between the landowner and the farmer. Similar sharing arrangements are commonly used to compensate workers in other employment relationships. For example, real estate brokers receive a share of the proceeds from a sale of property, some attorneys retain a percentage of any judgment received by their clients, and salespeople are often paid (at least in part) by a commission, computed as a percentage of gross sales. Although there is no obvious analog to a share contract in professional sports, at least not in modern times,[1] we will argue that incentive clauses serve the same purpose.

Returning to the agricultural context, it will be useful to compare share contracts to two other contractual forms: namely, *fixed wage contracts* and *fixed rental contracts*. Under a fixed wage contract, the farmer is paid a pre-set wage rate for his labor input, and the landowner then retains the entire crop yield. In contrast, under a fixed rental contract, the farmer pays a pre-set rent to the landowner for the right to cultivate the land, and the farmer then retains the entire crop yield. We will see that these contractual forms have very different implications with regard to risk-sharing and incentives. Although player contracts in sports are nearly always of the wage type (at least in terms of base pay), they vary considerably in terms of contract length (i.e., the period of time over which the wage is guaranteed), and whether or not different types of incentives are added on.

The preceding contractual forms can be seen as special cases of the following general contract, which conditions an employee's wage, w, on his or her measured output, q, but also possibly includes a fixed component:

$$w = aq + b \tag{9.4}$$

where a and b are constants. Under a fixed wage contract, $a = 0$ and $b > 0$; under a fixed rental contract, $a = 1$ and $b < 0$; and under a pure share contract, $0 < a < 1$, and $b = 0$. Which of these is optimal will depend on the particular circumstances of the employment relationship.[2]

PURE RISK-SHARING

We begin by examining optimal risk-sharing between the principal and the agent. To isolate this factor, we abstract here from the agent's effort choice and focus only on the impact of the random variable θ on output. The issue here is how to best allocate the unavoidable risk of uncertain performance. For purposes of the discussion, we will assume that the agent (player) is *risk-averse*, meaning that he suffers disutility from random fluctuations in his income. The assumption of risk aversion for individual economic agents is a standard one and is used to explain why most people buy insurance against unexpected losses. Formally, risk aversion turns out to be a consequence of the assumption that people receive diminishing marginal utility of income, meaning that each additional dollar yields a smaller positive benefit.

Consider, for example, the utility function $U = U(w)$, where w is the wage. For a risk-averse person, utility is increasing in w (i.e., the first derivative is positive, or $dU / dw > 0$) but at a decreasing rate (i.e., the second derivative is negative, or $d^2U / dw^2 < 0$). Such a utility function is shown in Figure 9.1.

For simplicity, we will suppose that the random variable here can have only two realizations: low and high, which translate into low income, w_L, and high income, w_H, given the person's fixed effort. Obviously, it is the case that $U(w_H) > U(w_L)$, as shown in the graph, so the person is better off if the high

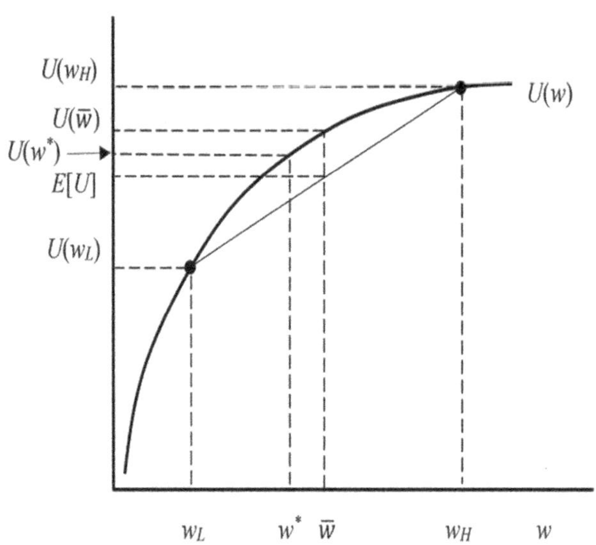

Figure 9.1 Utility of a risk-averse person

state of the world materializes. In the current formulation, however, the agent has no control over which state arises. Prior to the realization of the state, the person's *expected utility* is equal to the weighted sum of $U(w_H)$ and $U(w_L)$, or

$$E[U] = pU(w_H) + (1-p)U(w_L) \tag{9.5}$$

where p is the probability of the high state and $1-p$ is the probability of the low state. Similarly, the person's *expected income*, denoted $\bar{w}$, is computed as

$$E[w] \equiv \bar{w} = pw_H + (1-p)w_L \tag{9.6}$$

Expected utility is measured on the vertical axis in Figure 9.1, while expected income is measured on the horizontal axis. Because both are linear combinations of the two endpoints corresponding to the two possible realizations of the random variable, they are determined by the relevant point on the solid line segment connecting those endpoints. Note that as p gets larger, $\bar{w}$ moves closer to w_H, and correspondingly, $E[U]$ moves closer to $U(w_H)$.

Now suppose the person is offered a choice between receiving a guaranteed wage of $\bar{w}$ no matter what the state or the wage associated with the state that is actually realized (i.e., w_L in the low state and w_H in the high state). It should be clear from the graph that the employee would strictly prefer the guaranteed wage. This is true because, as the graph shows,

$$U(\bar{w}) > E[U] \tag{9.7}$$

This condition is the defining feature of risk aversion. Further, it should be clear that it is a consequence of the concavity of the utility function, which reflects the diminishing marginal utility of income.

In contrast to the agent, we will assume that the principal is *risk-neutral*, meaning that she only cares about expected output. For a risk-neutral person, expected utility and expected income are the same (i.e., utility is linear in income), and so the principal is indifferent between them. This assumption seems reasonable in the sports context because a team owner has the ability to diversify the uncertainty from random factors across the entire roster of players, assuming that the realizations of θ for different players are not correlated. In other words, a poor year by one player does not make it more likely that other players will have poor years. The situation is like an insurance company that sells policies to multiple customers under the assumption that the risk of claims is uncorrelated, thus allowing the insurance company to diversify the risk.

Like individual customers of insurance companies, however, players cannot diversify on their own because they are each subject to the realization of their own specific random variable. This is what creates the possibility of a mutually beneficial transaction between risk-averse individuals (agents) and risk-neutral insurance companies or employers (principals), whereby the latter absorb the risk in return for a premium that more than covers its expected payout. Risk-averse individuals are willing to pay such a premium because of the inequality in equation (9.6). In other words, they will accept a wage somewhat less than $\bar{w}$ so as to avoid the risk.

In the sports context, the team provides the player with insurance against performance risk by means of a guaranteed contract, in return for which the player is willing to accept a wage below his expected marginal revenue product. Note that this provides another reason, besides market power, for why a player's salary will understate his monetary value to the team.

PURE INCENTIVE CONTRACTS

The preceding analysis explained the preference among risk-averse agents for fixed (guaranteed) wage contracts. The downside of such contracts, however, is that they eliminate any incentive for agents to exert effort to increase expected output under the assumption that principals cannot observe effort, and hence cannot condition payment on it. Thus, principals would not generally find such contracts acceptable.

One might argue that in sports, effort, or at least performance, is readily observable because it occurs in the open, in contrast to the other contexts mentioned above (agriculture or sales). While this may be true of on-field actions, much of a player's effort involves preparation and conditioning, which are not done openly. As Krautmann and Solow (2009, pp. 7–8) note, "shirking may manifest itself in reduced intensity and dedication with which an athlete devotes himself to his off-season conditioning program. …For another, an unmotivated player may not prepare optimally for each game during the season."[3] In addition, actions do not always equate to effort, and what is truly in an athlete's heart is not observable and, in any case, is not easily written into a contract.[4] Finally, the team production problem, as will be discussed below, obscures the measurement of individual effort.

When only incentives matter (i.e., when the agent is risk-neutral), the optimal contract is a fixed rental type whereby the employee "rents" the capital or land from the owner and retains the full output. The literal analogy to this in a sports context would be for players to pay owners a fixed fee for the right to be on a professional team. This fee would cover the rental for the stadium, equipment, and other non-player costs. The players would then divide up the gate receipts among themselves. Such a structure would result in an efficient level of effort.

Obviously, this sort of contact is not seen in sports, primarily because most players would lack the resources to make the necessary rental payments. Presumably, players would demand a minimum income in all states of the world, including bad states, as a condition for accepting employment because even risk-neutral players would have a minimum income requirement.[5]

A second problem with the proposed rental contract is that the player is fully exposed to the risk of income variability. This is an inherent feature of an efficient contract because maintaining incentives requires the agent (player) to bear the full amount of actual output in all states of the world. This requirement stands in sharp contrast to the conclusion in the previous section that it was optimal to shift all of the risk to the principal (owner) for risk-sharing purposes. The inevitable conclusion is that if the agent is risk-averse at all, there is a fundamental conflict between incentives and optimal risk-sharing. In the next section, we ask how actual contracts in sports deal with this trade-off.

BALANCING RISK SHARING AND INCENTIVES

The preceding sections showed that consideration of risk sharing and incentives is necessarily in conflict with respect to the structure of player contracts. Whereas players want guaranteed wage contracts to insure them against performance risk, owners prefer contracts that tie compensation to performance as a means of creating strong incentives. Striking an optimal balance between these competing objectives routinely drives the negotiation process between players (or players' agents) and owners when engaged in collective bargaining.[6]

Actual contracts in other employment settings usually strike this balance by specifying that $0 < a < 1$ and $b > 0$ in equation (9.4), where a is the commission and b is the base salary. In contrast, recall that under the optimal risk-sharing contract (the analog to the pure wage contract), $a = 0$ and $b > 0$, thus shifting all of the risk to the principal but completely eliminating incentives for effort. Conversely, in the efficient incentive contract (the analog to the fixed rental contract), $a = 1$ but $b < 0$ (i.e., the agent pays a fee to participate). In addition, the agent bears all of the risk. Under the hybrid contract just described, there is partial risk-shifting (because $a < 1$), thereby providing some insurance while also preserving some incentives for the agent to invest effort, but there is also a floor on income given that $b > 0$ as a partial protection against risk.

In sports contracts, players are typically paid by fixed wage contracts, but rather than having a literal commission, other provisions are included as incentive devices. We consider three such devices here. The first involves variable contract length. Players obviously prefer multi-year contracts that guarantee salaries throughout the term of the contract, while owners want short-term contracts that allow adjustment in wages to reflect variable performance. For example, it is often conjectured that players perform better in the final year of their contracts (their "walk year") in order to increase their bargaining position for the next contract. Contract negotiations thus often hinge on the length of contracts as much as on the salary, with owners wanting shorter terms and players wanting longer terms.

A second incentive device is an explicit clause that conditions a player's compensation on some measurable performance goal, such as making the all-star team, achieving a certain number of wins, or playing in a minimum number of games. Typically, the player receives a base salary, which is then augmented by bonuses for reaching these goals. The overall structure of such a contract, therefore, looks a lot like the hybrid wage structure. Contracts heavily laden with incentive provisions are usually reserved for untried rookies and veteran players whose remaining skills are in question.

Finally, a contract can contain an option that allows one party, the player or the team, to add an additional year to an existing contract at a pre-set wage. How do these player or team options affect the player's incentives? Consider first a *team option*, which allows the team, at its discretion, to employ the player for an additional year at the current wage of w. It will exercise that option if the player's expected marginal revenue product (*MRP*) exceeds w, and decline to exercise it if the reverse is true. By exerting extra effort, the player will increase the chances that $MRP > w$, in which case the team will exercise the option and he will earn w. However, shirking increases the chances that $MRP < w$, in which case the team will not exercise the option, and he will earn *MRP* playing for some other team. Thus, the player's upside gain is limited to w, but he bears all of the downside risk. Thus, the player will have some incentive to exert effort to minimize that risk.

Now consider a *player's option*. In this case, the player will exercise the option if $MRP < w$, in which case he earns w, and not exercise the option if $MRP > w$, in which case he can earn up to *MRP*. Here, the player receives all of the upside benefit but is protected against the downside risk. The situation is therefore the reverse of that under the team option; that is, the player will have some incentive to exert effort to maximize his upside benefit.

The preceding reveals that either the team or the player options create partial but not fully efficient incentives for players to exert effort. As the current wage gets smaller, the player's option creates more powerful incentives, whereas as the wage gets larger, the team option is more powerful.[7] This makes intuitive sense. A lower wage makes it less likely that a player will exercise his option, so he expects to realize more of the return from his effort by going onto the free agent market. Thus, he has an incentive to work hard. At the same time, a lower wage makes it more likely that the team will exercise its option, which locks the player into the fixed wage for an additional year. Thus, he has less of an incentive to work hard. The opposite conclusions apply as the wage is increased. In sum, a low wage makes the player's option more conducive to effort, and a high wage makes the team option more conducive to effort.

THE TEAM PRODUCTION PROBLEM

The analysis to this point has focused on production technologies that involve a single agent working for the principal. This simplifies the issues but clearly abstracts from the case of team sports, where the actions of the team members combine to produce a single output—namely, wins. Study of the single-agent case would nevertheless be adequate to capture this situation if the "outputs" of the individual players could be separately observed, and if total output was simply the aggregate of the individual outputs; that is, if the production function was additive, or $Q = q_1 + q_2 + \ldots + q_n$. In that case, each player's contribution could be separately rewarded. In most team production contexts, however, sports certainly among them, this is not the case. ("Team chemistry," for example, introduces a non-additive element to team production.) Instead, individual effort levels combine to produce aggregate output in a non-separable way:

$$Q = g\left(e_1, e_2, \ldots, e_n\right) \tag{9.8}$$

where each input of effort contributes positively to the total output.

Team production, like random factors in the above single-agent model, complicates the incentive issue because individual members can, in essence, free ride on the efforts of teammates, given that, in the extreme case, compensation of all team members can only be conditioned on the common output level. The problem is similar to inducing individuals to contribute voluntarily to a public good in the sense that any effort by a team member that increases output benefits all members. Economists have studied the problem of team production and have proposed various incentive mechanisms for inducing effort.[8] Here, we focus on two mechanisms that seem most applicable to the situation on sports teams—peer monitoring and monitoring by a "residual claimant."

Peer monitoring involves members of the team policing each other's efforts through the use of peer pressure. In many cases, it is the players themselves who have the greatest ability to assess whether a teammate is exerting maximum effort, and to persuade those who are not to work harder.[9] As a general proposition, Putterman (1984) noted that:

> Some activities allow individuals to work and observe one another's performance simultaneously ... so that output and monitoring are joint products. While ... monitoring is made difficult by technologically non-separable activities, the implication

> that a third party can better assess the effort level of team members cannot be asserted to hold universally. (Putterman, 1984, pp. 173–174).

This characterization would seem to be especially applicable to sports teams. To be sure, there will be a free rider problem in carrying out this monitoring, as each team member benefits when someone else takes on the job. However, successful teams usually have one or a few team leaders, typically respected veterans, who take on the role of mentoring young players on the proper way to conduct themselves. In his study of the secrets that contribute to the success of great sports teams, Walker (2017) identified the role of team leaders in maintaining team unity and discipline as one critical factor. Effective leaders, Walker noted,

> engaged with the teammates constantly—listening, observing, and inserting themselves into every meaningful moment. They didn't think of communication as a form of theater. They saw it as an unbroken flow of interaction, a never-ending parade of boxing ears, delivering hugs, and wiping noses. (Walker, 2017, p. 169)

The other mechanism for policing shirkers in team production, first proposed by Alchian and Demsetz (1972), is the appointment of a specialized monitor who is also made the residual claimant. That means the monitor receives as his or her reward the net earnings of the enterprise after all inputs are paid. In this way, it is argued, the monitor has a strong incentive to induce team members to contribute optimal effort toward the team's success. Alchian and Demsetz argue that the capitalist firm, with the employer acting as the specialized monitor and residual claimant, epitomizes this solution to the team production problem.

There is no literal analog to this arrangement in sports, but the head coach/manager of a team plays a similar role in the sense that he is the chief monitor of player behavior and is also the residual claimant in the sense that it is ordinarily his job that is on the line if the team fails to perform well. This idea reflects the common lament among sports writers that when a team fails, it is usually not the coach's "fault," but the owner has to fire him because the whole team can't be fired. The coach takes the job knowing this risk and therefore has a strong incentive to get the most out of his team. Seen in the light of the team production problem, it seems that firing the coach of a poorly performing team may have a certain economic logic after all.

SUMMARY

This chapter continued the analysis of player salaries by examining the structure and function of contracts. The theoretical paradigm we used was the principal–agent model, which characterizes optimal contracts between an employer (principal) and an employee (agent) under various conditions. The two main issues that contracts address are risk-sharing and incentives. In a pure risk-sharing context, it is usually assumed that the principal is risk-neutral and the agent is risk-averse, which implies that it is optimal for the agent to receive a fixed wage, thereby shifting all of the risk to the principal. When agent inputs also matter and those inputs cannot be directly monitored, however, such a contract will not give the agent any incentive to exert effort, precisely because his compensation is independent of actual output. In this case, a contract that conditions payment on output is preferred, but this necessarily imposes some risk on the agent. When both risk-sharing and incentives matter, the optimal contract will therefore consist of a fixed payment combined with a conditional component tied in some way to measured output. Most contracts in professional sports resemble this structure, with players receiving a base salary augmented by bonuses linked to performance targets.

The chapter concluded by discussing the team production problem, which arises in any production setting where the inputs of several workers combine in a non-additive way to produce a single output. This complicates the incentive issue because it is difficult to measure the marginal contribution of each member. Even in a sports context, where individual statistics are generally available, many of those measures are dependent on the actions of other team members. We discussed two methods by which teams deal with this problem: peer monitoring, usually carried out by a player who takes on the role of "team leader," and monitoring by a manager or coach, whose job security is tied to overall team performance.

EXERCISES

9.1. Suppose that a player's salary is tied to his performance on the field in the following way. If he has a "good" season, he earns \$100,000, and if he has a "bad" season, he earns \$50,000. Suppose the probability of each outcome is 0.50. Also, suppose the player's utility function over his wage is given by $U = \sqrt{w}$.
   (a) Derive the player's expected utility.
   (b) Derive the player's expected income.
   (c) Show that the player enjoys higher utility than in (a) if he receives a guaranteed wage equal to his expected income as calculated in (b).

9.2. Suppose the player can exert either "high" or "low" effort during the season, which translates in a probabilistic way into either a good or a bad season. The impact of each of these on the *MRP* (marginal revenue product) of the player for his team is shown in Table E9.1, as is the probability of each outcome for each choice of effort.

Table E9.1

Season outcome	*MRP*	Probability of low effort	Probability of high effort
Good	$100,000	.30	.70
Bad	$ 50,000	.70	.30

Thus, when the player chooses "low" effort, the probability of a good season is .30 and the probability of a bad season is .70. When the player chooses "high" effort, the probabilities are reversed.

(a) Compute the expected *MRP* associated with each effort choice by the player.

Now suppose the cost of low effort to the player is $5,000, while the cost of high effort is $10,000.

(b) Suppose the player is paid a straight salary of $40,000, regardless of what type of season he has. What choice of effort maximizes the player's net return (i.e., salary less cost of effort)? Compute the expected profit for the team under each effort choicc. What choice would the team like the player to make?
(c) Now suppose the team offers the player a base salary of $35,000, but pays him a bonus of $20,000 if he has a "good' season. What effort choice maximizes his expected net return? What choice maximizes the team's expected profit?
(d) If the player is risk-averse, which type of salary structure would he like, holding the expected dollar payment the same? Explain.

NOTES

1. In the earliest days of professional baseball, some teams in the National Association, a precursor to the National League, were "co-op teams," which meant that players were compensated by receiving a share of the gate receipts. See Baker et al. (2004).

2. Some technical details of the pure risk-sharing and pure incentive contracts are provided in Appendix 1 to this chapter. Also see Eswaran and Kotwol (1985).
3. Also see Berri and Krautmann (2006) and Krautmann and Donley (2009).
4. As an example, in the aftermath of the Black Sox scandal, when the Chicago White Sox conspired with gamblers to throw the 1919 World Series (more about which in Chapter 12), it was asked how the players could intentionally have lost games without showing it. One of the players said that it was not a problem because they were "expert ballplayers" and "it's just as easy for a good player to miss a ball as to catch it" (Fountain, 2016, pp. 88–89). Of course, shirking is not the same thing as intentionally losing, but if anything, shirking—giving less than 100 percent—presumably would be even easier to conceal.
5. Note that this "participation constraint" is more restrictive than requiring *expected* income to be above a certain level. It specifically requires that realized income in each state must be above a certain level. Sappington (1983) calls this a *limited liability condition.*
6. When players themselves employ agents to negotiate on their behalf, there exists a multi-tiered principal–agent problem. See, for example, Mirrlees (1976).
7. The proof of this claim is provided in Appendix 2 to this chapter.
8. See, for example, Alchian and Demsetz (1972) and Holmstrom (1982) for classic treatments. Bolton and Dewatripont (2005, Chapter 8) survey the literature.
9. See Kandel and Lazear (1992) for a formal analysis of peer monitoring.
10. More generally, such a transaction would be possible as long as the owner is less risk-averse than the player.

APPENDIX 1: CONTRACT TYPES

This appendix provides some details regarding the contract types discussed in this chapter.

Pure Risk-sharing

To examine pure risk-sharing more specifically, let the value to the principal of the agent's output in state *j* (corresponding to the player's marginal revenue product) be v_j where $v_H > v_L$. In this formulation, the expected value of output in equation (9.2), $P{\cdot}E\left[f\right]$, takes the following form:

$$PE\left[f\left(e,\theta\right)\right] = pv_H + \left(1-p\right)v_L \tag{A9.1}$$

If the agent were paid his full value in each state, as would be true in a perfectly competitive labor market, $w_H = v_H$ and $w_L = v_L$. This would result in expected utility of $E\left[U\right]$ (the expression in equation (9.5)) for the agent, and zero expected profit for the principal:

$$E\left[\pi\right] = p\left(v_H - w_H\right) + \left(1-p\right)\left(v_L - w_L\right) = E\left[v\right] - \bar{w} = 0 \tag{A9.2}$$

But now let w^* be a fixed wage such that

$$U\left(w^*\right) > E\left[U\right] \text{ and } E\left[\pi\right] = E\left[v\right] - w^* > 0 \tag{A9.3}$$

(See Figure 9.1.) The first inequality says that the agent prefers the fixed wage to the uncertain income gamble, while the second says that the principal earns a positive profit because she pays a wage that is less than the expected value of the agent's output. Thus, both parties benefit from the contract. Note that this mutual benefit is a consequence of equation (9.7), reflecting the agent's risk aversion combined with the principal's risk-neutrality.[10]

Pure Incentives

To capture the impact of incentives, let us reintroduce effort in the following way. Suppose that in the simple two-state model, the agent's effort, *e*, increases the probability that the high state will occur. Specifically, let the probability of the high state be $p\left(e\right)$, which we assume is increasing in *e* at a decreasing rate (i.e., effort has diminishing marginal productivity). It necessarily follows that the probability of the low state, $1-p\left(e\right)$, is decreasing in *e*. We will also assume (for now) that both the principal and the agent are risk-neutral. Thus, the agent chooses effort to maximize his expected wage net of effort costs:

$$p(e)w_H + (1 - p(e))w_L - ce \tag{A9.4}$$

where w_H and w_L are the wages paid in the high and low states. The condition determining the agent's optimal effort is, therefore,

$$\frac{dp}{de}(w_H - w_L) = c \tag{A9.5}$$

where the left-hand side is the marginal benefit of effort and the right-hand side is the marginal cost. Clearly, the agent will only choose a positive level of effort if $w_H > w_L$. Further, the agent's effort will be increasing in the differential $w_H - w_L$. Intuitively, the agent will only exert effort to increase the likelihood of the high state if he expects to receive a wage premium in that state, and the greater that premium is, the more effort he will exert.

The socially optimal level of effort maximizes expected output less the agent's cost, or $p(e)v_H + (1 - p(e))v_L - ce$. The resulting condition for an optimum, corresponding to equation (9.3) in the text, is

$$\frac{dp}{de}(v_H - v_L) = c \tag{A9.6}$$

Comparing equations (A9.5) and (A9.6) shows that efficient effort by the agent requires

$$w_H - w_L = v_H - v_L \tag{A9.7}$$

Thus, the wage differential must match the differential in the value of output in the two states. One obvious solution is to set $w_H = v_H$ and $w_L = v_L$; that is, pay the agent the full value of his output in each state. The only way for this scheme to be profitable for the principal, however, is if the agent is required to pay the principal an up-front fee for the right to participate. In effect, the agent has to "buy out" the principal. In the agricultural context, this situation in fact corresponds to the fixed rental contract, under which the farmer pays the landowner a fixed rent for the right to cultivate the land and then retains the full harvest. In particular, we would set $w_H = v_H - R$ and $w_L = v_L - R$, where R is the rental payment that must be made in both the high and low states. (Obviously, R would be negotiated such that both parties expect to earn a positive profit.) Such a contract provides the optimal incentives for farmers to invest effort while giving the landowner a positive return on their land.

APPENDIX 2: INCENTIVE EFFECTS OF OPTION CONTRACTS

This appendix formally examines the incentive properties of the team and player options as discussed in the text. Let

w = option wage;

$m(e)\theta$ = marginal revenue product of a player, where $m' > 0$ and $m'' < 0$;

e = player effort;

θ = random variable with distribution function $F(\theta)$ and density function $f(\theta)$;

c = marginal cost of player effort.

This formulation captures the random nature of a player's value (through the effect of θ) as well as the positive effect of player effort on performance.

Under the team option, once θ is observed, the team will exercise the option if $w < m(e)\theta$, or if $\theta > w / m(e)$, and not exercise the option if the reverse is true. The resulting expected net income of the player is

$$\left[1 - F\left(\frac{w}{m(e)}\right)\right]w + \int_0^{w/m(e)} m(e)\theta f(\theta)\,d\theta - ce \tag{A9.8}$$

which the player maximizes by choosing e. The resulting first-order condition is

$$\int_0^{w/m(e)} \theta f(\theta)\,d\theta m'(e) = c \tag{A9.9}$$

Under the player option, in contrast, once θ is observed, the player will exercise the option if $w > m(e)\theta$, or if $\theta < w / m(e)$, and not exercise it if the reverse is true. The player's expected net income in this case is

$$\int_{w/m(e)}^{\infty} m(e)\theta f(\theta)\,d\theta + F\left(\frac{w}{m(e)}\right)w - ce \tag{A9.10}$$

Maximizing this expression with respect to e yields the first-order condition

$$\int_{w/m(e)}^{\infty} \theta f(\theta)\,d\theta m'(e) = c \tag{A9.11}$$

Finally, we derive the level of player effort that maximizes the value of the player to the team:

$$\int_0^\infty m(e)\theta f(\theta)\,d\theta - ce \tag{A9.12}$$

The resulting first-order condition for e is

$$\int_0^\infty \theta f(\theta)\,d\theta\, m'(e) = c \tag{A9.13}$$

Comparison of equations (A9.9) and (A9.11) with (A9.13) shows that the player exerts less than the efficient level of effort under both the team and player options, but it is ambiguous as to which induces more effort. As noted in the text, however, we can see that as w increases, effort under the team option approaches the efficient level while effort under the player option approaches zero. Conversely, as w gets small, effort under the player option approaches the efficient level while effort under the team option approaches zero. Thus, the team option is more conducive to effort when w is large, and the player option is more conducive to effort when w is small.

10. Player training: the minor leagues

This chapter turns to the role of the minor leagues as a training ground for prospective professional players. The focus will therefore be largely on baseball, where, more than any other sport, minor league training is essential for the vast majority of players who aspire to play at the major league level. The first part of the chapter examines the history of the minor leagues with particular emphasis on the economic relationship between major and minor league clubs. While early in their history, minor league teams were independent economic organizations, throughout the course of the twentieth century, a process of affiliation with major league clubs began to take place. We will argue that this reflected a rational economic response to the growing importance of the training function of the minor leagues. In other words, the organizational structure of the minor leagues co-evolved with its principal function in a predictable economic way.

The discussion then turns to the financing of training costs and shows that in order for teams to be willing to invest in players whose prospects of making the majors are uncertain, they need to retain exclusive rights to those players who make it for some extended period of time, during which they can pay them less than their value to the team. In this way, players effectively "repay" their training costs during this reserve period. This result explains why the players' union does not demand full free agency for all major league players. The insights from this discussion are then applied to the situation of ordinary job training and the financing of college, which is a form of job training.

The chapter concludes by examining the screening function of the minor leagues. The argument here is that screening is necessary to maintain a high quality of play on the field. However, a paradoxical consequence of this is that, as overall league quality rises, the measured performance of the best players actually declines. This is attributed to the higher level of average talent against which these stars must compete.

THE RELATIONSHIP BETWEEN THE MAJOR AND MINOR LEAGUES IN PROFESSIONAL BASEBALL

The modern era of Major League Baseball is usually dated to 1903 when the American and National Leagues signed the National Agreement, establishing the existing hierarchical structure of professional baseball. This structure consists of two separate but equal major leagues and a minor league system consisting of different levels.[1] Importantly, this agreement recognized the contractual rights of teams with respect to their players, as well as the reserve system that tied players to the teams that first signed them, even after any contracts expired (more about which later). Minor league teams had existed prior to the National Agreement, but the boundary between the majors and minors had been somewhat fuzzy.

A Brief History of the Minor Leagues

Although the game of baseball in the early years of the twentieth century, the so-called "dead-ball era," would be clearly recognizable to modern-day fans, it was played in a different way, with more of an emphasis on pitching, defense, and "small-ball" (to use a modern phrase). The manner in which players were scouted and signed was also quite rudimentary, with many players often moving directly from amateur teams to major league rosters with little or no minor league training.[2] To be sure, the minor leagues served as a training ground, but this was almost secondary to their role of providing local entertainment in small-town America in the days before television. Indeed, the available attendance data from this era shows that many teams drew impressive crowds, and most were therefore able to operate independently as viable economic organizations.

Because minor league teams were independent, however, if a major league team identified a talented player on one of these teams, it had to purchase that player's contract in an arm's-length transaction. As late as the 1930s, more than 75 percent of eventual major league players were initially signed by minor league teams, which then sold their contracts to a major league team. In fact, the sale of players was an important source of revenue for minor league teams during this era. And it was not uncommon for players to remain with their minor league teams well beyond the time when they were ready for the majors simply because they were more valuable to their current club, a situation that is inconceivable today (Hanssen, et al., 2016, pp. 531–532).

The situation began to change in the 1930s, however. The game on the field had changed dramatically with the arrival of Babe Ruth in the 1920s, and the consequent shift in emphasis to offense and power hitting brought an end to the dead-ball era. The importance of better training was also being recognized, and the relationship between the major and minor leagues began to reflect that change. The pioneer in these changes was Branch Rickey, who, as general manager of the St. Louis Cardinals in the 1920s, began to affiliate with minor league teams so that he could control the development of players as they refined their skills.[3] The success of the Cardinals on the field during the late 1920s and early 1930s[4] prompted other teams to copy Rickey's strategy (recall the discussion of the diffusion of innovations in Chapter 8). By 1936, 107 out of 180 (59 percent) minor league teams were affiliated with a major league team, either through outright ownership or by contractual agreement (Hanssen et al. 2016, p. 533). These agreements gave the parent major league team control over player development decisions as well as the right to acquire a player for a fixed payment rather than having to negotiate with the minor league team for purchase of his contract.

By the 1950s, the economic relationship between the majors and minors had to account for another trend: the declining attendance of minor league games. As Lamb (1994) observed

> [T]he advent of television and air-conditioning made staying home an appealing alternative to a night at the ballpark. By 1952 … minor league baseball had become an endangered species. Leagues were folding like afternoon newspapers, sometimes in mid-season, and attendance was tumbling. (Lamb, 1994, p. 147)

The televising of major league games, which began in 1939, only reinforced the trend. This introduced another reason for affiliation between major and minor league teams, namely, to subsidize the minor leagues so that they remained financially viable as a training ground. In recognition of the importance of the minor leagues, in the early 1960s, Major League Baseball (MLB) standardized the relationship between major league teams and their farm systems. This included the parent major league team's assuming complete control over player training decisions by means of "player development agreements." At the same time, business (non-baseball) decisions were often left in the hands of local officials, who presumably had better knowledge of what would draw fans to the ballpark.

A final change began occurring in the 1980s, when minor league attendance started to rise again. A renewed interest in supporting local sports teams seemed to be emerging, and many minor league franchises once again became profitable enterprises. Zimbalist (1992, p. 112), for example, reported that franchises which were being sold for as little as $5,000 in the 1970s were worth several million dollars by the 1990s. The result was a reduction in the subsidies paid to minor league teams, and, in some cases, minor league teams had to pay a percentage of their gate receipts into a central fund. Nevertheless, major league clubs retained total control over the baseball aspects of their affiliates. As Hanssen et al. (2016) observed,

> [A]lthough the minors have again become viable in economic terms, as they were in the early decades of the 20th century, the organizational relationship between the major and minor leagues did *not* revert to what it was in that earlier period. (Hanssen et al., 2016, pp. 538–539, emphasis in original)

This reflects the significantly greater role of the minor leagues for training at this time as compared with the earlier era, and, as we will show, the consequent need for major league teams to maintain control of that function.

The Economics of Player Training and League Organization

Against the preceding historical backdrop, this section develops a simple model of player training in an effort to rationalize the evolving organizational structure of the minor leagues. To that end, we define $V(x)$ to be the value of a player to a major league team (i.e., his marginal revenue product), written as a function of the dollar investment in the training of that player, x. We assume that V is increasing in x (i.e., $dV/dx > 0$) but at a decreasing rate (i.e., $d^2V/dx^2 < 0$), reflecting diminishing marginal productivity. The optimal investment in training is the choice of x that maximizes the player's net value, given by

$$V(x) - x \tag{10.1}$$

Thus, the condition defining the optimal investment, denoted x^*, is

$$\frac{dV}{dx} = 1 \tag{10.2}$$

Now, suppose that the player is initially owned by a minor league team that operates as an independent, profit-maximizing enterprise, as was true in the early years of the game. Further, suppose that the minor league team's revenue comes from two sources: gate receipts from the production of games, and revenue from the sale of players to major league teams. However, it has to incur the full cost of training those players. Let R be the value of the player in question to the minor league team, which, for simplicity, we will assume does not depend on x.[5]

The minor league team will decide how much to spend on training (i.e., it will choose the input x) to maximize its profit from the player. If the team expects to sell the player to a major league team for a price P, it will choose x to maximize $P - x$. The question is how that price will be determined. With an independent minor league, this will depend on bargaining between the major and minor league team once it has been determined that the player is of sufficient value.

After x has been spent, the value of the player to the major league team is $V(x)$, whereas his value to the minor league team is R. A sale is therefore mutually beneficial if $V(x) > R$. Assuming the sale occurs in this case, the price will be somewhere between these two values; that is, $V(x) \geq P \geq R$. If we suppose that the parties split the difference,[6] the price will be

$$P = R + \frac{V(x) - R}{2} = \frac{V(x) + R}{2} \tag{10.3}$$

That is, it will be the average of the two values.

As asserted above, the minor league team will choose its level of training, denoted by $\hat{x}$, to maximize its net return from a future sale of the player, or

$$P - x = \frac{V(x) + R}{2} - x \tag{10.4}$$

The resulting optimal condition is

$$\frac{dV(x)/dx}{2} = 1 \tag{10.5}$$

Comparing this to condition (10.2) shows that the team underinvests in training; that is $\hat{x} < x^*$.[7] This result is shown graphically in Figure 10.1. Intuitively, the minor league team underinvests in training because it only expects to capture a share (in this case, half) of the value of that investment in subsequent bargaining with the major league team.

In the industrial organization literature, the inefficiency here is said to be due to a *holdup* problem, which means that the buyer (the major league team) is able to capture a share of the seller's sunk investment in training.[8] The only way the minor league team would invest efficiently is if it expected to receive the full value of the player to the buyer; that is, if $P = V(x)$. This seems highly unlikely because it supposes no bargaining power on the side of the major league team.

The preceding analysis shows why independent minor league teams will not generally invest efficiently in training and thus explains why, as training became more important in professional baseball, major league teams sought to affiliate with minor league teams. The objective was to obtain control over player development decisions so as not to have to bargain in the manner described above. Once the major league team took ownership, it had complete

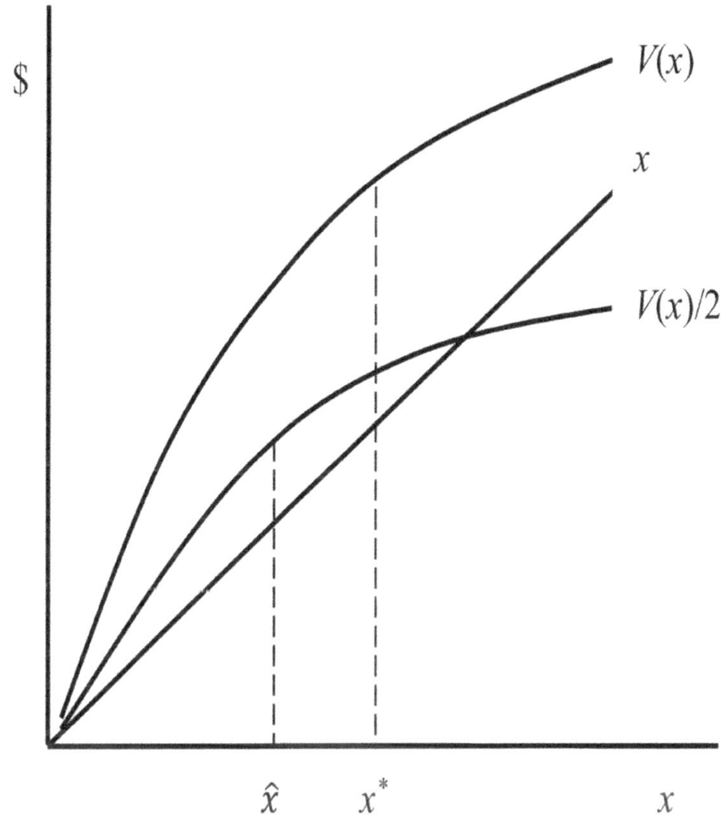

Figure 10.1 *The investment in player training*

control over all decisions regarding baseball and would therefore choose x efficiently. Specifically, it would choose x to maximize the expression in condition (10.1) for all players.

As we noted, however, major league teams did not always go so far as to acquire full ownership rights, especially when the minor league teams were financially viable (as many are today). Even in that case, however, the major league team nevertheless retained full control over *baseball* decisions, including the right to train players and to claim them for a set price at their discretion. Crucially, this price is *predetermined*, and so not subject to bargaining after x has been invested. Under this arrangement, the major league team will choose the level of training to maximize the following expression:

$$V(x) - \bar{P} - x \tag{10.6}$$

where $\bar{P}$ is the predetermined price.[9] The solution to this problem is x^*, the efficient level of training. Note that the sale price has no effect in this case precisely because it was determined independently of x.

WHO PAYS TRAINING COSTS?

This section inquires further into the training of professional athletes, with an emphasis on how it is financed—that is, who pays? The particular focus here will be on the allocation of costs between the team and the athlete, rather than between major and minor league teams. We will continue with the example of minor league baseball, but the issues are quite general and apply to any sport, and indeed to any employment setting in which workers need to be trained in job-specific skills.[10] Here is where we finally provide a rationale for the persistence of a partial reserve system that ties players to their original teams until they have a certain number of years of major league service. At the conclusion, we will use the analysis to draw insights into the problem of financing high and rising college costs.

The only change from the above model of player training is that we will now explicitly recognize the small fraction of minor league players who actually make it to the majors. Specifically, let $p(x)$ be the probability that a drafted player makes it, which we will treat as an increasing function of the level of the team's investment in training. Specifically, we will assume that $dp/dx > 0$ and $d^2p/dx^2 < 0$. To keep the model simple, we will now treat the player's value if he makes it, V, as fixed. We also continue to let R be the player's value while in the minors, where $V > R \geq 0$. (For the purposes of the current analysis, we assume that the major league team owns the minor league team or at least controls the relevant decisions.) Finally, let w^* be the wage paid to a player who makes the majors, and let w_T be the wage paid to a minor league player, i.e., the wage during a player's training phase.

As above, we begin by deriving the socially optimal level of investment, which coincides with the level of investment that the minor league player himself would choose if he were *self-financing* his training costs. In that case, he would choose x to maximize

$$p(x)V + R - x \tag{10.7}$$

The resulting level of investment, x^*, solves the condition

$$\frac{dp}{dx}V = 1 \tag{10.8}$$

which is the analog to equation (10.2). As in that case, the efficient level of training equates the expected value of the last dollar spent (which in this case increases the chances that the player will make it) to the marginal cost.

At the optimum, the probability that the player will make it equals $p(x^*)$. For the average player, this is very low—a back-of-the-envelope calculation puts it at less than 12 percent.[11] This, coupled with the very high cost of training, makes it practically impossible for players to self-finance their training costs. Thus, teams finance that cost up-front and also pay players' salaries during the training phase of their careers, which may well exceed their value while in the minors. They do this even though they know that fewer than one in eight players on a minor league roster will ever make it to the majors.

Under this team-financing arrangement, for each player, the team will choose x to maximize

$$p(x)(V - w^*) + (R - w_T) - x \quad (10.9)$$

where $V - w^*$ is the net value of a player if he makes it, while $R - w_T$ is his value while in the minors. Although we have noted that minor league teams are increasingly profitable, for at least some, it will be true that $R - w_T < 0$. In any case, the team's optimal investment, denoted $\hat{x}$, will solve the following equation:

$$\frac{dp}{dx}(V - w^*) = 1 \quad (10.10)$$

Several implications follow from this condition. First, for $\hat{x}$ to be positive, it must be true that $V > w^*$. That is, teams must pay players who make the majors *less than their full value to the team* (their *MRP*s). Second, comparing equation (10.10) with (10.8) shows that $\hat{x} < x^*$ for $w^* > 0$. That is, teams underinvest in players relative to the social optimum (i.e., they invest less than what the player would have chosen under self-financing). A third implication of the analysis so far is that, for the team to be willing to take on the task of financing player training, it must expect a positive return. Thus, at the optimal investment level, expression (10.9), the expected value of a minor league player, must be positive:

$$p(\hat{x})(V - w^*) + (R - w_T) - \hat{x} \geq 0 \quad (10.11)$$

At the same time, the expected income for a minor league player is

$$p(\hat{x})w^* + w_T \quad (10.12)$$

which must be larger than his next best opportunity. It follows from equation (10.12) that the player himself is better off as w^*, w_T, and $\hat{x}$ all increase. That is not possible, however, given the team financing of training costs. This is true, first, because, as we have seen, equation (10.10) implies that w^* and $\hat{x}$ are necessarily inversely related. Second, as w_T rises, the team's expected return in equation (10.11) decreases, which makes it less likely that the team will participate in the current arrangement, given that it bears the full cost of training. Thus, the interests of players and teams are opposed.

The other factor we need to account for in assessing this arrangement is the impact of free agency. Under the extreme case of full free agency, any team can bid for players who make the majors. A team that invested nothing in a player's training would therefore bid up to V for that player's services and so would be able to outbid the player's original team, which *has* invested in his training. But under such a system, no team would find it worthwhile to invest in training in the first place. If they did, they would either lose any players who turn out to be good enough to make the majors, or they would have to match the highest bid by offering $w^* = V$. Either way, their incentive to invest in training would be eliminated. Thus, players would be worse off than under a system that does provide teams with an incentive to invest. This logic explains why a limited reserve system, which ties players to their original teams for some number of years after they make the majors, is actually in the players' collective interests. Such a system ensures that $w^* < V$ for a sufficiently long period of time that teams can expect to recoup the training costs they incurred for that player.[12]

But the story is actually more complicated than that. Because so few players make the majors, the players who do make it have to, in effect, reimburse the team for their own training costs *plus the training costs of all those players who don't make it.* To illustrate, let us suppose that minor league players exactly cover their salaries, or that $R - w_T = 0$. Further, suppose that major league teams just break even. Thus, from equation (10.11) we have

$$p(\hat{x})\left(V - w^*\right) - \hat{x} = 0 \tag{10.13}$$

We can solve this for the wages of major league players (those who make it) to get

$$w^* = V - \frac{\hat{x}}{p(\hat{x})} \tag{10.14}$$

The term $\hat{x} / p(\hat{x})$ represents the minimum *wage discount* the player must accept during his reserve period with that team in order to satisfy the team's participation constraint. Note that this premium is larger than $\hat{x}$ (since $p(\hat{x}) < 1$), reflecting the need for the team to recover the costs incurred for all minor leaguers from the few who make the majors. Using the above calculation, $1/p(\hat{x}) = 1/.12 = 8.3$, which means that each player who makes it has to "repay" more than eight times his own training cost.

But why would those players who make it be willing to repay the costs of those who don't? The reason is that, at the point where the team has to make the initial investment, the average player doesn't know if he will be one of the lucky ones who make it to the majors. Thus, during his minor league career, a prospective major leaguer is, in effect taking a "loan" of $\hat{x}$ from the team, while simultaneously entering into an implicit bargain with all other minor leaguers, who are also taking loans, such that those who do make it, comprising a fraction $p(\hat{x})$ of the total, will "pay back" the loans for everyone. It is like a group insurance plan, which the players' union implicitly negotiates with team owners on behalf of all players.

Consider the following numerical example as an illustration. Suppose it costs \$1 million each to train 10 minor league players, of whom only one will make the majors. Also, suppose that those who make it produce a gross value of \$12 million each for the team over the six years that they are reserved. The team will therefore just break even if

$$\$12 - w^* = \$10$$

The result is that w^* = \$2 million, which translates into a yearly salary of \$333,333 over six years. Thus, in aggregate, each major leaguer "repays" \$10 million in training costs, which equals the difference between his gross value to the team and his actual salary during the reserve period. This total breaks down into his own cost of \$1 million, plus the \$9 million it cost to train those nine who did not make it.

Accounting for Differences Across Players

The discussion so far has assumed that all minor league players are identical in terms of their chances of making it, but what about the case of "can't miss" or highly rated prospects? Such players are clearly disadvantaged by the system as we have described it so far because they expect to pay back a disproportionate share of training costs. The situation is like that of a low-risk driver who implicitly subsidizes higher-risk drivers in a group insurance plan. To the extent they can identify lower-risk customers, competitive insurance companies will therefore find ways to offer discounts to them. The analogy in the current context is signing bonuses paid to highly-rated draftees.

To see this formally, suppose that, as above, $p(\hat{x})$ represents the probability that an "ordinary" minor leaguer will make the majors, while $p(\hat{x})+\varepsilon$ is the probability that a more talented player will make it, given the common investment levels $\hat{x}$. We assume, however, that both types of players have the same value while in the minors (which we continue to set at zero) and the same value once they make the majors (V). This allows us to focus exclusively on the training-cost issue. (Obviously, a player with higher value to the team will also probably command a higher salary once he makes it.) In this example, the expected value of the ordinary player is given by equation (10.13), while the expected value of the more talented player is

$$\left(p(\hat{x})+\varepsilon\right)\left(V-w^*\right)-b-\hat{x} \tag{10.15}$$

where b is the signing bonus.

With w^* given by equation (10.14), we can set equation (10.15) equal to zero and solve for b to obtain the maximum signing bonus the team would pay:

$$b^* = \frac{\varepsilon}{p(\hat{x})}\hat{x} \tag{10.16}$$

The bonus, in effect, serves as a "prebate" of the extra amount of training costs that the high-talent player is expected to contribute by virtue of his higher probability of making the majors.

To illustrate, return to the above numerical example where the probability of making it for ordinary players was one in ten, implying that $p(\hat{x})$=.10. Now suppose that the probability of a more talented player making it is .15, so that ε=.05. Recalling that $\hat{x}$=$1 million, the formula in equation (10.16) yields a bonus of (.05/.10)×($1,000,000)=$500,000.

The gist of the preceding argument is that a limited reserve system, which ties players to their initial teams for the first six years of their major league careers, actually benefits players because it creates an incentive for teams to invest in training, thereby enhancing all players' chances of making the majors. As a consequence, however, players have to be "underpaid" during the initial phase of their careers in order to "pay back" their training costs. We argued that this system has emerged in professional baseball principally because most players would not have sufficient resources to self-finance their training.

One might argue that players could overcome this problem by seeking third-party financing, which would then make full free agency feasible. Players would then pay back lenders out of their earnings once they make the majors. Under this scheme, players would have an incentive to invest in the efficient level of training, as dictated by equation (10.8), rather than teams' underinvesting, as they do under the limited reserve system. The problem, however, is that lenders would not likely be willing to participate in such an arrangement because the success rate is too low, resulting in default by the vast majority (88 percent) of borrowers. And if lenders did take this arrangement on, they would have to pass their losses on to those who do pay back their loans, which essentially replicates the scheme described above.

As a final point in this section, we note that the high earning potential of professional athletes in the era of free agency has created a new investment opportunity for third parties who are willing to take a gamble that combines high risk with high return. In fact, in 2015, a group of investors began doing just that. In particular, they offered to pay certain minor league players up-front money in return for a share of their earnings when and if they make the major leagues.[13] For example, a contract would offer a minor league player a sliding scale that would pay, say, $100,000 in up-front money in return for each 1 percent of the player's future earnings. Thus, the player could take $200,000 in return for 2 percent, $300,000 in return for 3 percent, and so forth. Further, the player would not be obligated to pay back *any* money if he didn't make it (as would be true under a loan). Thus, investors bear all of the risk. However, they would presumably only offer this deal to the best prospects, and they would "pool" these players so that the chance of some of them making it becomes much higher. Of course, the logic underlying this scheme exactly mirrors the group insurance argument offered above. It remains to be seen, however, how popular this investment opportunity will become.

Application of the Analysis to College Financing

In seeking to apply the foregoing logic to college financing, the question is why lenders *are* willing to make loans to cover college costs but aren't willing to do so for budding professional athletes. The main reason would seem to be the high "success rate" of college graduates in finding jobs (probably better than 90 percent), compared with minor league ballplayers (about 10 percent). Thus, lenders face a much lower rate of default on college loans than would be true of loans to finance the training of a professional athlete. However, the soaring costs of a college education in recent times, coupled with the increasing default rate on college loans, have made this arrangement more tenuous, and most lenders are only willing to continue participating because of government guarantees of college loans (which is likely one cause of the high default rate).

Recently, some politicians have begun calling for free college tuition. Under such a proposal, college costs would be publicly financed (or at least heavily subsidized), and taxpayers would foot the bill. It is interesting to note that, if such a plan were enacted, it would resemble the situation in professional baseball in the sense that young people would go to college for "free," and then, once employed, effectively "pay back" their college costs through taxes assessed on their incomes. In both situations, therefore, the "successful" trainees would finance the costs of everyone. The only real difference would be the substantially higher success rate of college grads as compared with minor league ballplayers, resulting in most of the former eventually contributing to the cost.

SCREENING OF PLAYERS AND THE AVERAGE QUALITY OF PLAY

Another important function of the minor leagues, in addition to training, is to assess talent and weed out players of inferior ability. In this sense, the minor leagues serve an important sorting or screening function aimed at maintaining a minimum quality of play at the professional level. Many professional groups also establish minimum quality standards for the right to offer their services for sale. Leland (1979), for example, has argued that licensing requirements in fields such as medicine, law, and accounting are intended to ensure a high average quality of service among practitioners by limiting the entry of inferior providers.

This practice is a response to the so-called adverse selection, or "lemons," problem that arises in markets where consumers are not able to judge the quality of products or services being offered. In the absence of some sort of quality assurance, it is argued, the price will reflect the average quality in the market, which will disproportionately drive out high-quality providers and thereby lower average quality overall (Akerlof, 1970). Quality assurance mechanisms are meant to counteract this sort of market failure.

In the sports context, team owners have similarly developed various methods of screening players to weed out low-quality performers. These include scouting networks and player evaluation methods designed to identify the best players and eliminate the worst. As these methods have improved, the average quality of play has increased. (One of the key improvements, as we have discussed, is the Moneyball revolution and the resulting development of analytical tools.)

As an illustration, suppose that in the population of professional players in a particular sport, ability can be represented by an index q, which is distributed uniformly on the interval from zero to 100, with zero being the lowest ability and 100 the highest.[14] The quality of play is therefore determined by the average ability level, denoted by $\bar{q}$, which in this simple example is equal to $50 = 100/2$. Players' abilities are not directly observable; however, only some measurements of performance, such as a batting average. In a team sport, the measured performance of a particular player i, denoted P_i, will be positively related to the player's own individual ability, q_i, but it will be negatively related to the average ability of all players in the league against whom player i must compete. To be specific, let us suppose that

$$P_i = \frac{q_i}{\bar{q}} \tag{10.17}$$

In our numerical example, $P_i = q_i / 50$. Thus, for the average player in the league, for whom q=50, P=1 (by construction), whereas for the best player in the league, for whom q=100, P=2.

Now suppose that the screening of players results in the weeding out of the lowest quality players in the league. Specifically, suppose that players with q between zero and twenty are removed. As a result, the average quality of play rises to $\bar{q}$=(100+20)/2=60. Notice, however, that this screening process will actually cause the measured performance of all players to *decrease* because the denominator in equation (10.17) has increased. The measured performance of the best player in the league, for example, which was equal to 2 before the change, is now equal to 100/60=1.67. The reason is that players are competing against players of higher average ability, resulting in more intense competition.

An interesting and paradoxical consequence of this conclusion is that, as a sport gets better at screening out inferior players, extreme performances at the high end should decline. Using an analogy to biological evolution, Gould (2003, pp. 151–173) has argued that such an explanation can account for one of the perennial conundrums among baseball historians—namely, the "disappearance" of the .400 hitter. According to his argument, .400 hitters, which were relatively common in the early days of major league baseball but have since become "extinct," represented instances where exceptional players exploited the relatively low quality of overall play in the early days of the game. Gould specifically argued that

> Variation in batting average must decrease as improving play eliminates the rough edges that great players can exploit, and as average play moves toward the limits of human possibility and compressed players into an ever-decreasing space between average play and the immovable right wall [of human ability]. (Gould, 2003, p. 163)

Zimbalist (1992) similarly argued:

> The fact that a smaller proportion of a more athletically talented population is playing baseball produces … compression of talent at the top end. The variation among players in performance statistics has narrowed steadily over the years. (Zimbalist, 1992, p. 144)

As an illustration of this point, consider Table 10.1, which shows the league batting average and the number of .400 hitters by decade since 1876, the first year of the National League. Notice first that the league average has remained relatively steady over time, reflecting the performance of the "average" player. This is consistent with the above theory, which showed that, as average quality in the league improves, the measured performance of the average player should, by construction, remain unaffected. However, the number of .400 hitters has declined precipitously. This is also consistent with the theory, which predicts that the measured performance of the best player should decline. Specifically, in equation (10.17), the best player's performance would be $P^{max} = 100/\overline{q}$, which is decreasing in $\overline{q}$.

The disappearance of the .400 hitter, therefore, does *not* imply that players of the caliber of Ty Cobb no longer exist.[15] Rather, it is a paradoxical consequence of the overall *improvement* in the quality of players throughout the league.

As a final point, this analysis implies that extreme performances can only arise if there is an increase in talent at the top end of the distribution—that is, if the best players get better. Few would deny that this probably has been happening over time in most sports as a consequence of better conditioning, better training, better equipment, and an overall better understanding of the game

Table 10.1 League batting average and number of .400 hitters by decade, 1876–2020

Decade	League average	No. of .400 hitters
1876–1890	.259	12
1891–1900	.280	10
1901–1910	.253	1
1911–1920	.259	4
1921–1930	.288	7
1931–1940	.277	0
1941–1950	.261	1
1951–1960	.259	0
1961–1970	.250	0
1971–1980	.258	0
1981–1990	.259	0
1991–2000	.266	0
2001–2010	.264	0
2011–2020	.252	0

itself. In team sports, however, these effects will tend to balance out as long as the improvements equally benefit offense and defense. Further, if these two aspects of the game do fall out of balance due to innovations that unequally benefit one or the other (for example, the invention of the slider in baseball), rule makers will usually intervene to restore the balance. As we discussed in Chapter 6, for example, this seemed to have happened in Major League Baseball in the late 1960s, when the dominance of pitching resulted in several rule changes aimed at restoring the balance between offense and pitching.

Two other possible sources of extreme performances are "cheating"—as was the case with the steroid-fueled home run boom in the 1990s—and the emergence of uniquely talented players, such as Babe Ruth, Wayne Gretzky, or Serena Williams. Individual sports such as golf are a bit different because players are not really competing against each other but against "the course." Thus, innovations in equipment, increased strength and conditioning of players, and the appearance of a once-in-a-generation figure such as Tiger Woods, who changed the way the game was played, allow extreme performances to occur. Course designers have responded, however, by lengthening courses and making holes more difficult, thereby restoring measured performances to acceptable levels. For sports where the "opponent" is time, such as track and swimming, this sort of adjustment is not possible. Thus, extreme performances in these sports are only limited by what is possible according to physical laws and the limits of the human body. Therefore, extreme performances may persist but should become less common.

SUMMARY

This chapter considered the training of professional players, with particular emphasis on the minor leagues. The focus was principally on baseball because that is a sport where, for reasons that are unclear, more extensive minor league training is required for the vast majority of players to make it to the highest level. This raises the question of how the minor leagues will be financed.

Our discussion of that question began with a brief history of the minor leagues, with special attention to their economic relationship to the major leagues. Early on, the leagues were independent of one another, which was possible because minor league teams were economically viable on their own as suppliers of baseball games. In this setting, if a major league team wanted a minor league player, it had to purchase him from his current team. This system began to break down for two reasons: the first was that, by the 1950s, minor league teams were no longer able to operate as self-sustaining ventures; and second, independent minor league teams underinvested in player training. The result of these two factors was that major league teams either purchased or entered into long-term contracts with minor league teams. This allowed the major league team both to subsidize its minor league affiliates and, more importantly, to direct the training of its players. The affiliation of major and minor league teams continues today, even as some minor league franchises have again become economically viable.

The next topic concerned the financing of training costs between teams and players. Players lack the resources to self-finance their training, but team financing raises another source of inefficiency—if a player can become a free agent once he makes the majors, his salary will be bid up to his marginal revenue product. Thus, the team that trained him will not be able to recoup its training costs. This insight accounts for the continued existence of a reserve period for players in Major League Baseball, despite a powerful players' union. During this reserve period (the first six years of a player's career), a player is "underpaid" by a sufficient amount to allow the team to recover the costs of training for him as well as for all those players who don't make it. The logic of this argument was then related to the problem of financing college costs.

The final topic in the chapter concerns the screening function of the minor leagues. This provides an important source of quality assurance by screening out players of inferior ability and, in this sense, is similar to quality assurance mechanisms such as licensing in ordinary markets. An interesting consequence of quality screening, however, is that it predicts a decline in the observation of extreme performances. This is true because as the average quality of the league improves, players at the top end of the talent distribution have fewer weaknesses to exploit. As an example, we chronicled the decline and eventual extinction of the .400 hitter in Major League Baseball in the early decades of the twentieth century.

EXERCISES

10.1. A team chooses between two levels of investment in newly drafted players: "low" or "high." Table E10.1 shows the cost of these two options and the effect on the probability (p) of the player making the major leagues. It also shows the value of the player to the team (MRP) if he "makes it.

(a) What level of investment maximizes the net expected value of the player to the team?

Table E10.1

Level	Cost	p	MRP
low	\$1,000	.10	\$100,000
high	\$10,000	.25	\$100,000

(b) Would this outcome arise under full free agency (i.e., if players who make it are free to negotiate with any team)? Explain why or why not.

10.2. When a league expands, each new team usually gets to select players from the rosters of existing teams. Existing teams, however, get to "protect" a certain number of players on their rosters from such a draft. Assuming players differ in "quality," explain why such an expansion draft virtually guarantees that the new team(s) will be of inferior average quality compared with existing teams. What will happen to the overall league average in terms of quality?

NOTES

1. Much of this section draws on Hanssen et al. (2016).
2. See the classic book by Ritter (2002 [1966]), which relates stories of this sort told first-hand by early ballplayers.
3. It was Rickey, of course, who also integrated baseball in 1947, as the general manager of the Brooklyn Dodgers.
4. Between 1926 and 1934, the Cardinals won five pennants and three World Series.
5. This is not a critical assumption. The argument we will make here only requires that training be *more valuable* to the major league team than to the minor league team. This seems sensible and, in fact, is really what differentiates major and minor league teams.
6. This is the outcome that would occur under the Nash bargaining solution, assuming equal bargaining abilities.
7. If R also depends positively on x, condition (10.5) would be $\left[(dV/dx)+(dR/dx)\right]=1$. This results in $\hat{x}<x$ as long as $dV/dx > dR/dx$.
8. See, for example, Klein et al. (1978). The solutions usually proposed for the holdup problem are vertical integration and contracts, both of which, as we have seen, were employed in professional baseball.
9. Major league teams, therefore, have a "call option" on minor league players owned by their affiliates, meaning that they can obtain those players at any time at the pre-set option price of $\bar{P}$.
10. A particularly comparable employment situation is the development of talent in the entertainment industry. In the early decades of filmmaking, it was common for studios to sign budding actors to exclusive contracts while they honed their skills, thus creating a kind of reserve system for actors. Basinger (2009) refers to this as the "star machine." See Miceli (2022) for a discussion of the similarities between the baseball reserve system and the star machine.
11. As of this writing, there are 256 minor league teams and 30 major league teams. Assuming that there are 25 players on each team's roster, the fraction of minor leaguers who will make it to a major league roster is 30/256 = .117. Of course, the percentage is not the same for every level of the minors. The higher up a player progresses, the greater his chances of making it. This

calculation also ignores players who go directly to the majors from college or from teams in foreign countries. Thus, the actual success rate of those in the minors is probably lower than this figure.

12. See Daly (1992), Miceli (2004, 2022), and Bradbury (2007, pp. 195–198).
13. See Diamond (2021).
14. This discussion is based on Miceli (2007). Also see Bradbury (2007, Ch. 8).
15. Ty Cobb topped the .400 mark three times in his career and finished with a lifetime batting average of .366, the highest of any player of all-time.

11. College sports

The National Collegiate Athletic Association (NCAA), although a non-profit organization, is essentially a cartel for college-level athletics, and in that capacity, it imposes very substantial restrictions on the behavior of member schools. For example, it limits the number of athletic scholarships that schools can offer; it puts limits on the kinds of recruiting activities coaches can engage in; and, until recently, it limited compensation of student-athletes to the in-kind benefits of a free college education (including room and board). The stated reason for these limits has always been to preserve the amateur status of the athletes, which, it is believed, results in a "purer" form of competition because it is unsullied by the profit motive.[1]

There is no denying, however, that college athletics, especially football and basketball at the Division I level, are a big business that generates significant revenues for schools. Indeed, coaches are often paid more than college presidents. Star players are therefore extremely valuable to these schools, but until recently, they were prevented from receiving any financial compensation outside of their scholarships. The situation looked a lot like the monopsony model of the determination of professional athletes' salaries, as discussed in Chapter 8, and for that reason, the NCAA has perpetually been subject to accusations of violating antitrust laws.

Then, in 2021, a unanimous ruling from the US Supreme Court held that it was a violation of antitrust laws for schools to profit from the name, image, and likeness (NIL) of players while denying them compensation.[2] This opened the door for players to receive "education-related" payments (broadly defined) for their NIL, while stopping short of requiring an outright "pay-for-play" system.

The purpose of this chapter is to examine some aspects of the current system of collegiate sports from an economic perspective. The objective is not to pass judgment on the merits of the amateurism-versus-professionalism debate, or to offer definitive answers to the various issues swirling around college athletics. Rather, it is to think carefully about the relationship between academic studies and athletics, particularly with respect to how these activities are financed at the collegiate level, and how the financing structure affects incentives and allocative decisions.[3] The particular focus will be on how academics and athletics are "bundled" at the collegiate level and what the implications of that arrangement are.

For the vast majority of college athletes, participation in sports is an extracurricular activity that is an important, but secondary, component of their college experience. However, for some small number of elite players, mostly at the Division I level, it is also a potential pathway to a professional sports career, and in this capacity, college sports effectively serve as a minor league for certain professional leagues. Particularly for football and basketball, those players who aspire to a professional career have little choice but to play at the collegiate level. This strange bundling of academics and athletics creates some interesting economic issues that we will explore. The discussion will not attempt an exhaustive analysis of the economic issues surrounding college sports, but will instead offer a sampling of ideas aimed at revealing the insights that economics can shed on this complex topic.

PAY-FOR-PLAY AND COMPETITIVE BALANCE

As a preliminary issue, we note that one argument against paying college athletes has to do with the goal of promoting competitive balance, which has been a recurrent theme of this book. Recall that team owners at the professional level have historically claimed that limiting competition in sports labor markets is necessary to prevent the rich teams from acquiring all the best players, and this same logic could be used as a supplemental reason, along with the amateurism rationale, for preventing schools from directly paying college athletes. Although NCAA rules place restrictions on recruiting practices, they apply uniformly to schools and so do not "disadvantage" richer programs the way reverse-order drafts are designed to do at the professional level. The greatest limitation, however, has been the inability of schools to compensate recruits beyond the value of their scholarships. This prevents outright bidding for players, which clearly is aimed at disadvantaging richer schools.

But let's think more carefully about how a move toward pay-for-play would likely affect the allocation of playing talent. Under the old rule, where athletes could not be directly compensated at all, schools competed for top talent by offering in-kind benefits—for example, by spending on lavish facilities and top-caliber coaches, both to enhance the college-sports experience and to increase a recruit's chances of a pro career. Thus, schools willing and able to spend the most on these attributes got the best talent. Clearly, this gave an advantage to richer schools. As a result, even in the absence of pay-for-play, there has existed a substantial imbalance at the Division I level in most sports (Peach, 2007).

The switch to pure pay-for-play would effectively turn the recruiting system into a free agent market, with teams bidding for top prospects in an auction-like manner. The current system, based on name, image, and likeness, is something of a compromise between the extremes of no pay-for-play and free agency. It will, therefore, likely produce results similar to those described in our discussion of the players' labor market when players maximize utility rather than income. Specifically, some players will mainly be interested in maximizing their income and thus will go to the school offering the highest financial benefit, while others will be attracted by non-monetary benefits. In any case, the rich schools will continue to have an advantage in attracting the best players. Thus, it is not clear that moving to pay-for-play would substantially worsen the situation in terms of competitive balance. Note that this conclusion reflects the logic of the Rottenberg Invariance Proposition.

COLLEGE ATHLETICS AS A "BUNDLED GOOD"

College is principally concerned with the provision of education (career training), but as a by-product, it offers students athletic opportunities along with other extracurricular activities. For certain sports, however, the highest caliber of college athletics supplies a product that is also very marketable to consumers. In fact, some fans prefer college sports to professional sports. In addition, as noted above, college athletics serves as the de facto minor leagues for professional football and basketball leagues, and to a lesser extent for soccer, hockey, and baseball. Thus, college sports are also valued as a training ground by the relevant professional leagues.

This is an odd arrangement in the sense that, in football and basketball particularly, prospective athletes have little choice but to go to college as the best route to a professional career, whereas baseball and hockey players have the option to go into a well-developed minor league system rather than college, and those leagues are entirely financed by the parent major league, as discussed in Chapter 10, or are self-sustaining. This section discusses the economic consequences of this bundling of academics and athletics in three contexts: college budgets, the allocative impacts with respect to college attendance and sports participation, and the training function of college sports.

Budgetary Impacts of Bundling

Consider a college that jointly provides two goods: education and athletic competition, where some of the consumers of education are simultaneously the providers of the athletic competition (student-athletes). Athletics, therefore, simultaneously serve as an extracurricular activity, or consumption good, for some students, and as a revenue source for the college.

In terms of the overall budget, students pay tuition for education, which generates a gross revenue of R_A, while fan interest generates revenue from ticket sales, television coverage, and the sale of merchandise, which generates a gross revenue of R_S. Finally, the school receives outside revenue of S in the form of government subsidies and alumni donations. On the cost side, the school incurs academic costs of C_A and athletic department costs of C_S. Assume that the college is a non-profit institution, and so it needs to satisfy a balanced-budget condition. In addition, assume that the academic and athletic budgets are completely intermingled, so we write the balanced-budget condition as

$$R_A + R_S + S = C_A + C_S \tag{11.1}$$

where the left-hand side is revenue, and the right-hand side is costs.

It will be instructive to rewrite this condition as follows:

$$R_A = C_A + \left(C_S - R_S\right) - S \tag{11.2}$$

The left-hand side is revenue from tuition, while the right-hand side consists of academic costs plus the athletic department's "deficit," net of outside money. It will perhaps surprise many readers to learn that the vast majority of athletic budgets are in deficit. Indeed, based on data from 2019, fewer than 10 percent of Division I athletic budgets (and certainly no Division II and III athletic budgets) showed a surplus. Even in the highest revenue-generating sports, only 68 of 351 (19 percent) of men's Division I basketball programs covered their costs in 2019, and only 73 of 252 (29 percent) of Division I football programs covered their costs in 2016. Across all three divisions of college athletics, revenue covered only 56 percent of costs, where the bulk of the latter consisted of scholarships and coaches' compensation (McGinty, 2021). According to equation (11.2), this shortfall has to be made up from tuition revenue and/or outside money. Thus, in most schools, academics subsidize athletics, not the other way around.

In contrast to the above arrangement, unbundling of academics and athletics would require each activity to cover its own costs, with some apportionment of outside money to each, as dictated, perhaps, by donor preferences or targeted grants. Given that most athletic departments run a deficit, this would almost certainly require a reduction in athletic scholarships, particularly in sports that do not generate significant revenue, which is most sports. Further, it is very likely that this would disproportionately affect women's sports, particularly in schools with football programs, which would conflict with Title IX requirements. Thus, to remain in compliance with this mandate, schools would likely have to institute across-the-board scholarship reductions and/or find new sources of revenue to cover the budget shortfall.

In the end, the group most harmed by these changes would likely be athletes participating in non-revenue-generating sports, for whom the number of scholarships will almost certainly have to decline. By contrast, non-athletes would benefit to the extent that tuition revenue would no longer have to subsidize athletic budgets.

Allocative Effects of Bundling

The unbundling of budgets will also have allocative effects, meaning they will affect the participation decisions of would-be student-athletes—both the decision to attend college and to participate in sports. First, consider the decision to attend college. For non-athletes, we just saw that the unbundling of academics and athletics would probably result in lower tuition because tuition revenue would no longer have to subsidize the athletic deficit. This change would improve the efficiency of the college attendance decision because prospective students would now confront the true marginal cost of attendance.

It is efficient for an individual to attend if the value of a college education, denoted by V_A, exceeds the marginal cost, c; that is, if $V_A > c$.[4] The individual will actually decide to attend if V_A exceeds the tuition (price), T. The decision is therefore only efficient if $T = c$. Thus, too few individuals will attend college if $T > c$, as is often true when the athletic and academic budgets are mingled.

The resulting welfare loss under a system in which tuition revenue subsidizes athletics is illustrated in Figure 11.1, which shows the academic benefit of college, V_A, as a downward sloping demand curve, reflecting a diminishing marginal benefit across prospective students. For example, think of prospective students as being lined up along the curve from the highest to the lowest valuers of a college education. The efficient outcome occurs at the point where $V_A = c$; that is, where the academic value of college for the marginal student equals its cost. As noted above, the efficient level of attendance, Q^*, occurs under the proposed unbundling plan because $T = c$, whereas too little attendance ($\hat{Q}$) occurs under the status quo, where $T = \hat{T} > c$. The resulting welfare loss is shown by the shaded triangle in Figure 11.1, which represents the forgone gains to those who are inefficiently deterred from attending college under the current system.

Now consider student-athletes. For them, there are actually two choices: whether to attend college for academic purposes, and whether to attend for the athletic opportunity. From an efficiency perspective, the two decisions should be made separately. However, because college athletics is an activity that is limited to college students, this necessarily becomes a joint decision. For current purposes, we will let V_S be the overall value of the athletic opportunity, including the utility from participation plus any future income prospects.

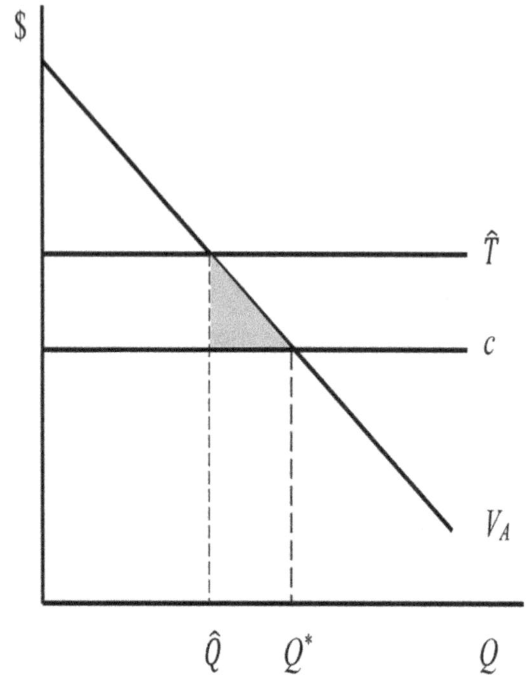

Figure 11.1 *College attendance decision by non-athletes*

In terms of efficiency, the decision of an athlete to attend college for academic purposes is the same as for non-athletes—that is, it is efficient to attend if $V_A > c$. As for athletic participation, it is efficient to participate if $V_S > x$, where x is the per-athlete cost. With these activities bundled, however, a prospective student-athlete who is offered a full scholarship will attend college if

$$V_A + \alpha V_S > 0 \tag{11.3}$$

where α is the fraction of the athletic benefit that the athlete actually expects to capture, while $1-\alpha$ is the fraction retained by the college. For the athlete, αV_S consists of the value of participation (the utility gain), plus any future income prospects. For non-revenue-generating athletes and those with no chance of a professional career, V_S consists purely of the utility benefit. Further, $\alpha = 1$ for those athletes since the school can appropriate none of this value. However, for some revenue-generating athletes, a large portion of V_S may be monetary, and the school can appropriate a substantial share of it (i.e., $\alpha < 1$).

In any case, equation (11.3) implies that a scholarship recipient will choose to attend college, even if V_A is low, because the cost is zero.[5] (This assumes that the athlete meets the school's admission standard, which for some schools is not much of a barrier.) The constraining factor is therefore the decision of whether or not the school grants a scholarship. This is presumably under the discretion of the appropriate coach. If we suppose (for simplicity) that coaches only offer "efficient" scholarships, then the constraint becomes $V_S > x$ (or possibly $(1-\alpha)V_S > x$). It follows that under the current system, *any student-athlete who receives a scholarship offer will attend, even if the net value of academics for that individual is negative.* In other words, athletes for whom participation in college athletics is deemed desirable by the school will attend even if it is inefficient for them to consume the education component (i.e., even if $V_A < c$).

The consequences of this are represented graphically in Figure 11.2, which measures the value of academics (V_A) on the vertical axis and the value of athletics (V_S) on the horizontal axis. Based on efficiency, students in regions A+B+C (the region where $V_A > c$) should attend college for academic reasons, while those in regions C+D+E (the region where $V_S > x$) should participate in college athletics. When the two choices can be made separately, the overlap is region C. These are the "efficient" scholar-athletes. However, when academics

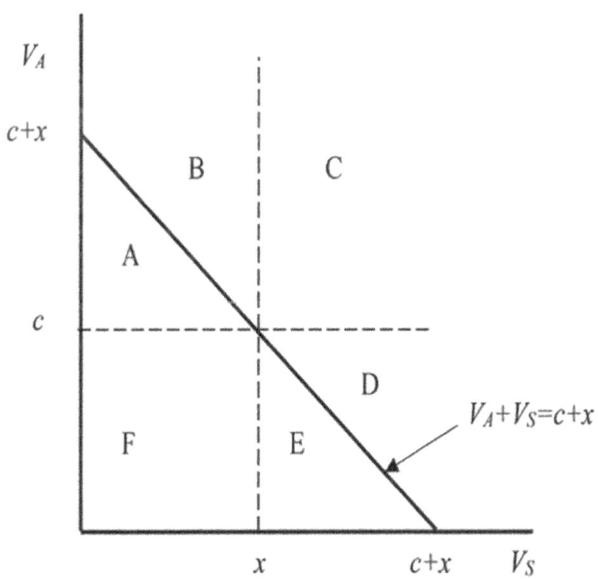

Figure 11.2 *Decision to attend college and participate in athletics*

and athletics are bundled, individuals in regions C+D+E will attend college under the assumption that scholarships are offered to all those prospective athletes who should efficiently participate in college sports. Thus, those student-athletes in regions D+E inefficiently attend college. Even if the coach's criterion does not exactly match efficiency, and some prospects fail to meet admission requirements, there will still be some individuals in regions D+E who attend college for athletic purposes but should not for academic purposes.[6]

Now consider the situation in which prospective student-athletes would have to confront the actual costs of college attendance (including the athletic department cost) but also expect to receive the full benefits (as under pay-for-play). However, assume college athletics remains linked to college attendance. This is a step closer to the way that a market would allocate these activities, but does not fully unbundle them. An athlete will now choose to attend college if

$$V_A + V_S > c + x \tag{11.4}$$

Here, athletes are required to pay for both the academic and athletic costs of college, but also expect to receive the full benefits. We will continue to assume that, although athletic scholarships are no longer given, coaches still act as efficient screeners for would-be athletes; i.e., they require $V_S > x$ in order to recruit a player. Combining this with condition (11.4) implies that all student-athletes in regions C+D now attend college. Thus, compared with the current situation, individuals in region E, who by hypothesis are offered a spot on a college team, now choose not to attend because the net positive value of athletics is not sufficiently large to offset the net loss from the academic component of college, which they are now required to purchase. The outcome is therefore more efficient than under the status quo system. However, too many athletes still choose to attend college—specifically, those in region D for whom $V_S > x$ but $V_A < c$.

We have so far maintained the assumption that it is only possible to be a "college athlete" by attending college—that is, by also becoming a student. The proposed "unbundling", therefore, only concerns the allocation of revenues and costs. A more radical proposal would allow athletes to opt out of the academic portion of college altogether, in which case, college athletics would become more like a true minor league. In other words, colleges would have affiliated "professional teams," some members of which may also choose to be students. In this case, the choices of participation in the two activities would be truly separate and thus presumably more efficient, assuming students and athletes each faced the actual benefits and costs of those activities.

Under such an arrangement, one supposes that the relationship between professional sports and college teams would also change accordingly, with pro sports leagues likely subsidizing those college teams that would not be able to cover their costs under such a system. The situation would begin to look more like that between the major and minor leagues in baseball, as discussed in Chapter 10. This proposal, however, will likely remain hypothetical, at least for the foreseeable future.

The Impact on Training of Players

Consider finally the impact of bundling on the training function of college sports, which picks up on the discussion from Chapter 10. The analysis of college sports to this point has treated the athletic budget as fixed. However, both the revenue generated by athletics and the probability that a player will make the pros are likely dependent on how much a school invests in athletics (i.e., in coaches and facilities). Thus, schools and athletes alike have an interest in how this spending is determined.

The crucial issue concerns who has control over the amount of investment in athletics. The thrust of the argument in the previous chapter was that as training became more important in professional baseball, the organizational structure of the minor leagues changed in a way that shifted property rights over the player's value from the minor league team to the major league team, thereby resulting in a more efficient investment choice. In the current context, if we assume that colleges will retain control over training under any proposed payment scheme, any move in the direction of pay-for-play will likely *reduce* a school's incentive to invest in training because players would be able to claim a larger share of the financial gains that they generate while in college (i.e., α would become larger).

The situation can be usefully compared with the case in Chapter 10 of an independent minor league team that owned its players. We saw that its incentive to invest was based on two sources of revenue: the return from its own ticket sales while the player remained with the minor league team, and the prospect of being able to sell the player to a major league team at some time in the future. In the current context, a college will similarly invest based on its share of the value of a player while he or she is in college, which we measured by $(1-\alpha)V_S$, but it will likely ignore the expected future value of the player as a professional, αV_S. This is true because, unlike the independent minor league team, colleges have no hope of being able to sell their players to professional teams. As a result, colleges will most likely underinvest in players relative to the efficient level, particularly those with professional prospects. Thus, college athletes who aspire to a professional career have some interest in keeping $\alpha < 1$ so schools will invest in their training. It is the same interest that minor league baseball players have in the maintenance of a limited reserve system.

Of course, this situation could be changed as part of any reform, but the most radical change—requiring professional teams to compensate schools for drafted players—seems highly unlikely. In any case, the point of the analysis in this section is that college players and their advocates have to be aware not just of the distributional (static) aspects of any proposed change in compensation rules. They also need to recognize the possible incentive (dynamic) aspects of the change on their future earnings, and training at the college level in certain sports is an essential component of any future success.

PROPOSED REFORMS IN COLLEGE BASKETBALL

In recognition of the serious financial issues surrounding big-time college athletics, a commission was formed to study the situation specifically as it relates to men's college basketball. The Report of the Commission on College Basketball was issued in April of 2018 (Report, 2018). Its assessment was that, while the "state of men's college basketball is deeply troubled" (p. 1), there are concrete steps that could be taken to significantly improve matters without dramatically altering the current system. Thus, in making its recommendations, the Commission emphasized its commitment to the status quo with respect to the non-compensation of student-athletes. The Report specifically stated that

> Intercollegiate athletics is a trust based on a promise: athletes play for their schools and receive a realistic chance to complete a college degree in return. Any policy or action that violates that trust is morally wrong. (Report, 2018, p. 2)

Within the confines of this viewpoint (which obviously emphasized issues besides economic factors), the report proposed several changes.

First, it is recommended that the National Basketball Association (NBA) make 18-year-olds eligible for the NBA draft. The idea is to allow elite high school players to go directly into the NBA rather than spending a year or two in college simply as a stop-off on the way to the pros. A side effect of such a change is that the NBA would likely have to develop a true minor league for the development of such players. (The NBA's current G League is such a league.) This change would be a move in the direction of reducing the role of college basketball as a minor league and would perhaps be a way of partially unbundling the academic and athletic components of college sports. College sports would then be largely limited to athletes who have little or no prospect of playing professionally.

The Report also recommended that high school and college players who declare for the NBA draft, and/or sign with an agent, be allowed to retain college eligibility so that if they are not drafted, they can still play in college. The idea is not to penalize players who either misjudge their readiness for the NBA or who seek advice about their best course of action. Finally, the Report recommended that the NCAA establish a fund for the use of those athletes who leave school early but then seek to return to complete their degrees.

The foregoing proposals represent some small steps in the direction of unbundling the academic and athletic components of college attendance, while stopping short of fully severing the linkage. The proposals would at least leave young athletes the option of testing the professional waters, thus bypassing a possibly unproductive or unwanted investment in higher education for some, but without entirely foreclosing the possibility of participating in college athletics if that turns out to be the best option down the road.

A Broader View of Athletic Department Spending

The analysis of athletic department spending in the previous section was narrowly focused on the training of those collegiate athletes with pro potential. Obviously, the objective of athletic directors and college presidents is more broadly focused on the overall success and reputation of the athletic program, with the hope that such success will produce ancillary benefits for the institution as a whole, particularly in the form of a larger and higher quality applicant pool and greater alumni donations. There is some evidence for the existence of these benefits.

Humphreys and Mondello (2007), for example, found that post-season appearances by the football and basketball teams of Division I schools enhance giving. As for the intermediate link between athletic department spending and program success, Beaudin (2018) found that there is a positive and significant impact, but that further benefits could be obtained by reallocating existing spending. In particular, she showed that a dollar spent on women's programs might be more effective than a dollar spent on men's programs.

SUMMARY

This chapter examined college sports with specific reference to the "bundling" of college attendance and participation in athletics. This would not be a particularly important issue if college athletics were truly amateur and hence purely extracurricular, but certain sports—notably football and basketball—have become big businesses that generate huge amounts of money for the schools and for broadcasters, so it is relevant to ask whether the players should get a share of the proceeds. In addition, college teams serve as de facto minor leagues in these and other sports, and so those college athletes who aspire to a professional career, and the relevant professional leagues, have a strong interest in how the college teams are managed. This chapter took some steps toward addressing the various questions surrounding these issues.

The analysis began by tracing the budgetary implications of unbundling the academic and athletic components of college budgets, including paying athletes at least a share of their worth. The conclusion was that non-athletes and revenue-generating athletes would probably benefit from such a change, but non-revenue-generating athletes would likely be worse off because they would no longer be subsidized. As for attendance decisions, this would likely increase college attendance among non-athletes, but the situation is more complicated for student athletes. If participation in college sports remains tied to college attendance, even if the costs are unbundled, there will be some athletes who inefficiently go to college because that is their best route to a professional career in sports. Proposed reforms to college basketball would retain that linkage but would offer alternative routes to participating in athletics, and in some cases, a path to the professional ranks for those who have the skills but for whom college is not an efficient option.

The final issue we addressed was the training function of college sports. As athletes are able to claim a larger share of the financial benefits that they generate for their schools, the incentive for the latter to invest in training would likely be proportionately curtailed because they would receive fewer of the returns. Elite players might therefore find that they are trading greater immediate gains for diminished long-term prospects.

EXERCISES

11.1. Suppose the demand curve for college attendance for purely academic purposes is P=1000–.2Q, where P is the amount a student is willing to pay, and Q is the number attending college. Let the marginal (=average) cost of attendance be \$500.

(a) Assuming that the tuition is set equal to \$500, what is the equilibrium number of college attendees?

Now, suppose that at this same college, there are 500 student-athletes on scholarship. Also, suppose that the athletic budget is in balance so that revenues from sports exactly cover the costs. However, the academic costs of these students must be covered by the tuition charged to non-athletes. Thus, the total cost of \$250,000 (=500×\$500) is spread over the Q non-athletes. This makes the per-student tuition for non-athletes

$$T = 500 + 250{,}000 / Q$$

(b) Show that the number of non-athlete college attendees now equals (approximately) 1809. (Hint: equate the demand curve to the above formula for T and show that Q=1809 approximately solves the equation.) How does this compare with your answer to (a)?

NOTES

1. This notion is epitomized by the word "amateur," which comes from the Latin verb *amare,* "to love." Thus, amateurs play purely for the love of the game.
2. *National Collegiate Athletic Association v. Alston*, 141 S.Ct. 2141 (2021).
3. For a provocative study of athletics at academically elite colleges (Ivy League and highly selective liberal arts colleges), see Bowen and Levin (2003).
4. The value of college, V_A, includes the opportunity cost of attending, meaning the forgone income during the time in college.
5. Remember that the opportunity cost of attending college is already included in V_A.
6. Another issue, not discussed here, is that bundling academic and athletic components might induce some athletes to attend college who should but otherwise would not have. In other words, an athletic scholarship acts as a subsidy for academics. Ideally, however, this subsidization would be done independently of athletics by means of academic scholarships and student loans.

PART IV

Public Policy and Sports

12. Policy issues

This chapter examines four public policy issues related to the sports industry: the application of antitrust law to sports, public financing of sports facilities, gambling on sports, and discrimination in sports. The issue with respect to antitrust law is whether sports leagues should be treated like other industries with respect to cooperative or collusive behaviors. In ordinary markets, collusion among firms is nearly always detrimental to consumers and is, therefore, subject to antitrust scrutiny. In sports, by contrast, we have argued that some amount of cooperative behavior among teams, as coordinated by the league, is essential to the provision of sporting contests. Thus, the key question concerns the "optimal" amount of cooperation.

The second policy issue we address is the question of whether local governments should subsidize some or all of the construction of sports facilities as part of a regional economic development plan. The rationale advanced for such public involvement in what is principally a private venture is the claim that a professional sports team provides spillover benefits to the host city in the form of jobs and taxes. Economic theory provides some justification for this argument based on the role of the government in providing public goods, but the question is ultimately an empirical one that turns on the magnitude of the purported spillover benefits relative to the costs. We review the theory and the available evidence.

The third issue concerns gambling, which has become a particularly prominent issue in recent times with the widespread legalization of sports gambling. Gambling and sports, however, have always been intertwined because, from the perspective of consumers/fans, both seemingly derive from the same impulse: namely, a preference for contests involving an uncertain outcome. Our analysis examines the traditional economic explanation of gambling as a manifestation of risk-preferring behavior, and then proposes other possible explanations not based on risk preferences. It concludes by discussing the critical issue of how gambling on sports potentially threatens the integrity of sports leagues.

The final policy issue we will discuss concerns discrimination in sports, both racial and gender-based. This is an extension of the larger issue of discrimination in employment generally. Our discussion will consider how discrimination is detected and measured, and what the consequences of it are in a labor-market setting.

ANTITRUST LAW AND SPORTS

The legal foundation of antitrust law in the United States is the Sherman Act, which was passed by Congress in 1890 with the intention of making illegal "every contract, combination in the form of trust or otherwise, or conspiracy, in the restraint of commerce" (Section 1), as well as any "attempt to monopolize any part of the trade or commerce among the several States, or with foreign nations" (Section 2). Enforcement of the law is left to courts based on the so-called *rule of reason* test, which is based on a "balancing of the likely competitive harm from a restraint of trade against its likely pro-competitive benefits" (Gilbert and Williamson, 1998, p. 83). This test is particularly appropriate for application of the law to sports leagues because, as we have argued in previous chapters, significant cooperation among member teams is a necessary component of providing sports competition. The key question, then, is "where does one draw the line between a legal and an illegal agreement?"(Szymanski, 2009, p. 59).

Numerous legal challenges have been made against sports leagues on antitrust grounds, but with little success. One notable challenge, filed against Major League Baseball back in the 1920s, resulted in a US Supreme Court ruling that exempted the league from antitrust laws, a decision that remains in place today. The genesis of the challenge was the formation of the Federal League in 1913 as a rival to the existing American and National Leagues. The new league was able to attract many top stars by offering salaries above those paid by the existing owners under the reserve clause, which, recall, was an agreement among owners not to compete for each other's players, thereby effectively capping salaries (see the discussion in Chapter 6).

Despite some initial success, the new league was short-lived, but it left a legal legacy when the owners of a Federal League franchise in Baltimore pursued an antitrust challenge to the existing two major leagues, which is the case that eventually made it to the US Supreme Court. The Court held for the existing leagues by finding that their actions did not constitute restraint of interstate commerce, and hence were not a violation of antitrust laws. Writing for the majority, Justice Oliver Wendell Holmes asserted that

> The business [of the leagues] is giving exhibitions of baseball, which are purely state affairs. It is true that, in order to attain for these exhibitions the great popularity that they have achieved, competitions must be arranged between clubs from different cities and States. But the fact that in order to give the exhibitions the Leagues must induce free persons to cross state lines and must arrange and pay for their

> doing so is not enough to change the character of the business ... the transport is a mere incident, not the essential thing.[1]

On the face of it, this argument seems silly, but more importantly it never really addresses the core issue—namely, whether cooperative agreements among league owners that have the effect of preventing entry of rival leagues meet the rule-of-reason test for anti-competitive behavior. Thus, the ruling, and the resulting antitrust exemption, may or may not have been legally justified.[2] The next section examines the question from an economic perspective.

The Impact of Free Entry of Teams

A hallmark of competitive markets is the free entry of firms, which ensures that prices will fall to the minimum average cost, thereby maximizing consumer welfare. Figure 12.1 illustrates the effect of entry and the resulting decline in price in an ordinary market with a fixed marginal (=average) cost. Suppose that the initial price and quantity are P_1 and Q_1, reflecting a situation of restricted entry (see the discussion of market power in Chapters 2 and 3). At

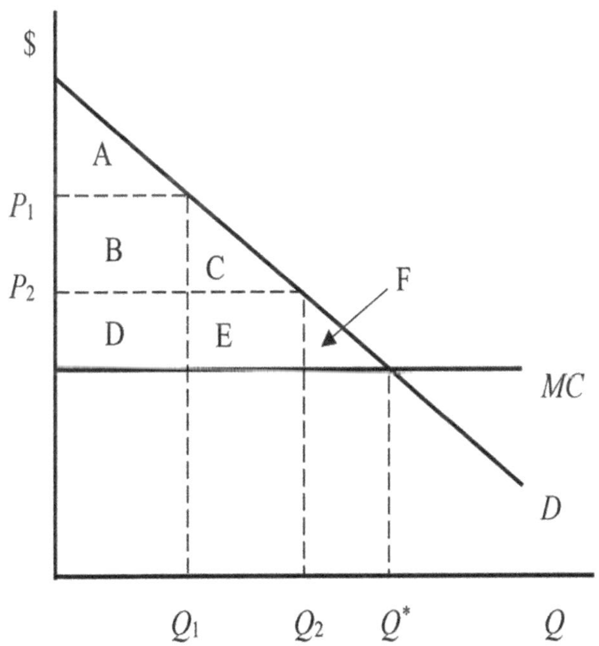

Figure 12.1 *Impact of entry on welfare*

this point, consumer surplus is the triangle labeled A, producer surplus is area B+D, and the welfare loss is area C+E+F.

Now, starting from this initial point, suppose some new firms enter, causing output to rise to Q_2 and price to fall along the demand curve to P_2. As a result, there is an increase in consumer surplus of area B+C, making the total surplus area A+B+C. Area B is a transfer of producer surplus (profit) to consumer surplus, and area C is a net gain resulting from the expansion of output from Q_1 to Q_2. Producer surplus is now area D+E, and the welfare loss is area F. Overall, welfare is therefore increased as a result of the change by area C+E. The limit of this process of expanding output is the efficient level of output, Q^*, which occurs at the intersection of the demand and marginal cost curves. When this point is reached, welfare attains its maximum, which in this case would entirely consist of consumer surplus.[3]

The unambiguously beneficial effect of entry in the preceding discussion, however, relied on the implicit assumption that product quality remained constant as output expanded. In other words, new firms were assumed to be able to perfectly replicate the quality of the product offered by the incumbent firms. As we argued in Chapter 10, however, this will not generally be possible in professional sports because the supply of elite athletes who can perform at the highest level is limited. Thus, as new teams enter, team owners will have to dig deeper into the talent pool to fill their rosters, thereby diluting the average quality of play in the league. And since consumers value quality as well as quantity, the demand curve will not remain fixed as this talent dilution occurs. In particular, we would expect it to shift downward, reflecting a lower willingness to pay for games of decreasing quality.

The likely result is depicted in Figure 12.2, which again considers the impact of the entry of teams, starting from the initial point of (P_1, Q_1). In this case, however, we suppose that demand depends on average league quality. Thus, as new teams enter, average quality declines, causing the demand curve to shift downward from D_1 to D_2. There is now associated with each output level a new demand curve reflecting the average quality at that level of output. In Figure 12.2, for example, the price P_2, which in Figure 12.1 corresponded to the quantity Q_2 along the original demand curve, D_1, now produces the quantity $\hat{Q} < Q_2$ along the new demand curve, D_2. The resulting welfare impacts of entry are indicated by the arrows. As drawn, consumer surplus appears to decline on net (i.e., the loss exceeds the gain), while producer surplus appears to increase (the gain exceeds the loss). The point is, however, that the overall effect will generally be ambiguous. This is in contrast to the above case in which quality was held constant, and so entry unambiguously caused welfare to increase.

Figure 12.3 shows the case where entry occurs continuously until the team profit is driven to zero. The original demand curve, reflecting league quality at

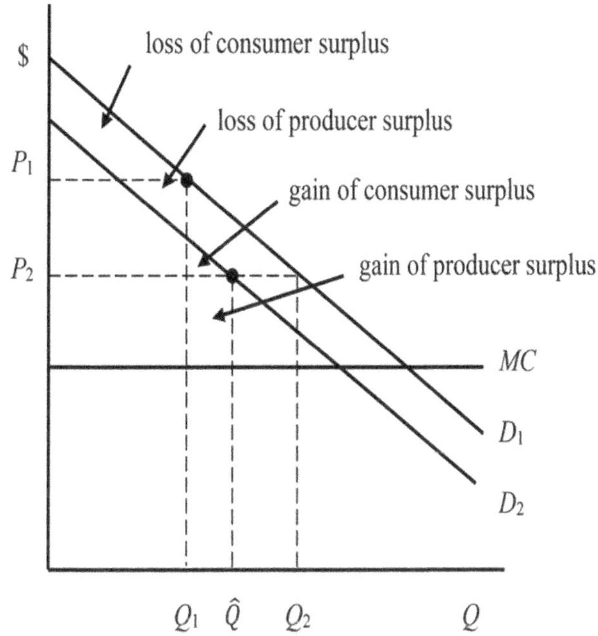

Figure 12.2 *Impact of entry when demand depends on league quality*

the starting point (P_1,Q_1), is D_1, while the demand curve after entry is complete is labeled D_0. The dashed curve shows the path of price–output combinations as entry occurs and demand continually shifts down in response to declining league quality. At the final point, Q_0, welfare consists entirely of consumer surplus, which is shown by the shaded area. This is clearly less than the total surplus that would be attained by free entry if quality were held constant, which is the triangle under the original demand curve D_1 and above the marginal cost curve up to the intersection point Q^*. The relevant comparison, however, is with the original limited-entry point (P_1,Q_1). Specifically, it is between the shaded area in Figure 12.3 (after entry) and area A+B+D in Figure 12.1. Consumer welfare may have increased (compare the shaded area in Figure 12.3 with area A in Figure 12.3), but producer surplus has definitely declined from area B+D in Figure 12.1 to zero in Figure 12.3. Thus, the overall impact is ambiguous.

Also, it is possible that the demand curve after entry is more elastic (flatter), as shown in Figure 12.3. This reflects the idea that, as league quality declines, professional sporting events lose some of their unique appeal and,

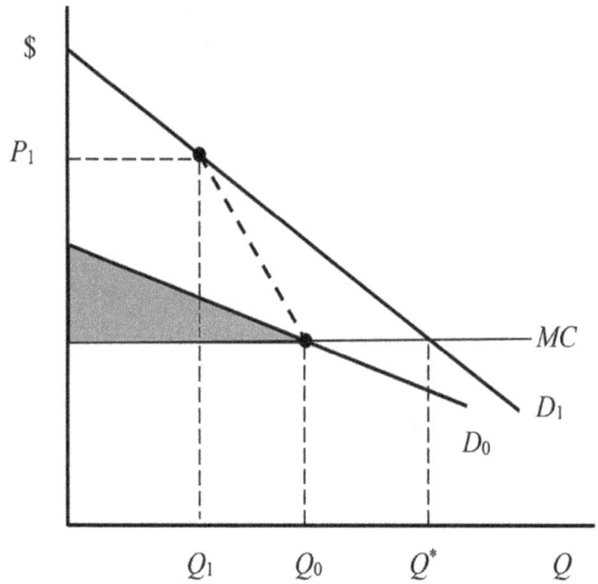

Figure 12.3 *Outcome under fully free entry*

as a result, other entertainment options become closer substitutes. This will further reduce the amount of consumer surplus as a result of free entry. The foregoing argument implies that once the quality of play is accounted for, free entry is not necessarily desirable.

Another line of argument, suggested by the theory of "contestable markets," is that an existing league, even if it limits entry, has an incentive to supply games efficiently in order to forestall the entry of a competing league. There have, in fact, been several attempts by upstart leagues to form in various sports, so the threat is not an idle one.[4] In the case of Major League Baseball, Bradbury (2007, pp. 226–227) concludes that

> …MLB's actions are consistent with the economic model of contestable markets, in which the threat of competition is sufficient to cause [the existing league] to properly supply the market.

For example, MLB has countered credible threats of entry by expanding to satisfy consumer demand. Thus, the appearance of a monopoly does not always signify the *exercise* of monopoly power.

Relocation of Franchises

Another restriction imposed by professional leagues is that relocation decisions must be approved by the league. For example, in 1980, the Oakland Raiders in the National Football League (NFL) sought to relocate to Los Angeles, where there already was an NFL franchise (the Rams). The league opposed the move (a three-fourths vote of owners would have been needed to approve it), but the Raiders sued and ultimately won the right to move.[5]

The league argued that it needed to have veto power over any moves so as to prevent "unwise" relocations, while the Raiders claimed that the requirement violated the Sherman Act. The court agreed with the Raiders. It pointed out that the market for NFL games would itself effectively sort out wise from unwise moves under the presumption that owners are interested in maximizing profits and would therefore not enter the market of another team if they believed that it could not support two teams. Further, the league provided no evidence that the move would otherwise adversely affect the league. Thus, the balance of factors favored allowing the team to move.

Note first that relocation is very different from entry in the sense that the average quality of play presumably would *not* be adversely affected. Thus, the only detrimental effect would be that Oakland fans would lose their team, but presumably this loss should be more than offset by the new fans in Los Angeles if the move was, in fact, efficient. In addition, the increased competition in this city would be beneficial to fans overall.

There is one possible unaccounted loss, however, consisting of the subjective, or sentimental value, of a long-standing team to home fans, which is not necessarily offset by the value of the team to "new" fans in the destination city. This reflects the distinction between willingness-to-accept and willingness-to-pay measures of value. The difference is sometimes attributed to the so-called "endowment effect," which is the idea that possession of an asset creates a kind of attachment to it that increases the amount that a possessor would accept in payment for giving it up, as compared with what that person would pay to acquire it in the first place.[6] This is a genuine economic value, but one that is very hard to measure. The same issue will arise in connection with public financing of sports facilities, a topic to which we now turn.

PUBLIC FINANCING OF SPORTS FACILITIES

Public financing of sports facilities has become an increasingly important component of economic redevelopment policies across the United States and throughout the world. Sports stadiums provide highly visible (one might say "concrete") evidence of public efforts to revitalize cities and hence are attractive to politicians. The purported benefits of the policy include the creation of new jobs, enhanced tax revenues, and civic pride from hosting a major sports franchise or a major event, such as the Olympics. The question is whether these claims are supported by any evidence. This section first develops the economic theory of public financing—specifically, whether there is a sound basis for the use of the policy—and then reviews the available evidence.

Theoretical Basis for Public Financing

Building (or renovating) a facility represents a large, up-front expense for a sports franchise. Let this cost be denoted by F. The team will then generate a stream of profits, reflecting its monopoly power, the present value of which equals π. For the facility to be a profitable investment for the team owner, it must be true that the profits are expected to cover the initial investment, or $\pi > F$. In theory, the team would not need a subsidy if this condition is satisfied. (We will see, however, that competition among cities might still result in one.)

The basis for a subsidy, as discussed above, is the possible spillover of economic benefits to the city or the region. Let these benefits be denoted B. (Below, we will discuss how to actually calculate both π and B.) When these benefits are accounted for, the condition for the facility to be *socially* beneficial is $\pi + B > F$. Thus, if the following condition is satisfied

$$\pi + B > F > \pi \tag{12.1}$$

the facility is socially optimal but not privately optimal for the team owner. This is the prototypical case where some public financing is both necessary for the facility to be built and socially desirable.

Bargaining Between the Team and the City

Let us begin by considering the case of pairwise bargaining between a team owner and a city when equation (12.1) holds. This reflects the situation of a team that is immobile, and so negotiating with the current host city for a renovation is its only option.[7] In this case, the project will only proceed if the city subsidizes construction. Let the amount of the subsidy be S, where it must be true that $B - S > 0$ for the city to expect a benefit, and $\pi + S - F > 0$ for the team to expect a benefit. Thus, together it must be true that

$$B > S > F - \pi \tag{12.2}$$

for a mutually beneficial bargain to be possible. Note that this condition will always be met if the first inequality in equation (12.1) is satisfied—that is, if the facility is socially optimal.

The exact amount of the subsidy, however, will depend on bargaining between the team and the city. The joint surplus from a bargain equals $\pi + B - F$, which we will assume the parties split evenly, as under ordinary Nash bargaining. In that case, the amount of the subsidy the city would pay to the team equals[8]

$$S^* = \frac{B + F - \pi}{2} \tag{12.3}$$

which is increasing in B and F and decreasing in π. Given this subsidy, each party would receive a net benefit of

$$\frac{\pi + B - F}{2} \tag{12.4}$$

from the bargain, which, as noted, is half of the overall surplus.

As an example, suppose a stadium would cost \$100 million to renovate, the expected profits for the team are \$50 million, and the anticipated spillover benefits to the city are \$80 million. The project is therefore socially beneficial, producing a net social gain of \$30 million, but it is not profitable for the team. Under the proposed bargain, therefore, the city would pay the team a subsidy of \$65 million toward the cost of the renovation, which would result in a net benefit of \$15 million for each, and a joint gain of \$30 million. The example is summarized in Table 12.1.

Competition Among Cities

In some cases, multiple cities will bid against one another, either to attract a new team or one that is willing to relocate. In either case, this situation creates a surplus that a team owner can exploit to increase the amount of subsidy

Table 12.1 Stadium subsidy example

Party	Net return (\$ millions)
Team	$50 + 65 - 100 = 15$
City	$80 - 65 = 15$
Joint	$50 + 80 - 100 = 30$

that a city will pay, possibly resulting in complete public financing of a new stadium. To examine this scenario, suppose that the cost of a stadium, F, is the same in all cities, but the profitability of the team and the spillover benefits can vary. Let π_i be the profit an owner expects to earn in city i, and let B_i be the spillover benefits to city i. Given the fixed cost of construction, it is optimal for the team to locate in the city for which $\pi_i + B_i$ is maximized. Let $\pi^* + B^*$ be this maximized sum.

We now examine where the team actually ends up locating as a result of the bidding process, assuming that the team is perfectly mobile and the owner chooses where to locate by maximizing the sum of his own profit plus the subsidy from the city. The situation is similar to our analysis of team bidding for a free agent in Chapter 8, except that here, the city offering the highest subsidy will not necessarily win. Rather, it will be the city whose bid, in combination with the team's profit in that city, is largest.

Note first that the maximum amount each city will bid is its expected spillover benefit, B_i. If this is the highest in the city where the team should efficiently locate, then that city will clearly get the team. However, the city need not bid B_i to win. As we argued in our discussion of free agent bidding, the winning bidder will bid at most the bid of the second-highest bidder. Further, if the team will also maximize its profit in that city, the city can reduce its bid by the profit differential.

To examine the outcome more specifically, suppose that city k has the second highest sum, $\pi_k + B_k$. Then, by assumption

$$\pi^* + B^* \geq \pi_k + B_k \tag{12.5}$$

If city k makes its highest bid, $S_k = B_k$, the winning city's bid, S^*, must satisfy $\pi^* + S^* \geq \pi_k + B_k$, or

$$S^* \geq B_k + \pi_k - \pi^* \tag{12.6}$$

Now, assuming that the winning city offers the lowest subsidy that just allows it to outbid the second-highest bidder, we obtain

$$S^* = B_k + \pi_k - \pi^* \tag{12.7}$$

Finally, for the winning city to expect a net benefit, it must be true that $B^* \geq S^*$. However, with S^* given by equation (12.7), this requirement must be true by equation (12.5), which holds by assumption. According to equation (12.7), the winning bid equals the second-highest spillover benefit (B_k) plus the profit differential relative to the second-best city (which may be positive or negative).

Notice several things about the expression in equation (12.7). First, *it is independent of the winning city's benefit,* B^*. This is a consequence of the need for the winning city only to outbid the next most favorable city. Second, S^* *is also independent of the cost of building the stadium,* F. Both of these conclusions are different from the calculation above, where the subsidy was determined by bargaining between the team and a single city. In that case, the subsidy was increasing in both B and F (see equation (12.3)). This again is a consequence of bidding among cities, which forces the winning bidder to compete away some of the gains from attracting the team relative to the above case of pairwise bargaining between the team and one city. In the case where the value of the team in the second-best location is nearly as large as that in the optimal location, the winning city may have to forgo most of its gains. An implication of this result is that the subsidy could end up covering more than the full cost of the stadium, even if the team could have afforded to pay this cost on its own.

To illustrate the preceding conclusions, consider the following elaboration of the example in Table 12.1. Suppose that, in addition to the city in that example, there are two other cities competing for the team. Table 12.2 summarizes the relevant data. In particular, for each city, the table shows the team's expected gross profit if it locates in that city, the resulting spillover benefit to that city, and the net social benefit, including the stadium cost of $100 million. Note that, based on the net social benefit, it is optimal for the team to locate in city 1, even though the team's gross profit in that city is the lowest. In the absence of a subsidy, however, only locating in city 2 would allow the team to self-finance the stadium cost and still make a profit.

The process of bidding among the three cities, as described above, should result in the team locating in city 1, as this is where the joint surplus is largest. Since city 2 is the second-best location, equation (12.7) predicts that the winning bid by city 1 will be equal to $70 million (=$10 mil + $110 mil – $50 mil). Thus, city 1 will end up paying 70 percent of the $100 million stadium cost. The expected net surpluses for the two parties under this arrangement are $20 million for the team and $10 million for the city. For the team, this consists of profit of $50 million minus the $30 million net cost of the stadium; for the

Table 12.2 Example of competition for a team among three cities

City:	1	2	3
Team's gross profit	$50 mil	$110 mil	$70 mil
Spillover to city	80 mil	10 mil	40 mil
Joint benefit	30 mil	20 mil	10 mil

city, this consists of the spillover benefit of \$80 million less the subsidy of \$70 million. Finally, note that if the stadium's cost were less than \$70 million, the winning city would end up paying its full cost and then some.

Calculating Profits and Spillover Benefits

Prior to approving such a large-scale project, municipalities typically conduct economic impact studies to determine the projected benefits. This section briefly reviews some of the tools and considerations needed to perform the necessary calculations.

First, because a stadium project, or any large-scale investment, produces a flow of net benefits over time, these benefits must be appropriately discounted in order to calculate the *net present value* (*NPV*) of the project. In the above analysis, π represented the present value of future profits to the team, and B represented the present value of the spillover benefits. Adding these and subtracting the up-front cost, F thus yields the *NPV*:

$$NPV = \pi + B - F \tag{12.8}$$

The calculation of present value reflects the simple idea that \$1 today is worth more than \$1 received a year from now. The reason is that the dollar today can be invested at the prevailing interest rate, which allows it to grow over time. If, for example, r is the interest rate, then \$1 invested today will yield \$(1+r) after one year. For income that will be received more than one year in the future, simply repeat the process. Thus, after two years, the future value of \$1 today is $(1+r)^2$, after three years, it is $(1+r)^3$, and so on, so that after n years, it is $(1+r)^n$.

One can use this same logic to ask what \$1 to be received one year in the future is worth today. Let x be that amount. Then, applying the above formula, we have that $x(1+r)=1$, or

$$x = \frac{1}{1+r} \tag{12.9}$$

This is defined to be the *present value* of \$1 to be received in one year. Following the above approach, \$1 to be received n years from now has a present value of

$$\frac{1}{(1+r)^n}$$

When the income from a project is a flow over time, the individually discounted yearly amounts are simply added up. Thus, for example, if π_t is the team's profit from a new stadium in year t, and B_t is the city's spillover benefit in year t, then for a stadium with an expected life of T years, equation (12.8) can be written as

$$NPV = \sum_{t=1}^{T} \frac{\pi_t + B_t}{(1+r)^t} - F \tag{12.10}$$

Note that this assumes F is spent in year zero, and the flow of benefits commences in year 1.

Not surprisingly, the actual calculation of this expression involves some further complications. The first is the choice of the discount rate, r. It should represent the opportunity cost of capital for the investor, which is not necessarily the same as the prevailing market interest rate. Second, the calculation of the spillover benefit B reflects the economic impact of a stadium above and beyond the profit to the team. The pecuniary element of these benefits represents spending outside of the stadium—on restaurants, hotels, etc. These can be difficult to estimate because they involve a counterfactual situation. Specifically, how much will a typical fan spend outside of the stadium, and how does that spending ripple through the local economy? This *multiplier effect* of spending on sports, or any other investment, is a critical calculation, but one that requires substantial speculation.

Further complicating matters is that spending at a new stadium will not necessarily be net new spending because some fraction of it will be a substitute for spending on other entertainment options that would have occurred anyway. This *substitution effect* must be accounted for so as not to overestimate the magnitude of B. These considerations suggest that there will generally be a wide margin for error in determining the true value of B.

The final issue in calculating the net benefit of a new stadium is the non-pecuniary benefits, such as civic pride in having a professional team. This is the most difficult factor to account for precisely because it is non-monetary and therefore hard to quantify, but it has real economic value, as evidenced by the hysteria following championships won by hometown teams or the loss fans feel when their team relocates. The issue is similar to the problem of putting a monetary value on preserving an environmental resource or protecting an endangered species. Economists usually resort to the use of surveys to ascertain the importance people attach to these non-monetary values, but this so-called *contingent valuation* approach suffers from some obvious difficulties, including the likelihood of over-valuation when no actual payment from respondents is required, and determining the scope of the relevant market (i.e., whose opinion matters?).[9]

With these considerations in mind, we now turn to an evaluation of the evidence on public financing.

Evidence

To get a sense of the scope of public financing of sports facilities in the United States, Coates and Humphreys (2003) provide a summary of all new facilities built for professional baseball, basketball, and football from 1998 to 2003. Over that period, 26 facilities were built at an average cost (in 2003 dollars) of $321 million. The average subsidy was $208 million, or 65 percent of the total. Seven facilities were completely publicly financed, while only two received zero public money. Based on these studies, the authors found no evidence of positive economic benefits. More recent assessments reinforce this negative assessment. For example, Humphreys (2019, p. 269) concludes:

> Despite continued claims by subsidy proponents, research in peer-reviewed journals finds no evidence supporting the idea that professional sports events generate tangible new economic benefits for host cities. Subsidies for the construction of new professional sports facilities cannot be justified by these claims.

There are several possible explanations for this surprising conclusion. First, the substitution effect may be larger than planners expected (if they accounted for it at all). Perhaps various entertainment options are highly substitutable for one another. Second, public spending on sports may have less of an impact on worker productivity in the affected region compared with spending on other public goods, such as public transportation, police, etc. Third, much of the income earned by professional athletes may flow out of the city, thus substantially lowering the expected multiplier effect of sports spending relative to other spending. Finally, the finding of little or no net public gain is consistent with the argument above that cities compete away much of the expected benefits.

A crucial caveat, as noted above, is that there may be substantial nonpecuniary benefits from having a sports stadium in a city, and these benefits represent real economic gains. (Note that the above quote referred to "tangible" benefits.) If these gains are large, they may more than offset the pecuniary losses. The problem is finding a way to quantify them in a consistent and believable way.

As a final point, Matheson (2019) notes that localized benefits may exist. In particular, he concludes that "…the evidence is fairly clear that [stadium construction] can generate significant neighborhood effects, and policymakers may have good reason to make a conscious decision to prefer one area over another" (p. 275). Thus, the use of public funds to attract a sports team may be justified as part of a larger effort to conduct targeted urban redevelopment policy.

SPORTS AND GAMBLING

Gambling and sports have always been closely linked. For some fans, wagering on games enhances the experience of watching a contest and thus increases the demand for sporting events. In this sense, sports and gambling are complementary activities. For many fans, gambling is itself a form of sport in the sense that it fulfills the same desire for an uncertain outcome as does the underlying contest. In this sense, gambling and sports are more like substitutes.

Whatever role gambling plays, sports and betting have historically had an uneasy relationship, as the US Supreme Court recently observed:

> Opponents [of sports gambling] argue that it is particularly addictive and especially attractive to young people with a strong interest in sports, and in the past gamblers corrupted and seriously damaged the reputation of professional and amateur sports.[10]

The Court's ruling struck down as unconstitutional a 1992 federal law, the Professional and Amateur Sports Act (PASPA), that had effectively banned commercial betting on sports in most states. The full results of that decision remain to be seen, but the massive tax revenues that sports betting promises for state coffers suggest that it will almost certainly become the norm. Our discussion in subsequent sections will first examine the economics of betting and will then use the resulting insights to examine the likely impact of betting on sports.

Betting on Sports

We begin by reviewing the basis for betting in consumer preferences.[11] Most of the time, economists assume that individual consumers are averse to risk, which is why they buy insurance against uncertain events, such as accidents and illness, which might entail a large and unexpected cost. (It is also why we argued in Chapter 9 that professional athletes prefer fixed wage contracts.) One of the puzzles associated with gambling of any kind, whether it involves betting on sports, buying lottery tickets, or going to a casino, is that it seems to be inconsistent with risk aversion, or even risk neutrality, because the expected return must be negative in order for the bet to be profitable for the bookie or the house, or for a lottery to generate revenue for the state. We will focus only on sports betting here, and in this context, we will later suggest a couple of resolutions to this paradox.

For now, however, we will consider a consumer who has no particular rooting interest in sporting contests but only views them as opportunities for betting on uncertain events. The particular wagering opportunity is therefore unimportant—all that matters is that the outcome is uncertain. The unique aspect of sports betting is that the probability of winning a particular bet depends on the specific teams competing, which is why the odds vary by event.

To be specific, consider a contest between two teams, A and B, in which, prior to the contest, the probability of A's winning is put at p. If the amount of the bet is x dollars and the payoff for a winning bet on A is R dollars, then a *fair bet* satisfies the equation $-x+pR=0$, which yields the payoff.

$$R=\frac{x}{p} \tag{12.11}$$

Thus, the odds are determined by the multiplier $1/p$, which is the amount that a bet of \$1 returns if the chosen team wins.[12] The odds can also be expressed by the ratio $p/(1-p)$, or inversely by $(1-p)/p$. Table 12.3 shows some examples. Note that in the cases where $p<½$ the chosen team is the "underdog," and where $p>½$ it is the "favorite."

A risk-neutral person—someone who maximizes expected wealth—would be indifferent between making a fair bet and making no bet at all, while a risk-averse person would avoid a fair bet. However, a risk-preferrer will actually derive positive utility from a fair bet and even some losing bets precisely because they introduce uncertainty. To see this, consider a person whose utility over wealth is given by $U=U(w)$, where $dU/dw>0$ and $d^2U/dw^2>0$. Thus, utility is increasing at an increasing rate; that is, it is a convex function of wealth. This is in contrast to a risk-averse person, whose utility is assumed to be concave in wealth.[13] For current purposes, the key characteristic of a convex utility function is that the person actually benefits from uncertainty over wealth, which is what makes betting attractive.

Table 12.3 Ways of expressing odds

p	$1/p$	$p/(1-p)$	$(1-p)/p$
¼	4	⅓	3
⅓	3	½	2
½	2	1	1
⅔	1.50	2	½
¾	1.25	3	⅓

To be specific, consider a person with an initial wealth of W who makes a fair bet of x dollars, which returns R if the bettor's team wins. The bettor's expected utility is therefore

$$EU = pU(W - x + R) + (1 - p)U(W - x) \tag{12.12}$$

His or her corresponding expected wealth from the bet is given by

$$p(W - x + R) + (1 - p)(W - x) = W - x + pR = W \tag{12.13}$$

where the last equality follows after substituting for R from equation (12.11). The defining feature of a risk-preferrer is that he or she is strictly better off by making a fair bet:

$$EU > U(W) \tag{12.14}$$

The inequality, as noted, is a consequence of the convexity of $U(\cdot)$. This is shown graphically in Figure 12.4 by the vertical distance between EU and $U(W)$.

The inequality in equation (12.14) is what makes betting both desirable for the bettor and profitable for the "bookie" (the person taking the bet). To see

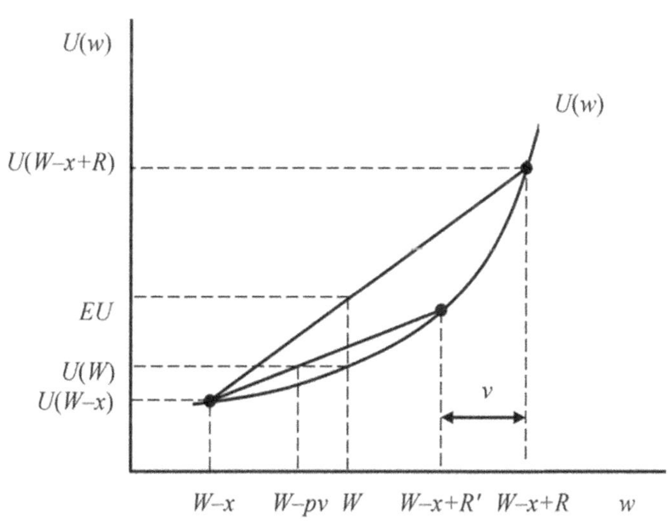

Figure 12.4 Betting behavior of a risk-preferrer

why, suppose that the bookie promises a payoff slightly below the amount in equation (12.11) so that the bettor's expected wealth from the bet is less than W (i.e., the bet has a negative expected value). Condition (12.14) ensures that the bettor will still be willing to make the bet, while the bookie retains this extra wealth as profit.[14] The maximum amount of this return is determined by adjusting the winning payoff downward in equation (12.12) until equation (12.14) holds with equality. The resulting payoff, denoted R', solves the following equation:

$$pU(W - x + R') + (1 - p)U(W - x) = U(W) \tag{12.15}$$

The bookie's profit is then determined in relation to R' according to the equation

$$v = R - R' = \frac{x}{p} - R' \tag{12.16}$$

The determination of v in equation (12.16) is shown graphically in Figure 12.4. Starting with a fair bet, the winning payoff is reduced, causing the chord connecting the bettor's minimum and maximum wealth levels to rotate downward around the minimum point, $(W - x)$, until equation (12.16) holds for the fixed odds $p/(1 - p)$. Note that at this point, the bet is no longer "fair" in the sense that the winner's expected wealth, $W - pv$, is less than his initial wealth. In this case, he is indifferent between making the bet and not making it, and the bookie retains all of the gains from the transaction. The bookie's expected profit in this case is[15]

$$E[\pi] = p(x - R') + (1 - p)x = pv \tag{12.17}$$

where the last equality follows from equation (12.16). More generally, if v is smaller than the value in equation (12.16), so that the left-hand side of equation (12.15) is greater than $U(W)$, the parties share the benefit. The specific division of the surplus depends on the competitiveness of the betting market. The following example illustrates the preceding analysis.

Example 12.1: Utility and profit from betting on sports.

Suppose the bettor has a utility function over wealth given by $U = w^2$, which satisfies the conditions for risk-preferring behavior. In addition, suppose the person has initial wealth of W =\$10, and wishes to bet \$5 on a sporting event with even odds; that is, each team has a probability of winning of p =½. From equation (12.11), a fair bet would have a winning payoff of R =\$5/.5=\$10, which yields the bettor an expected utility of

$$EU = (.5)(10-5)^2 + (.5)(10-5+10)^2 = (.5)(25) + (.5)(225) = 125$$

Note that this is strictly greater than the utility the person would get if he did not place the bet.

$$U(10) = 10^2 = 100$$

To find the payoff that leaves the person just indifferent between betting and not betting, solve the following equation for R' :

$$(.5)(10-5)^2 + (.5)(10-5+R')^2 = 100$$

This yields R' =8.23<10. From this, we can calculate the expected profit for the bookie to be

$$E[\pi] = .5(5) + .5(5-8.23) = .885$$

Betting by Risk-neutral Individuals

The preceding analysis suggested that only risk-preferring individuals will ever bet, which seems contrary to everyday experience that some people both buy insurance (indicating risk aversion) and also make bets. Friedman and Savage (1948) famously explained this observation by supposing that individuals may be risk-preferring for small wagers, such as the purchase of lottery tickets, but risk-averse for large risks, such as the loss of their house. This is not really an explanation at all, however, but merely an assertion that people have a preference for both betting and buying insurance.

For the case of sports betting, other resolutions of this paradox are possible. One is related to the idea, explored in Chapter 6, that fans receive utility from the uncertainty of outcome associated with sporting events.[16] We may thus conjecture that the taste for betting, which in standard economic theory is justified as arising out of risk-preferring preferences, is related to the attraction people have for watching sports. Indeed, the establishment of betting odds and point spreads can be seen as restoring competitive balance in contests between unequal contestants, thereby promoting uncertainty of outcome. Thus, risk-averse people who also receive utility from the suspense of sporting contests may find it attractive to engage in betting as a way to maximize that utility (Miceli, 2023).[17]

Another explanation for sports betting is that, unlike a lottery or casino games, which have truly objective odds, people can hold differing beliefs about the possible outcome of a sporting contest.[18] For example, they might believe that they have better knowledge or insight about the quality of the two contestants than the "market" does, or they might hold irrational beliefs based on a partisan interest, and these beliefs can create profit opportunities.

Consider, for example, point-spread betting. In such a wager, the bookie announces a point spread, *PS*, reflecting the amount by which the favorite is expected to win. A bet on the favorite will therefore be a winner only if the actual point differential, *DP*, exceeds *PS*. For such a wager, a bet of $\$(1+v)$ will return \$1, where v is the bookie's take. If we let p be the probability, from the bookie's point of view, that $DP>PS$, then the bookie's expected return from such a bet is

$$p\cdot(-1)+(1-p)(1+v)=(1+v)-p(2+v)$$

which will be non-negative if

$$p\leq\frac{1+v}{2+v} \tag{12.18}$$

When $v=.1$, as is typical, the right-hand side equals .524. Thus, if the point spread is set to create even odds, or $p=.5$, which is the objective, the bookie will expect to make a profit. It must follow, however, that if the bettor holds the same beliefs, she will expect a negative return from the bet. Specifically, the bettor's expected return will be

$$p\cdot1-(1-p)(1+v)=p(2+v)-(1+v)$$

which will only be non-negative if the reverse inequality holds in equation (12.18). That is, p must be greater than .524. Thus, if *PS* is set to produce even odds, the bet must be a loser on average.

But now suppose that some bettors have subjective beliefs that exceed the bookie's assessment of the *PS* that will produce $p=.5$. Suppose, in particular, that an individual believes that for the announced *PS*, the favorite has a chance of winning equal to $\hat{p}>p$ where

$$\hat{p}>\frac{1+v}{2+v}>p \tag{12.19}$$

In this case, both parties will expect to gain from the wager.

Of course, we would expect the bookie to be a better predictor on average; otherwise, he or she will not be able to stay in business. Thus, some bettors must be wrong in their subjective beliefs, but others will also be right. The ones that are correct more often than not will possibly become repeat bettors, while systematic losers will presumably drop out of the pool, leading to a selection effect that weeds out those who hold incorrect beliefs. However, as long as there is a steady inflow of new bettors, some of whom will turn out to be losers, an equilibrium with betting can be sustainable.

Gambling and the Integrity of Competition

As noted above, one of the problems associated with betting on sports is the concern that bettors will try to influence the outcome of contests to their benefit, thereby undermining fair competition. The odds of a contest reflect the belief that all of the contestants are exerting maximum effort to win. The worry, therefore, is generally not that bettors will try to incite *greater* effort by contestants on whom they have placed a wager, but rather that they will try to influence the contestant against whom they have bet to "throw" the contest. If this sort of "game fixing" is successful, it will increase the fixer's probability of winning the bet, which will increase the expected utility for any given payoff, R, while obviously lowering the return for the party accepting the bet. If this becomes known, people will therefore refrain from making bets.

Note that game fixing need not always involve arranging for a contestant to lose. It can also involve "point shaving" in contests where the odds are stated in terms of point spreads. For example, if a team is favored by ten points, a bet on the opponent will be a winner for any contest in which the favored team wins by less than ten. A bettor may, therefore, arrange for a member of the favored team to take steps to ensure that the winning margin falls below the ten-point threshold. Such behavior would presumably be harder to detect and thus easier to sustain.

Probably the most famous episode of the corrupting influence of gambling on sports was the so-called "Black Sox Scandal" of the 1919 World Series.[19] The Series that year pitted the heavily favored Chicago White Sox against the Cincinnati Reds. Odds makers had put the Sox as a 5 to 1 favorite, but the Reds ended up winning the series 5 games to 3.[20] Rumors swirled during and after the series that the games had been fixed, but the extent of the corruption was not revealed until the next season, when eight players and several professional gamblers were indicted for conspiracy to defraud the public. No one was ever convicted, but the eight players were banned from the game for life, the most famous of whom was Shoeless Joe Jackson.[21]

The motivation for the players to participate in the conspiracy was the reserve clause, which, as discussed at various points in this book, bound players to their teams for life and thereby kept salaries low. Thus, when gamblers approached players offering sums substantially larger than their salaries, it was not hard to find several willing takers. The high salaries of modern players, coupled with the harsh penalty for being caught, therefore suggest that nowadays the risk of gamblers colluding with players to throw games is substantially reduced.[22] The greater remaining threat may therefore be college sports, where players are not fully compensated for the value of their participation.

The larger result of the Black Sox Scandal was that in 1920, professional baseball was on the brink of losing public trust—a disaster for any sports league which, as we have emphasized, relies on uncertainty of outcome to attract fans. Fortunately, two events intervened to avert the crisis—one by design, the other fortuitous. The first was the appointment of Kenesaw "Mountain" Landis, a tough-minded and uncompromising judge, as commissioner. He immediately handed out lifetime bans to the eight players as a strong deterrent to future such actions. The other fortuitous event was the emergence of Babe Ruth, who single-handedly changed the way the game was played.

DISCRIMINATION IN SPORTS

Before discussing discrimination in sports *per se*, it is important to distinguish between *prejudice* and *discrimination*. Prejudice is a preference for or against something or someone, while discrimination is an action based on that preference. When defined at this level of generality, it should be apparent that not all instances of prejudice and discrimination are bad or unacceptable. For example, consumer choice in a market setting involves a decision based on a kind of "prejudice" for or against some good or service, and the efficient operation of markets is based on the ability of consumers to act based on that prejudice. Indeed, this is the basis for market competition.

In a sports context, partisanship by fans—a form of discrimination—is also a manifestation of consumer preferences and therefore is the basis for sports competition. The goal of competitive balance, which has been a cornerstone of our study of policies related to professional sports, is not a desire for the elimination of partisanship among fans, but rather that the partisan interests of fans be equally served by the league. This involves each team having the ability to put the best possible product on the field.

The question then becomes, what sort of prejudice/discrimination is *not* acceptable, in sports or any other context? This is a question largely outside of economics because it depends on what characteristics society deems as being acceptable as a basis for treating people differently. For example, athletic ability or product characteristics are acceptable, but race is not.

For the remainder of this section, we will focus on an employment context. The key question is, what factors can employers legitimately use to make hiring decisions and to determine wages, whether in a sports or any other employment setting?

Discrimination in Employment

From our previous discussion of labor markets, we determined that in a competitive market setting, wages are equated to the marginal productivity of workers. Any factors aside from that, such as race, gender, ethnicity, or religious beliefs, are irrelevant because they do not affect a worker's productivity. Employers may harbor prejudices about these personal characteristics, but it is generally considered unacceptable—and indeed it is illegal—to make hiring and wage decisions based on them. That would represent an illegitimate form of discrimination.

In his classic study of racial discrimination in a market setting, Gary Becker (1971) argued that determining employment or pay based on factors other than productivity will be costly to the party undertaking the discrimination. In other words, an employer with a prejudice against a certain group will incur an implicit cost, on top of the wage, of hiring members of that group. In effect, prejudice acts like a tax on employment. The result of this is illustrated in Figure 12.5.

In Figure 12.5, MRP is the marginal revenue product for workers in a given industry, and S is the supply curve of workers, representing their reservation wage (i.e., the lowest wage at which they would accept employment). We have seen that in a competitive market where employers have no prejudice, the equilibrium wage and employment levels would be w^* and Q^*, which are determined at the intersection of these curves. But now suppose that the owner of a firm (or team) experiences a cost x (measured in dollar terms) of hiring a person from a certain group. This causes the "perceived" demand curve for members of that group to shift downward by the vertical distance x. The resulting curve is labeled $MRP - x$. If the prejudiced owner can set the wage for his or her workers, the employment of members of the disfavored group by that owner would fall to Q', the point where the new demand curve intersects S, and the wage for those individuals would correspondingly fall to w'.

Becker argued, however, that competition will reduce the extent of this sort of discrimination, not because of any change in the preferences of employers, but because market pressures will tend to drive prejudiced employers out of business due to their failure to hire the best-qualified workers. Suppose, in the above diagram, that the owner cannot set the wage but must take the market-determined wage as w^*. Then, he or she would employ even fewer members of the disfavored group. Specifically, only Q'' workers would be hired, as

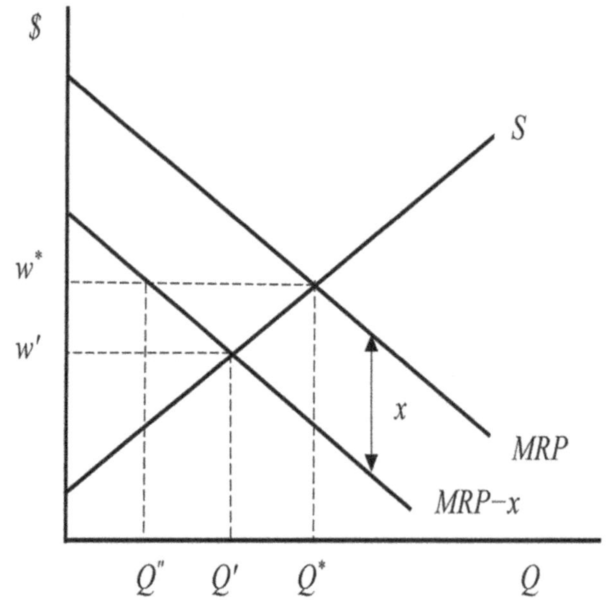

Figure 12.5 *Impact of discrimination on employment and wages*

determined by the point where $MRP - x = w^*$. This refusal to hire some otherwise qualified workers will cause the quality of the product being produced to decline, resulting in a loss of the firm's market share.

In the sports context, teams unwilling, or less willing, to hire minority players will likewise be less competitive. The fact that professional sports teams have market power for reasons we have noted provides scope for this sort of discrimination to persist. For example, not all MLB teams integrated right away following Jackie Robinson's debut in 1947. (This is one cost of market power that we did not mention above.) Eventually, however, fans will respond to a team's inferior performance on the field by staying away (unless, of course, it is *their* prejudice that the team is manifesting), and this may induce a prejudiced owner to sell out to an owner who has no such prejudice and hence can make a larger profit by not discriminating against certain groups.

Testing for Discrimination in Labor Markets

The foregoing theory offers various predictions that can be tested empirically. For example, data on wages and observable measures of performance can be used to see if there is evidence of racial discrimination in a particular labor market. Sports markets are a particularly fruitful area for undertaking this sort of study because performance measures are abundant, something that is not generally true in most industries.

In terms of methodology, a researcher could regress wages on observable measures of worker (player) performance along with personal characteristics, such as race or gender, to determine if wages are lower for minorities or women, while holding all other measures fixed. Such a regression equation would look like this:

$$w = \beta_0 + \beta_1 X + \beta_2 R + \varepsilon \tag{12.20}$$

where

w = a player's wage or salary;

X = a set of performance measures;

R = a dummy variable that indicates a worker's race or gender;

ε = an error term.

If R is specified to equal one if a worker is African American, say, and zero if he or she is white, then a negative and significant value for β_2 would be evidence of racial discrimination. The same would be true of gender differences. There are, of course, many econometric issues that have to be addressed in conducting analyses of this sort, such as what measures to include in X.[23]

An early survey of the literature on racial discrimination in sports by Kahn (1991) found little evidence of discrimination in salaries or hiring in Major League Baseball (MLB), but it did find evidence of fan prejudice in favor of white players by fans in the National Basketball Association (NBA) (as evidenced by ticket sales). And, perhaps as a consequence, it found that white players were paid more than comparable black players in that league. Using more recent NBA data (from 1990–2008), by contrast, Groothuis and Hill (2013) failed to find evidence of either "exit discrimination" (i.e., whether a player is cut from a team) or wage discrimination between white and black players. If anything, they found slight evidence that white players were paid less than black players, all else being equal.

Hanssen and Meehan (2009) asked the question of whether winning or losing teams were more likely to integrate in the MLB following the elimination of the color barrier in 1947. They found slight evidence that losing teams integrated first, which is consistent with the above argument that prejudiced owners excluded qualified players from the league, but that losing teams would feel pressured to reverse that practice.

Volz (2017) found that black quarterbacks were benched sooner than their comparable white counterparts in the National Football League (NFL), and that teams improved more when a white quarterback was benched. Finally, Volz (2013) found that black former players were less likely to be hired as managers in the MLB than white former players with similar credentials. Additionally, Hispanic former players were less likely to be hired as major league coaches and minor league managers, compared with white former players. Interestingly, however, he also found that minority managers were *more likely* to return for another year as compared with white managers, all else being equal (Volz, 2009).

Gender Discrimination

A pay gap between men and women in the labor market is an issue that has received a lot of attention from economists, primarily aimed at determining whether such a gap exists and, if it does, how large it is once all factors aside from gender are accounted for. In the case of professional sports, where gender segregation is the norm, a pay gap clearly exists between men and women, thus raising the question of whether this gap reflects discrimination or a genuine difference in the nature of men's and women's sports. Simply comparing pay levels cannot answer this question because the product is fundamentally different. In addition, professional sports for women are newer, and so they have had less time to develop a fan following and to receive media coverage at a comparable level to that given to men's professional sports. The question, then, is whether observed pay differences reflect a fundamental difference in fan preferences for men's versus women's sports or are an example of growing pains.

This is obviously a difficult question to answer because of the absence of "natural experiments" in which everything besides the gender of the competitors can be held constant. Conducting empirical studies comparing men's and women's golf, basketball, or tennis, say, to determine if pay gaps reflect gender discrimination *per se* rather than fundamental differences in style of play, speed, strength, etc.—things that are very hard to quantify—would be exceedingly difficult. Thus, for now, the question remains an open one.

At the amateur level, the principal issue has not been equality of pay between the genders but rather equality of opportunity. This is a different question because it does not involve assessing whether observed wage and employment differences are driven by market competition, gender discrimination, or some combination. It is, instead, a question of civil rights, and that is appropriately dealt with by government intervention. To that end, in 1972, the US Congress passed Title IX, which prohibited discrimination based on gender for any educational programs receiving federal funds. The implementation of this law with respect to scholastic sports has clearly offered girls and women greatly expanded athletic opportunities. And although it has unavoidably resulted in diminished opportunities for boys and men, given limited athletic budgets for schools and colleges, most would agree that, on the whole, this has been a worthwhile and highly successful policy initiative.

SUMMARY

This chapter addressed four policy issues related to sports. The first was the application of antitrust laws to sports leagues. The purpose of antitrust laws is to protect consumers from anti-competitive actions by firms, and, from a purely business perspective, there is no reason why the same scrutiny should not be applied to sports leagues. The complication is that some amount of cooperation is necessary for leagues to supply contests in a predictable way, most obviously because individual teams cannot provide contests on their own. Still, excessive cooperation is potentially detrimental to consumers, such as restricted entry of teams. We showed, however, that because entry erodes quality for reasons discussed in Chapter 10, allowing completely free entry may not be desirable either. The challenge, therefore, is to allow beneficial cooperation without fostering collusive practices that are detrimental to fans.

The second policy issue concerned public funding of sports facilities, which is increasingly becoming a standard component of city and state economic redevelopment plans. The question is whether it is a wise policy. We reviewed the economic basis for subsidizing stadiums, which largely turns on the extent of spillover benefits to the public. The key, therefore, is estimating these benefits, many of which may reside in the non-pecuniary value associated with having a professional sports team. The available evidence suggested that, at least in terms of the pecuniary gains (jobs and taxes), the benefits do not seem to be sufficient to justify the extent of subsidization that has occurred.

The third topic we examined was gambling and sports. We reviewed the economics of gambling in general, which derives from the risk-preferring preferences of consumers. The taste for gambling and the demand for sporting events are no doubt closely linked through the desire for uncertain outcomes. For some fans, gambling is itself a form of sport, while for others, the ability to bet on a game merely enhances the value of the event. Thus, on one hand, sports leagues benefit from the legality of sports betting, but on the other, betting has the potential to undermine the integrity of sports if gamblers are able to collude with competitors to alter the outcome of contests. Sports leagues, therefore, generally favor some amount of legal oversight of sports betting.

The final policy issue we examined was discrimination in sports leagues. We first reviewed the economics of discrimination in the labor market generally. Specifically, we saw that owners who have a prejudice against a certain group will hire fewer members of that group, even when they are equally (or better) qualified, and, when feasible, will pay them lower salaries. Market competition limits the extent to which business owners can engage in this sort of practice, whereas firms with market power—such as sports teams—may be able to engage in it. Ultimately, however, acting on such prejudices will manifest itself in the inferior performance of a team on the field, which may cause fans to demand a change of ownership (unless the fans themselves are prejudiced). We then discussed how evidence of discrimination based on race or gender can be detected using salary and performance data, and reviewed the evidence from some recent studies in the sports context.

The discussion concluded with some comments on gender discrimination in sports. The key issue here is whether obvious differences in pay between male and female athletes reflect gender discrimination or are a manifestation of fan preferences. This remains an open question.

EXERCISES

12.1. The demand for games supplied by a sports league is given by $P = 500 - .5Q$, where Q is the number of games. Let the number of games per team be fixed at 50, so $Q = 50n$, where n is the number of teams.

- (a) Suppose the league wants to maintain a price per game of \$100. Find the total number of games it should supply, Q^*, and the resulting number of teams it should allow in the league, n^*.
- (b) Holding the number of games fixed at 50, find the number of teams the league should allow if it wants the price to fall to \$50.
- (c) Finally, suppose that entry dilutes the quality of play, which causes the demand curve to shift down to $P = 475 - .5Q$. Find the number of teams that supports the price of \$50 in this case. How does it compare with (a) and (b)?

12.2. An expansion team in a professional sports league is considering locating in one of two cities, A or B. The team estimates that its profits in the two cities will be as follows:

$$\text{Profit in A} = \$100 \text{ million}$$

$$\text{Profit in B} = \$110 \text{ million}$$

This profit, however, is exclusive of the cost of building a new stadium, which is estimated to be \$50 million in either city. However, the team expects whichever city it chooses to subsidize some of this cost. Suppose that City A expects the team to generate \$40 million in economic activity for the region (over and above the team's profit), while City B expects the team to generate \$25 million in economic activity for the region.

(a) Accounting for all benefits and costs, in which city is it efficient for the team to locate?

(b) What is the least amount of a subsidy that the city from part (a) would have to bid to attract the team, assuming that the other city bids nothing?

(c) What is the least amount that that city would have to bid to outbid the other city?

(d) Given your answer to (c), does the winning city end up receiving a net gain? If so, how much?

12.3. A person considers placing a bet of \$10 on a team with a 1 in 5 chance of winning. A winning bet pays \$45.

(a) Is this a fair bet?

(b) Suppose the person has a utility function over wealth of $U = w^2$ and initial wealth of \$100. Will she place the bet?

(c) What is the expected return (in dollars) to the bookie?

(d) Now consider a person with a utility function of $U = w$. Would she place the above bet?

(e) Suppose the person in (d) believes she has special knowledge about the team, on which basis she believes it has a 1 in 4 chance of winning. Will she now make the bet?

NOTES

1. *Federal Base Ball Club of Baltimore v. National League*, 259 US 200 (1922).
2. Bradbury (2007, Ch. 14) argues that Major League Baseball, although uniquely protected among the major professional sports from antitrust scrutiny, does not appear to act more like a monopolist than the other sports in terms of limiting output, pricing games, or restricting the entry of teams.
3. This is a consequence of a constant marginal cost curve.
4. In fact, some rival leagues became so successful that the incumbent league eventually subsumed them. Two examples are the American League in professional baseball and the American Football League (AFL) in professional football.
5. See *Los Angeles Memorial Coliseum Commission v. NFL*, 726 F.2d 1381 (9th Cir. 1984). One legal tactic the city of Oakland sought to use to stop the move was to use its powers of eminent domain to "take'" the franchise. The California Supreme Court upheld the city's right to do so (see *City of Oakland v. Oakland Raiders*, 183 Cal. Rptr. 673 (1982)), but the subsequent appeals court ruling allowed the move.
6. See, Kahneman et al. (2000).

7. In this case, π and B should be interpreted as the *extra* profits and spillover benefits from the renovation.
8. In the Nash bargaining solution, the subsidy S would maximize the product of the surpluses, or $(B-S)(\pi+S-F)$, which yields the expression in the text.
9. Another issue is the distinction between the willingness-to-pay and the willingness-to-accept measures of value, as discussed above in connection with team relocation.
10. *Murphy, Governor of New Jersey et al. v. National Collegiate Athletic Assn. et al.* (2018).
11. See Sauer (1998) for an overview of the economics of sports betting.
12. Note that a fair bet is therefore not the same thing as an "even" bet; that is, a bet with even odds, or $p=1/2$.
13. Specifically, $d^2U/dw^2<0$.
14. We assume that the bookie is risk-neutral, which can be justified by supposing that he takes many bets that are uncorrelated and therefore, like an insurance company, can diversify away most of the risk.
15. In betting parlance, the bookie's profit is referred to as *vigorish*, or "vig" for short.
16. It was also one reason we suggested in Chapter 5 for why contestants enter a tournament with a negative expected value.
17. Also see Conlisk (1993) for a similar argument that does not appeal specifically to the utility from uncertain outcomes.
18. See, for example, Woodland and Woodland (1991).
19. This discussion is taken from Ward and Burns (1994, pp. 133–145). Also see Fountain (2016).
20. In those days, the World Series was a best-of-nine contest.
21. *Eight Men Out*, a 1988 movie, dramatizes the affair.
22. It is not eliminated, however. Some players will still gamble because of addiction—witness Pete Rose, an all-time great baseball player who in 1989 was banned from baseball for life for betting on games (Ward and Burns, 1994, pp. 453–454).
23. Such issues are beyond the scope of the current discussion. See, for example, Chapter 7 in Berri (2018).

Answers to end-of-chapter exercises

2.1 To maximize profit, the team sets $MR=MC$, or $210–40\,Q=10$. Solving for Q yields

$Q^* = 5$

Substituting Q^* into the demand function yields $P= 210–20(5) = \$110$.

Profit is given by $(110)(5) – 200 – (10)(5) = \$300$.

2.2 a) First set $MR=MC$ to maximize profit: $100–100WP=60$, which yields $WP^*= .400$

b) To maximize winning percentage subject to a balanced budget, set $TR=TC$ and solve for WP: $100WP–50WP^2 = 60WP$, which yields $WP^*= .800$

2.3 a) The first derivative of profit with respect to Q is $20 \cdot WP \cdot Q^{-\frac{1}{2}} - 10 \cdot WP$. Setting this equal to zero and solving for Q yields $Q^*=4$, which is independent of WP.

b) Substituting the answer to (a) into the profit expression gives $\pi^* = 40 \cdot WP \cdot (4)^{\frac{1}{2}} - 10 \cdot WP \cdot 4 - 60 \cdot WP^2$. Equating this to zero and solving for WP gives $WP^*=.667$.

3.1 For each market segment, set $MR=MC$. Thus, for segment 1, $25–.0002Q=5$, which yields

$Q_1^* = 100{,}000$

Substituting this into the demand function yields $25–.0001(100{,}000) = \$15$.

For segment 2, $50–.0004Q=5$, which yields

$Q_2^* = 112{,}500$

Substituting this into the demand function yields $50–.0002(112{,}500) = \$27.5$.

The higher price for market segment 2 implies that it has the more inelastic demand curve.

Formally,

$$\varepsilon_1 = -(dQ_1 / dP_1)(P_1 / Q_1) = -(10{,}000)(15/100{,}000) = -1.5$$
$$\varepsilon_2 = -(dQ_2 / dP_2)(P_2 / Q_2) = -(5{,}000)(27.5/112{,}500) = -1.22$$

3.2 a) If the team only sets a single game price of \$25, the total attendance will be 105 (i.e., all fans will attend exactly one game), and total revenue = (105)(\$25) = \$2,625

b) Multi-game fans will pay up to (25+20+15+10+5) = \$75 for a season ticket.

c) Now, 100 fans will attend exactly one game, but multi-game fans will each attend 5 games. Thus, total attendance will be 100+(5)(5) = 125, and total revenue = (100)(25) + (5)(75) = \$2,875.

3.3 a) If P=\$6, the five highest valuers will attend the event (10, 9, 8, 7, 6).

b) If P=\$3, eight people will want to attend (10, 9, 8, 7, 6, 5, 4, 3). The five seats will likely be allocated on a first-come, first-served basis.

c) Suppose the person who values a ticket at \$4 acquires one, while the person who values it at \$9 does not. A trade between them is mutually beneficial for some price between \$4 and \$9. If they divide the surplus evenly, they will settle on a price of \$6.50.

4.1 a) Under a monopoly, set $MR=MC$. For the demand curve given, $MR=200-2Q$. Thus, set $200-2Q=50$ and solve for Q to get $Q=75$. The resulting price is $P=125$. In a Cournot model, each firm will maximize $[200-(Q_1+Q_2)]Q_i - 50Q_i$. The resulting first-order condition for firm 1 is $200-2Q_1-Q_2-50=0$. Solving for Q_1 yields the reaction function: $Q_1=75-Q_2/2$. In a symmetric equilibrium $Q_1=Q_2$. Using this fact, we can solve this single equation for the common output per firm to be $Q_1=Q_2=50$. Total industry output is therefore $Q=100$, and market price is $P=100$. Finally, in a competitive market, set $P=MC=50$. The resulting output is $Q=150$.

b) See Figure A.1.

c) The Bertrand outcome would be identical to the competitive outcome, with the two firms sharing the total output of 150.

4.2 a) Attendance for Reds = 75,000, TR = \$50×75,000 = \$3,750,000
Attendance for Blues = 75,000, TR = \$50×75,000 = \$3,750,000
Gross revenue for the two teams = \$7,500,000

b) The Reds will attract all of the neutral fans. Thus, Attendance for Reds = 100,000, TR = \$40×100,000 = \$4,000,000 Attendance for Blues = 50,000, TR = \$50×50,000 = \$2,500,000 Gross revenue = \$6,500,000

c) Aggregate revenue is maximized when the teams both set their price at \$50, but each team acting alone benefits from unilaterally undercutting the other's price.

5.1 a) high effort: (.60)(\$50) – \$7 = \$23 *
low effort: (.40)(50) – \$4 = \$16

b) high effort: (.60)(\$30) + (.40)(\$20) – \$7 = \$19
low effort: (.40)(\$30) + (.60)(\$20) – \$4 = \$20 *

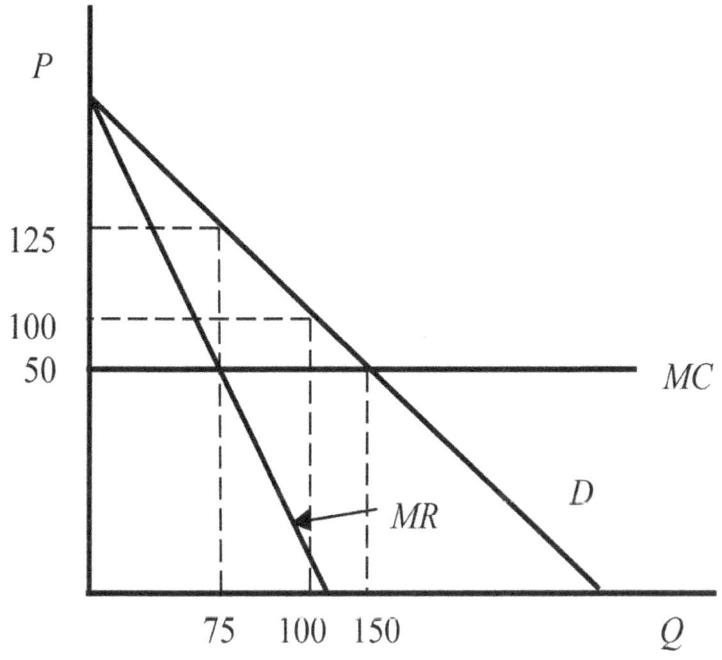

Figure A.1 *Answer to problem 4.1 (b)*

6.1 For year 1, σ=.129. For year 2, σ=.081. Thus, competitive balance has improved from year 1 to year 2 because the standard deviation is lower.

6.3 a) Form the equation 5−.1x=1 and solve for x to get x^*=40.

b) Form the equation 5−.1x=1.3 and solve for x to get x^*=37. Since this is above the threshold of 30, the team must pay a 30% luxury tax on the extra 7 million. The tax is thus equal to (.3)(7)=2.1 million.

c) If the team spends x=30 to avoid the tax, its profit would be $(5)(30)-(.05)(30)^2-30=75$. By contrast, if it spends x=37, its profit would be $(5)(37)-(.05)(37)^2-37-(.3)(7)=77.45$, which is higher. Finally, if it spends x=40, its profit would be $(5)(40)-(.05)(40)^2-40-(.3)(10)=77$, which is less than if it had spent 37.

7.1 a) The expected value of the strategy is (.1)(100)=10. The strategy thus provides the team a net benefit of 10−5=5.

b) The sanction must be at least as large as the net benefit. Thus, $s \geq 5$ to deter the strategy.

c) If the sanction is only imposed one fourth of the time, $s/4 \geq 5$, or $s \geq 20$.

d) If the value of winning increases to 150, the expected value of winning is now 15, and so the minimum sanction that deters the strategy when its use is detected with certainty is now s=10. When the sanction is imposed only one fourth of the time, the minimum sanction is s=40.

8.1 a) To find the competitive outcome, set MRP=w. Thus, 800,000–10,000q = 200,000 + 10,000q, which yields q=30. The resulting wage is w=200,000+10,000(30) = 500,000.

b) Under monopsony, set MRP=MFC, or 800,000–10,000q = 200,000+20,000q. This yields q=20, and a wage of w=200,000+10,000(20) = 400,000.

c) The wage gap when q=20 is equal to MRP–w= 600,000–400,000 = 200,000.

d) See Figure A.2.

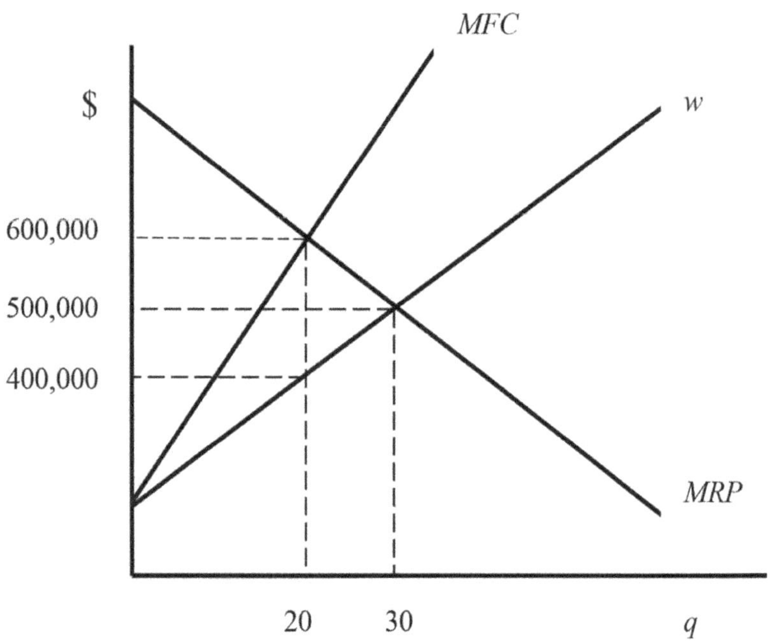

Figure A.2 Answer to problem 8.1 (d)

9.1 a) $E(U)= (.5)(50{,}000)^{1/2} + (.5)(100{,}000)^{1/2} = 269.9$
b) $E(I)=(50{,}000+100{,}000)/2=75{,}000$
c) $U(75{,}000) = (75{,}000)^{1/2} = 273.9 > 269.9$
9.2 a) Low effort: (.70)(50,000) + (.30)(100,000) = 65,000
High effort: (.30)(50,000) + (.70)(100,000) = 85,000
b)

Table A.1

Effort	Player's Income	Team's return
Low Effort	40,000-5,000=35,000	65,000-40,000=25,000
High effort	40,000-10,000=30,000	85,000-40,000=45,000

The player will choose low effort, but the team would like him to choose high effort (both as indicated by the underlined entries).
c)

Table A.2

Effort	Player's Income	Team's return
Low Effort	35,000+(.3)(20,000)–5,000=36,000	65,000–41,000=24,000
High effort	35,000+(.7)(20,000)–10,000=39,000	85,000–49,000=36,000

The player will now choose high effort, which also maximizes the team's profit.
d) A risk-averse player would prefer the fixed salary, all else equal, because it insulates him from risk due to random factors.
10.1 a) The expected value of a player is computed as follows:
Low training: (.10)(100,000) – 1,000 = 9,000
High training: (.25)(100,000) – 10,000 = 15,000
Thus, high training maximizes the player's value.
b) Under full free agency, the team will not invest in a high level of training because it would not be able to recoup the value of the extra spending.

10.2 Teams will obviously protect their best players, so only those on the low end of the quality scale will be available for the expansion draft. Thus, the new teams will necessarily be of lower than average quality in the league. Overall league quality will also likely decline because, to fill the additional roster sports, all teams will need to include players who previously were below the line for inclusion on a major league roster.

11.1 a) Set $1000 - .2Q=500$. Solving for Q gives $Q^{*}=2{,}500$.

b) Set $1000 - .2Q=500 + \frac{250{,}000}{Q}$ and show that 1809 solves this equation. Thus, there are fewer non-athletes.

12.1 a) Set $500-.5Q=100$ and solve to get $Q=800$. Thus, $n=800/50=16$ teams.

b) Now set $500-.5Q=50$, which yields $Q=900$ and $n=18$. Thus, two teams can enter.

c) Set $475-.5Q=50$, which yields $Q=850$ and $n=17$.

12.2 a) City A: 100+40–50=90

City B: 110+25–50=85Thus, the "social" value of the team is maximized if it locates in City A.

b) For City A to attract the team, it must offer to subsidize at least $10 million of the cost of the stadium to offset the higher team profit in City B.

c) City B would bid up to $25 million to attract the team. City A would therefore have to bid at least $35 million, which is the maximum bid of City B plus the profit differential of $10 million.

d) With a subsidy of $35, City A would still realize a net gain of $40–$35=$5 million.

12.3 a) A fair bet would require the payoff R to equal 10/.2=$50. Thus, this is not a fair bet.

b) Expected utility from the above bet is $EU=.2(100-10+45)^2+.8(100-10)^2 =10{,}125$, whereas not making the bet yields utility of $(100)^2= 10{,}000$, so the person will place the bet.

c) The expected return to the bookie if the bet were placed is $10-.2(45)=1$.

d) $EU=(.2)(135) + .8(90) = 99 < 100$. Thus, she would not place the bet.

e) $EU=(.25)(135) + .75(90) = 101.25 > 100$. Thus, she would place the bet.

References

Abrevaya, J. (2004). Fit to be tied: the incentive effects of overtime rules in professional hockey. *Journal of Sports Economics*, 5, 292–306.

Akerlof, G. (1970). The market for "lemons": quality uncertainty and the market mechanism. *Quarterly Journal of Economics*, 84, 488–500.

Alchian, A. & H. Demsetz (1972). Production, information costs, and economic organization. *American Economic Review*, 62, 777–795.

Baker, M., T. Miceli & W. Ryczek (2004). The old ball game: organization of 19th century professional base ball clubs. *Journal of Sports Economics*, 5, 277–291.

Basinger, J. (2009). *The Star Machine*. New York: Vintage Books.

Beaudin, L. (2018). Examining the relationship between athletic program expenditure and athletic program success among NCAA division I institutions: a dynamic panel data approach. *Journal of Sports Economics*, 19, 1016–1045.

Becker, G. (1968). Crime and punishment: an economic approach. *Journal of Political Economy*, 76, 169–217.

Becker, G. (1971). *The Economics of Discrimination*. Chicago: University of Chicago Press.

Berri, D. (2018). *Sports Economics*, New York: Worth Publishers.

Berri, D. & A. Krautmann (2006). Shirking on the court: testing for the incentive effects of guaranteed pay. *Economic Inquiry*, 44, 536–545.

Blair, R. (2012). *Sport Economics*. New York: Cambridge University Press.

Boldrin, M. & D. Levine (2008). *Against Intellectual Property*. New York: Cambridge University Press.

Bolton, P. & M. Dewatripont (2005). *Contract Theory*. Cambridge, MA: MIT Press.

Bowen, W. & S. Levin (2003). *Reclaiming the Game: College Sports and Educational Values*. Princeton, NJ: Princeton University Press.

Bradbury, J. (2007). *The Baseball Economist: The Real Game Exposed*. New York: Dutton.

Bradbury, J. & D. Drinen (2006). The designated hitter, moral hazard, and hit batters: new evidence from game-level data. *Journal of Sports Economics*, 7, 319–329.

Brocas, I. & J. Carrillo (2004). Do the "three-point victory" and "golden goal" rules make soccer more exciting? *Journal of Sports Economics*, 5, 169–185.

Brown, D., C. Link & S. Rubin (2017). *Moneyball* after ten years: how have major league baseball salaries adjusted? *Journal of Sports Economics*, 18, 771–786.

Cheung, S. (1969). *The Theory of Share Tenancy*. Chicago: University of Chicago Press.

Chong, A. & P. Restrepo (2017). Regulatory protective measures and risky behavior: evidence from ice hockey. *Journal of Public Economics*, 151, 1–11.

Coase, R. (1960). The problem of social costs. *Journal of Law and Economics*, 3, 1–44.

Coates, D. & B. Humphreys (2003). Professional sports facilities, franchises and urban economic development. *Public Finance and Management*, 3, 335–357.

Coates, D. & B. Humphreys (2012). Game attendance and outcome uncertainty in the National Hockey League. *Journal of Sports Economics*, 13, 364–377.
Coates, D. & B. Humphreys (2020). Outcome uncertainty, home win preferences, and econometric identification of the game uncertainty-attendance relationship. In P. Rodriguez, S. Kesenne & B. Humphreys (eds), *Outcome Uncertainty in Sporting Events*. Edward Elgar.
Coates, D., B. Humphreys & L. Zhou (2014). Reference-dependent preferences, loss aversion, and live game attendance. *Economic Inquiry*, 52, 959–973.
Congdon-Hohman, J. & J. Lanning (2018). Beyond Moneyball: changing compensation in MLB. *Journal of Sports Economics*, 19, 1046–1061.
Conlisk, J. (1993). The utility of gambling, *Journal of Risk and Uncertainty*, 6, 255–275.
Cooter, R. & D. Rubinfeld (1989). An economic analysis of legal disputes and their resolution. *Journal of Economic Literature*, 27, 1067–1097.
Cramer, R. (2000). *Joe DiMaggio: The Hero's Life*. New York: Simon and Schuster.
Daly, G. (1992). The baseball players' labor market revisited. In P. Sommers (ed.), *Diamonds are Forever* (pp. 11–28). Washington, DC: Brookings.
Diamond, J. (2021). An investment fund mines the diamond. *Wall Street Journal*, February 20–21.
Dietl, H. M., Franck, E., Lang, M. & Rathke, A. (2012). Salary cap regulation in professional team sports. *Contemporary Economic Policy*, 30, 307–319.
Dietl, H. M., M. Lang & A. Rathke (2011). The combined effect of salary restrictions and revenue sharing in sports leagues, *Economic Inquiry*, 49, 447–463.
Dietl, H. M., M. Lang & S. Werner (2009). Social welfare in sports leagues with profit-maximizing and/or win-maximizing clubs. *Southern Economic Journal*, 76, 375–396.
El-Hodiri, M. & J. Quirk (1971). An economic model of a professional sports league. *Journal of Political Economy*, 79, 1302–1319.
Ellickson, R. (2016). When civil society uses an iron fist: the roles of private associations in rulemaking and adjudication. *American Law and Economics Review*, 18, 235–271.
Eswaran, M. & A. Kotwol (1985). A theory of contractual structure in agriculture. *American Economic Review*, 75, 352–367.
Farber, H. (1980). An analysis of final-offer arbitration. *Journal of Conflict Resolution*, 24, 683–705.
Farmer, A., P. Pecorino, & V. Stango (2004). The causes of bargaining failure: evidence from Major League Baseball. *Journal of Law and Economics*, 47, 543–568.
Felber, B. & G. Gillette (2001). The changing game. In J. Thorn, P. Palmer, M. Gershman, M. Silverman, S. Lahman & G. Spira (eds), *Total Baseball* (pp. 79–103). Kingston, NY: Total Sports Publishing.
Fort, R. & J. Quirk (1995). Cross-subsidization, incentives, and outcomes in professional team sports leagues. *Journal of Economic Literature*, 33, 1265–1299.
Fountain, C. (2016). *Betrayal: The 1919 World Series and the Birth of Modern Baseball*. New York: Oxford University Press.
Friedman, M. & L. Savage (1948). The utility analysis of choices involving risk. *Journal of Political Economy*, 56, 279–304.
Garfinkel, M. & S. Skaperdas (2007). Economics of conflict: an overview. In T. Sandler and K. Hartley (eds), *Handbook of Defense Economics*, Vol. 2. Amsterdam: Elsevier.

Gilbert, R. & O. Williamson (1998). Antitrust policy. In P. Newman (ed.), *The New Palgrave Dictionary of Economics and the Law* (pp. 82–87). New York: Stockton Press.
Goff, B., W. Shughart & R. Tollison (1997). Batter up! Moral hazard and the effects of the designated hitter rule on hit batsmen. *Economic Inquiry*, 35, 555–561.
Goldfarb, R. (2013). Shortage, shortage, who's got the shortage? *The Journal of Economic Education*, 44, 277–297.
Gould, S. J. (2003). *Triumph and Tragedy in Mudville*. New York: Norton.
Groothuis, P. & J. Hill (2013). Pay discrimination, exit discrimination or both? Another look at an old issue using NBA data, *Journal of Sports Economics*, 14, 171–185.
Hakes, J. & R. Sauer (2006). An economic evaluation of the *Moneyball* Hypothesis. *Journal of Economic Perspectives*, 20, 173–185.
Hanssen, A. & J. Meehan (2009). Who integrated Major League Baseball faster? Winning or losing teams? *Journal of Sports Economics*, 10, 141–154.
Hanssen, A., J. Meehan & T. Miceli (2016). Explaining changes in organizational form: the case of professional baseball. *Journal of Sports Economics*, 17, 523–557.
Hart, H. L. A. (1961). *The Concept of Law*. London: Oxford University Press.
Holmes, O. W. (1897). The path of the law. *Harvard Law Review*, 10, 457–478.
Holmstrom, B. (1982). Moral hazard in teams. *Bell Journal of Economics*, 13, 324–340.
Hotelling, H. (1929). Stability in competition. *Economic Journal*, 39, 41–57.
Humphreys, B. (2002). Alternative measures of competitive balance in sports. *Journal of Sports Economics*, 3, 133–148.
Humphreys, B. (2019). Should construction of new sports facilities be subsidized? *Journal of Policy Analysis and Management*, 38, 264–270.
Humphreys, B. & T. Miceli (2019). The peculiar preferences of sports fans: toward a preference-based motivation for the uncertainty of outcome hypothesis. *Journal of Sports Economics*, 20, 782–796.
Humphreys, B. & T. Miceli (2020). Outcome uncertainty, fan travel, and aggregate attendance, *Economic Inquiry*, 58, 462–473.
Humphreys, B. & M. Mondello (2007). Intercollegiate athletic success and donations at NCAA division I institutions. *Journal of Sport Management*, 21, 265–280.
Kahane, L. (2006). The reverse-order-of-finish draft in sports. In V. Andreff & S. Szymanski (eds), *The Elgar Companion to Sports Economics*. Edward Elgar.
Kahn, L. (1991). Discrimination in professional sports: a survey of the literature, *Industrial and Labor Relations Review*, 44, 395–418.
Kahneman, D., J. Knetsch & R. Thaler (2000). Experimental tests of the endowment effect and the Coase Theorem. In C. Sunstein (ed.), *Behavioral Law and Economics*. Cambridge: Cambridge University Press.
Kandel, E. & E. Lazear (1992). Peer pressure and partnerships. *Journal of Political Economy*, 100, 801–817.
Késenne, S. (2000). Revenue sharing and competitive balance in professional team sports. *Journal of Sports Economics*, 1, 56–65.
Késenne, S. (2006). The win maximization model reconsidered: flexible talent supply and efficiency wages. *Journal of Sports Economics*, 7, 416–427.
Klein, B., V. Crawford & A. Alchian (1978). Vertical integration, appropriable quasi-rents, and the competitive contracting process. *Journal of Law and Economics*, 21, 297–326.
Knowles, G., K. Sherony & M. Haupert (1992). The demand for Major League Baseball: a test of the uncertainty of outcome hypothesis. *The American Economist*, 36, 72–80.

Krautmann, A. (1999). What's wrong with Scully?—estimates of a player's marginal revenue product. *Economic Inquiry*, 37, 369–381.
Krautmann, A. & T. Donley (2009). Shirking in major league baseball revisited. *Journal of Sports Economics*, 10, 292–304.
Krautmann, A. & J. Solow (2009). The dynamics of performance over the duration of major league baseball long-term contracts. *Journal of Sports Economics*, 10, 6–22.
Lamb, D. (1994). The minors. In G. Ward & K. Burns (eds), *Baseball: An Illustrated History* (pp. 146–149). New York: Alfred Knopf.
Leland, H. (1979). Quacks, lemons, and licensing: a theory of minimum quality standards. *Journal of Political Economy*, 87, 1328–1346.
Lewis, M. (2003). *Moneyball: The Art of Winning an Unfair Game*. New York: Norton.
Maennig, W. & S. Mueller (2023). Game outcome uncertainty revisited—a clustering analysis of team-specific game attendance predictions. *Applied Economics*, 55, 3487–3497.
Matheson, V. (2019). Is there a case for subsidizing sports stadiums? *Journal of Policy Analysis and Management*, 38, 271–277.
Meade, J. (1972). The theory of labor-managed firms and of profit sharing. *Economic Journal*, 82, 402–428.
McGinty, J. (2021). On sports, most schools swim in red ink. *Wall Street Journal*, March 13–24.
Meehan, J., R. Nelson & T. Richardson (2007). Competitive balance and game attendance in Major League Baseball. *Journal of Sports Economics*, 8, 563–580.
Miceli, T. (2004). A principal-agent model of contracting in professional baseball. *Journal of Sports Economics*, 5, 213–220.
Miceli, T. (2007). Minimum quality standards in professional baseball and the paradoxical disappearance of the .400 hitter. *Nine: A Journal of Baseball History and Culture*, 16, 99–103.
Miceli, T. (2022). Investing in talent development: theory and applications. *Managerial and Decision Economics*, 43, 1641–1650.
Miceli, T. (2023). On sports betting and the Uncertainty of Outcome Hypothesis. *International Journal of Sport Finance*, 18, 97–104.
Miceli, T. (2024a). A note on the preferences of sports fans: partisanship versus uncertainty of outcome. *Journal of Sports Economics*, 25, 155–168.
Miceli, T. (2024b). A note on externalities and revenue sharing in sports leagues. *International Journal of Sport Finance*, 19, 143–151.
Miller, M. (1991). *A Whole Different Ball Game: The Sport and Business of Baseball*. New York: Birch Lane Press.
Mills, B. & R. Fort (2018). Team-level time series analysis in MLB, the NBA, and the NHL: attendance and outcome uncertainty. *Journal of Sports Economics*, 19, 911–933.
Mills, B. & R. Fort (2023). Performance quality preference heterogeneity in Major League Baseball. *Journal of Sports Economics*, 24, 353–373.
Mills, B., S. Salago & S. Tainsky (2016). NBA primary market ticket consumers: *ex ante* expectations and consumer market origination. *Journal of Sport Management*, 30, 538–552.
Mirrlees, J. (1976). The optimal structure of incentives and authority within an organization. *Bell Journal of Economics*, 7, 105–131.
Nalbantis, G. & T. Pawlowski (2019). U.S. demand for European soccer telecasts: a between country test of the uncertainty of outcome hypothesis. *Journal of Sports Economics*, 20, 797–818.

Nalbantis, G., T. Pawlowski & D. Coates (2017). The fans' perception of competitive balance and its impact on willingness-to-pay for a single game. *Journal of Sports Economics*, 18, 479–505.

Neale, W. C. (1964). The peculiar economics of professional sports. *The Quarterly Journal of Economics*, 78, 1–14.

Nicholson, W. & C. Snyder (2017). *Microeconomic Theory: Basic Principles and Extensions*, 12th ed. Mason, OH: Thompson Higher Education.

Oi, W. (1971). A Disneyland dilemma: two-part tariffs for a Mickey-Mouse monopoly. *Quarterly Journal of Economics*, 85, 77–96.

Pawlowski, T. (2013). Testing the uncertainty of outcome hypothesis in German professional football: a stated-preference approach. *Journal of Sports Economics*, 14, 341–367.

Peach, J. (2007). College athletics, universities, and the NCAA: Western Social Science Association Presidential Address. *Social Science Journal*, 44, 11–22.

Peltzman, S. (1975). The effects of automobile safety regulation. *Journal of Political Economy*, 83, 677–726.

Phillips, C. (2019). *Scouting and Scoring: How We Know What We Know About Baseball*. Princeton, NJ: Princeton University Press.

Png, I. P. L. (1986). Optimal subsidies and damages in the presence of legal error. *International Review of Law and Economics*, 6, 101–105.

Putterman, L. (1984). On some recent explanations of why capital hires labor. *Economic Inquiry*, 22, 171–187.

Quirk, J. & R. Fort (1992). *Pay Dirt: The Business of Professional Team Sports*. Princeton, NJ: Princeton University Press.

Report (2018). *Report and Recommendations to Address the Issues Facing Collegiate Basketball*. Commission on College Basketball, April.

Ritter, L. (2002 [1966]). *The Glory of Their Times*. New York: Perennial.

Rottenberg, S. (1956). The baseball players' labor market. *Journal of Political Economy*, 64, 242–258.

Ryczek, W. (1999). *Blackguards and Red Stockings: A History of Baseball's National Association*. Wallingford, CT: Colebrook Press.

Ryczek, W. (2017). *Baseball on the Brink: The Crisis of 1968*. Jefferson, NC: McFarland and Co.

Sappington, D. (1983). Limited liability contracts between principal and agent. *Journal of Economic Theory*, 29, 1–29.

Sauer, R. (1998). The economics of wagering markets. *Journal of Economic Literature*, 36, 2021–2064.

Schreyer, D., S. Schmidt & B. Tergler (2018). Game outcome uncertainty in the English Premier League: do German fans care? *Journal of Sports Economics*, 19, 625–644.

Scully, G. (1974). Pay and performance in major league baseball. *American Economic Review*, 64, 915–930.

Shavell, S. (1995). The appeals process as a means of error correction. *Journal of Legal Studies*, 24, 379–426.

Szymanski, S. (2003). The economic design of sporting contests. *Journal of Economic Literature*, 41, 1137–1187.

Szymanski, S. (2009). *Playbooks and Checkbooks: An Introduction to the Economics of Modern Sports*. Princeton, NJ: Princeton University Press.

Szymanski, S. & S. Kesenne (2004). Competitive balance and gate revenue sharing in team sports. *Journal of Industrial Economics*, 52, 165–177.

Tullock, G. (1967). The welfare costs of tariffs, monopolies, and theft. *Western Economic Journal*, 5, 224–232.
Volz, B. (2009). Minority status in managerial survival in Major League Baseball. *Journal of Sports Economics*, 10, 522–542.
Volz, B. (2013). Race and the likelihood of managing in Major League Baseball. *Journal of Labor Research*, 34, 30–51.
Volz, B. (2017). Race and quarterback survival in the National Football League. *Journal of Sports Economics*, 18, 850–866.
Vrooman, J. (1995). A general theory of professional sports leagues. *Southern Economic Journal*, 61, 971–990.
Walker, S. (2017). *The Captain Class: The Hidden Forces Behind the World's Greatest Teams*. London: Elbury Press.
Ward, G. & K. Burns (1994). *Baseball: An Illustrated History*. New York: Alfred Knopf.
Wittman, D. (2006). *Economic Foundations of Law and Organization*. New York: Cambridge University. Press.
Woodland, B. & L. Woodland (1991). The effects of risk aversion on wagering: point spread versus odds. *Journal of Political Economy*, 99, 638–653.
Zimbalist, A. (1992). *Baseball and Billions: A Probing Look Inside the Big Business of Our National Pastime*. New York: Basic Books.
Zimbalist, A. (2002). Competitive balance in sports leagues: an introduction. *Journal of Sports Economics*, 3, 111–121.

Index

Abrevaya, J. 130
adverse selection problem 194
aggressive play 113, 115, 117, 124, 129–30
Alchian, A. 174
antitrust laws 1–2, 8, 28, 46, 201, 215–17, 221, 241
auction theory 6, 142

Babe Ruth 123, 183, 197, 236
barriers to entry 8, 28, 46, 63, 159
Beane, B. 153
Beaudin, L. 211
Becker, G. 114, 237
Benthamite welfare function 86
Bertrand model 47, 52, 54–6, 58–9, 64
Black Sox Scandal 235–6
Blair, R. 94
Bradbury, J. 158–9, 220

cartels 4–5, 46–7, 59–62, 64, 138, 159, 201
Coase, R. 2
Coase Theorem 2
Coates, D. 94, 96, 228
collective bargaining 141, 171
college sports 8, 193–4, 198, 201–12, 236
competition on the field 5, 47, 66–76, 78–81
competitive balance 2, 5, 62, 71, 77, 83–7, 89, 91–4, 96–104, 106–7, 124, 131, 157, 159, 202–3, 233, 236
competitive labor market 136–8
competitive pricing 27–8
concussion 5, 124, 127
conflict model of sports contests 5, 66–71, 78, 80
Congdon-Hohman, J. 155
contracts *see* player contracts

Cournot model 47–52, 59, 63–4, 69, 71
crime and punishment, economics of 3, 6, 64, 112–14, 121, 131

dead ball era 123, 183–4
"Deflategate" controversy 120
Demsetz, H. 174
designated hitter rule 123, 125, 127
DiMaggio, J. 146
discrimination in sports 8–9, 215, 236–42
domestic violence 113
doping 112–13, 115, 125, 157, 197
drug testing 112, 115, 124

economic concepts 2–4
Ellickson, R. 113
endowment effect 221
entrepreneur-run contests 74–5

fan loyalty 14, 57–8, 61, 64
final offer arbitration 146–9
fixed rental contracts 167, 171, 178
fixed wage contracts 167, 171, 229
folk theorem 61
Fort, R. 85, 96, 99
free agents 2, 6, 62, 99, 135, 138, 140–44, 146–9, 154, 160, 173, 182, 190, 193, 198, 203, 224
free-entry contest 73–4
free entry of teams 217–20, 241
free-rider problem 62
Friedman, M. 233

gambling 8, 74, 107, 113, 215, 229–36, 241
game outcome uncertainty 96; *see also* Uncertainty of Outcome Hypothesis
game theory 2–3, 61, 160

gender 9, 215, 237, 239–40, 242
Goff, B. 125
graduated reward schemes 71–3, 80

Hakes, J. 153
Hanssen, A. 184, 239
head contact 6, 125, 127
hit-by-pitch rate 125, 127
Hotelling, H. 53
Humphreys, B. 94, 96, 228

imperfect competition 46–7, 49
imperfect information 3, 34
incentive clauses 6, 79–80, 170–72, 175
invariance proposition 2, 99, 106–7, 203

Kahn, L. 239
Krautmann, A. 141, 170

Lamb, D. 184
Lanning, J. 155
law enforcement, economic theory of *see* crime and punishment, economics of
leagues as economic organizations 4, 46–64
Leland, H. 194
"lemons" problem 194
Leontief utility function 89
luxury taxes 63, 104–7

Major League Baseball 2
market sizes 19–21, 55–6
Matheson, V. 228
Meehan, J. 94, 239
Miceli, T. 96
Mills, B. 85, 96
minor leagues 7–8, 79, 160, 182–6, 188–94, 197–8, 203, 208–9, 211
Moneyball Hypothesis 6, 103, 135–6, 152–5, 157, 159, 161, 194
monopoly power 13–14, 24, 27–38, 46, 59, 138, 160, 220, 222
monopsony model 6, 135, 138, 140, 160, 201
moral hazard 125, 127

Nalbantis, G. 96
name, image, and likeness 201–2
Nash equilibrium 3, 52, 55, 60, 69, 148, 162, 223
National Collegiate Athletic Association (NCAA) 8, 83, 201–2, 210
Neale, W. C. 2, 84

oligopoly 46, 53
  Bertrand model 47, 52, 54–6, 58–9, 64
  Cournot model 47–52, 60, 63–4, 69, 71
opportunity cost 13, 75, 142, 227
optimal contest 73
optimizing behavior 2
overtime rules 129–30

partisanship 56, 83–7, 89–92, 94, 236
Pawlowski, T. 96
pay for play 8, 201–3
Peltzman Effect 127–9
player contracts 6, 79–80, 135, 165–75, 183–4, 193, 229
player salaries 6, 135–61, 201
  discrimination and 9, 239–41
  pay for play 8, 201–3
  salary caps 5, 63, 103–7, 216
players' unions 80, 135, 138, 160, 165, 198
player training 7, 182–98, 203, 209–10
point shaving 113, 235
policy issues 8–9, 29, 215–42; *see also* antitrust laws
price discrimination 4, 27, 29–37, 41
price theory 2
pricing of sporting events 4, 27–42
principal–agent model 6, 79, 165–7, 175
Prisoners' Dilemma 60–61
product differentiation 52–6, 64
Professional and Amateur Sports Act 229
professional leagues 75–6, 78, 84, 106, 135
profit maximization 11–16, 18–24, 27, 38, 41, 59, 97, 185, 224
property rights 2, 158, 209
public goods 62–4
Putterman, L. 173–4

quantity discounts 4, 27, 31, 34–7, 41
Quirk, J. 99

race 9, 215, 236–40, 242
Rate of Technical Substitution 155
relegation 106–7
relocation decisions 221, 224
rent-seeking 69
reserve system 2, 6–7, 63, 84, 97–100, 107, 138, 140, 154, 160, 183, 188, 190, 192, 209, 236
revenue functions 92–3
revenue sharing 5, 61, 63, 100–102, 104, 107
reverse-order drafts 5, 63, 106–7, 202
Rickey, B. 158, 183
risk-sharing 6, 80, 168–71, 175
Robinson, J. 238
Rottenberg, S. 1–2, 5, 9, 21, 84, 97, 99–100, 106–7, 203
rule of reason test 216–17
rules and enforcement 5, 112–25, 127 31, 197

safety equipment 127–9
salaries *see* player salaries
salary caps 5, 63, 103–7, 216
salary renegotiation and holdouts 144–6
sanctions *see* rules and enforcement
Sauer, R. 153
Savage, L. 233
Schreyer, D. 96
screening function of minor leagues 7, 79, 160, 182, 194–7
Scully, G. 6, 140–42, 160
season tickets *see* quantity discounts
second-degree price discrimination 30–37, 41
senior citizen discounts 27, 29–30, 41
sharecropping contract 167
Sherman Act 216, 221
sign stealing 121, 157
small-ball 123, 183
Solow, J. 170
spatial model of differentiated products 53–5, 64
spillover benefits 8, 215, 223–7, 241
sports economics, definition of 1–2
sports teams as business firms 4, 11–24, 41; *see also* pricing of sporting events
stadium capacity 16–17, 39–40
stadium financing 8, 17, 215, 221–9, 241
standard deviation 93–5, 99, 107
Supreme Court 1, 8, 201, 216, 229
Szymanski, S. 1, 74, 94

tanking 106–7
team production problem 7, 79, 165, 170, 173–5
third-degree price discrimination 30–31, 41
ticket-scalping 4, 27, 30, 37–42
Title IX 240
training costs 188–92, 198
travel distance 56–9, 96
tuition costs 203–5, 208
two-part pricing 4, 27, 31–4, 41

uncertainty 3
Uncertainty of Outcome Hypothesis 2, 5, 9, 20, 83–5, 92, 94, 96–7, 215, 230, 233
unequal fan bases 88–9, 92, 97

video replay 6, 112, 122–3, 131
Volz, B. 240

wage gap 140–42
Walker, S. 113–14, 174
win maximization 11, 17–20, 22–4, 27
winning percentage 17–21, 24, 66, 93–5, 97, 99, 107, 140, 150–51, 153–4
Woods, T. 73, 197

Zimbalist, A. 184, 195